DRUG WAR CAPITALISM

BY

DAWN PALEY

Drug War Capitalism

© 2014 Dawn Paley
Foreword © 2014 Guadalupe Correa-Cabrera

This edition © 2014 AK Press (Oakland, Edinburgh, Baltimore).
ISBN: 978-1-84935-193-5 | eBook ISBN: 978-1-84935-188-1
Library of Congress Control Number: 2014940826

AK Press	AK Press
370 Ryan Avenue #100	33 Tower St.
Chico, CA 95973	Edinburgh EH6 7BN
USA	Scotland
www.akpress.org	www.akuk.com
akpress@akpress.org	ak@akedin.demon.co.uk

The above addresses would be delighted to provide you with the latest AK Press distribution catalog, which features the several thousand books, pamphlets, zines, audio and video products, and stylish apparel published and/or distributed by AK Press. Alternatively, visit our websites for the complete catalog, latest news, and secure ordering.

Cover design by John Yates | stealworks.com
Index by Chris Dodge
Printed in the USA on acid-free paper

DRUG WAR CAPITALISM

DRUG WAR CAPITALISM

This book is dedicated to the memory of independent photographer and journalist Ali Mustafa, 1984–2014. His bravery, fighting spirit, and commitment live on in our hearts, in our work, and in our words.

Días antes de terminar este libro recibimos las primeras noticias de los 43 normalistas de Ayotzinapa desaparecidos en Iguala, Guerrero, el 27 de septiembre de 2014. Sus nombres aquí aparecen, con la firme esperanza de que sean encontrados con vida y con la profunda rabia e indignación por lo que les haya sucedido, ¡los tenemos presentes!: Abel García Hernández, Abelardo Vázquez Peniten, Adán Abrajan de la Cruz, Alexander Mora Venancio, Antonio Santana Maestro, Benjamín Ascencio Bautista, Bernardo Flores Alcaraz, Carlos Iván Ramírez Villarreal, Carlos Lorenzo Hernández Muñoz, César Manuel González Hernández, Christian Alfonso Rodríguez Telumbre, Christian Tomas Colon Garnica, Cutberto Ortiz Ramos, Dorian González Parral, Emiliano Alen Gaspar de la Cruz, Everardo Rodríguez Bello, Felipe Arnulfo Rosas, Giovanni Galindes Guerrero, Israel Caballero Sánchez, Israel Jacinto Lugardo, Jesús Jovany Rodríguez Tlatempa, Jonas Trujillo González, Jorge Álvarez Nava, Jorge Aníbal Cruz Mendoza, Jorge Antonio Tizapa Legideño, Jorge Luis González Parral, José Ángel Campos Cantor, José Ángel Navarrete González, José Eduardo Bartolo Tlatempa, José Luis Luna Torres, Jhosivani Guerrero de la Cruz, Julio César López Patolzin, Leonel Castro Abarca, Luis Ángel Abarca Carrillo, Luis Ángel Francisco Arzola, Magdaleno Rubén Lauro Villegas, Marcial Pablo Baranda, Marco Antonio Gómez Molina, Martín Getsemany Sánchez García, Mauricio Ortega Valerio, Miguel Ángel Hernández Martínez, Miguel Ángel Mendoza Zacarías, Saúl Bruno García.

Contents

FOREWORD

GUADALUPE CORREA-CABRERA

"To get rich, one must have but a single idea, one fixed, hard, immutable thought: the desire to make a heap of gold. And in order to increase this heap of gold, one must be inflexible, a usurer, thief, extortionist, and murderer! And one must especially mistreat the small and the weak! And when this mountain of gold has been amassed, one can climb up on it, and from up on the summit, a smile on one's lips, one can contemplate the valley of poor wretches that one has created."

—Petrus Borel, *Champavert, Immoral Tales*

CAPITALISM is defined as a socioeconomic system based on private ownership of the means of production and the exploitation of the labor force. According to Karl Marx, the capitalist mode of production "rests on the fact that the material conditions of production are in the hands of non-workers in the form of property in capital and land, while the masses are only owners of the personal condition of production, of labor power."[1] This is the system that rules most parts of our world today; and it is a system based on the accumulation of wealth/capital and exploitation of labor and natural resources by small elites—mainly transnational businesses. With these ideas in mind and with an aim of explaining the violent socioeconomic and political reality of Colombia, Mexico, and Central America today, Dawn Paley wrote *Drug War Capitalism*. Paley is one of the best and most serious journalists I have encountered in my own journey to understand the massive crisis these societies have undergone in recent times, and *Drug War Capitalism* is the best book I have recently read on this subject, by far.

I was born in Mexico in 1975, and witnessed the end of the Cold War and the fall of the Berlin Wall, which allegedly meant the triumph of capitalism over what was called at that time communism. I studied economics in the 1990s, during the Third Wave of democratization in the post–Cold War world, when scholars Samuel Huntington and Francis Fukuyama suggested that ideologies had come to an end, and that capitalism had won the ideological battle forever. For Fukuyama we were living the "end of history." As an undergraduate student of economics at a private university in Mexico City, I was trained in the tradition of neoclassical economics. I became familiar with the ideas of Milton Friedman, Ludwig von Mises, Friedrich Hayek, Ayn Rand, and Adam Smith, who are associated—by themselves or by others—with the ideology of capitalism. I was a student when the North American Free Trade Agreement (NAFTA) was signed; at school I was taught about the supposed benefits of economic liberalization, the compara- tive advantage, free markets, deregulation, and privatization; in other words, the benefits of capitalism. I began to understand the limita- tions of this socioeconomic system and structural economic reforms during Mexico's economic and devaluation crisis in 1994–1995, and the Zapatista uprising.

I worked for the Ministry of Finance and the Ministry of Agri- culture in Mexico and was present during the 2000 elections, when Vicente Fox became president of the country, after more than seven- ty years of one-party rule. I witnessed months of great expectations and enthusiasm by Mexican society, in the streets, in the universities, and elsewhere. Democracy amounted to a big promise in a still very unequal nation. But poverty and inequality, at that particular mo- ment, did not seem to matter for many, who thought that the prob- lems of our country would be solved through free and fair elections and the consolidation of democratic institutions. For many optimistic citizens, the new Mexican democracy and President Fox—a former employee of a transnational company (Coca Cola-México), a tall and unintelligent man who wore cowboy boots and ran a very successful presidential campaign—would save Mexico and bring prosperity and stability to our nation after serious economic and political crises in the 1980s and 1990s.

In August of 2000, I left my country to study for a PhD in political science at the New School for Social Research in New York City. It was there, at a progressive school in the United States, that I learned the basics of Marxism and understood the key limitations of capitalism in extremely unequal nations. During the years I spent in New York, I studied the contemporary political history of most Latin American countries and became very interested in the Central American region as well as in the massive violence and war on drugs in Colombia. The first years of the twenty-first century were determinant for the relative stabilization of the Colombian conflict, after many years, even decades, of intense violence and massive social and political crisis.

I returned to Mexico City in early 2006, some months before the most contested presidential election in the country's history. Mexican society was extremely divided and polarized over the issues and the selection of presidential candidates. I realized that Fukuyama was mistaken about the end of history and the end of ideologies. After a very tight election, allegations of fraud, and a period of intense social mobilization, Felipe Calderón became president of Mexico. Immediately after he assumed power on December 1, 2006, he declared a war on drugs and launched military operations against drug trafficking organizations—now known as transnational criminal organizations (TCOs). To some extent, certain elements of this episode of Mexico's history reminded me of recent violence and anti-narcotics efforts in Colombia.

Since that time, violence in Mexico has reached unprecedented levels. To date, Mexico's so-called "war on drugs" has claimed over 100,000 lives—probably many more, but we do not have access to the exact figure. During this period, more than 27,000 people have vanished, with many of these disappearances linked to organized crime. Thousands of citizens have become internal refugees, displaced within Mexico, or forced to move abroad. This momentous increase in violence has been accompanied by the widespread use of barbaric, terror-inflicting methods such as decapitation, dismemberment, car bombs, mass kidnappings, grenade attacks, blockades, and the widespread execution of public officials. These practices remind me of the late Cold War period in Central America.

At the same time, drug trafficking organizations diversified their operations and became involved in lucrative new businesses, such as kidnapping, extortion, migrant smuggling, human trafficking, weapons smuggling, video and music piracy, and trafficking of crude oil, natural gas, and gasoline stolen from Mexico's state petroleum company, among others. These activities have been made possible by a new relationship of organized crime with a new set of actors. New corruption networks have been built between criminal organizations, local police and law enforcement agencies, politicians at all levels, and federal authorities. Formal businesses, including transnational companies (e.g., financial firms, US oil companies, private security firms, arms-producing companies, and gambling companies) have also established new connections with TCOs.

A new model of organized crime has evolved in the last few years, and it seems to have been exported to other parts of the Americas, particularly to Central America. This new paramilitarized model of organized crime has coincided with the militarization of anti-narcotic operations in the region, which was furthered by the successor of Plan Colombia, that is, by Plan Mérida—a program that started officially about one year after Plan Colombia ended—and the Central America Regional Security Initiative (CARSI). These initiatives were advanced and supported by the government of the United States. The combination of these phenomena led to levels and types of violence that had not been experienced in a long time.

I now live in Brownsville, Texas, right across the border from the Mexican city of Matamoros. The area south of Brownsville—as many other regions along the Mexican side of the US-Mexico border—has been particularly affected by new and more extreme forms of violence, organized crime, militarization, and paramilitarization.

Experiencing violence so closely—and being aware of a disturbing transformation of Mexican society—I have become particularly interested in this phenomenon that has expanded to other regions of the hemisphere and seems to have transnational roots and explanations. For the past few years, I have conducted a large number of lengthy interviews with experts, journalists, and other key actors regarding drug violence and the activities of transnational organized crime syndicates. I have talked with many people and have read almost every trade book that has come out on this subject matter. Before reading *Drug War Capitalism*, I had not found any comprehensive text that offered a coherent explanation of these very complex phenomena that have affected entire communities and led to the loss of thousands of lives, sparking a human tragedy of considerable dimensions in Colombia, Mexico, and Central America—the Northern Triangle countries in particular (Guatemala, Honduras, and El Salvador).

The first time I talked to Paley was in April of 2011, when she was writing an article about violence in the northeastern Mexican state of Tamaulipas for *The Nation* magazine. We stayed in contact, and I started to follow her work and her trips to different parts of our hemisphere in her quest to understand violence, imperialism, and exploitation of poor communities in the context of what she calls a "war against people" (*guerra contra los pueblos*). I still remember a conversation we had in February 2012, in La Paz, Baja California, when we met briefly and talked about the situation in Mexico five years into a war that was allegedly declared to fight organized crime and to reestablish order and the rule of law in the country.

At that time, Paley expressed to me her intention to write this book and explained in detail what she meant by a "war against the people" that derives from the war on drugs in the United States. She stressed then (and stresses now) "the importance of critical research and writing on the conflicts in Colombia, Mexico, and elsewhere in the hemisphere that take into consideration resource extraction as a driving force behind whatever the current dominant explications of the conflicts are." For Paley, it is important to rethink what is called the war on drugs, which "isn't about prohibition or drug policy," but instead, is a war "in which terror is used against the population at large in cities and rural areas," while "parallel to this terror and the panic it generates, policy changes are implemented which facilitate foreign direct investment and economic growth." For the author of the present book, this is drug war capitalism, advanced through a war on the people and their communities. In her words, "The war on drugs is a long-term fix to capitalism's woes, combining terror with policymaking in a seasoned neoliberal mix, cracking open social worlds and territories once unavailable to globalized capitalism."

Paley is, in my opinion, one of the very few persons I know who understands the dynamics of drug-related conflicts in the Americas. She has traveled to the most important regions in the hemisphere afflicted by drug war violence and has carefully documented what she has observed. Her material is precise, well-documented, and provocative, and this book is the culmination of an extraordinary effort to understand a complex phenomenon that has affected thousands of persons and entire communities in the Western hemisphere.

Notwithstanding the numerous human and material resources spent by government agencies, NGOs, and civil society in general to explain the drug war crisis, recent studies on the drug war have been very limited and explain very little—particularly, the most popular ones.

From readings and conversations over the past years, I have concluded that there are essentially three types of analyses on the so-called drug wars in the Americas. One popular view on the subject—the one that is present in most trade books displayed in airports, popular bookstores, and shopping centers—is the one that sees this conflict as an issue of "drug lords" (*narcos*) and wars among "drug cartels" and of cartels fighting against the state for the control of drug trafficking routes. Another viewpoint focuses on prohibition and drug policy. These two perspectives do not seem to be very helpful to explain violence and organized crime in the hemisphere. Stories about *narcos* do not portray accurately the complex reality of transnational businesses involving a variety of extremely powerful actors and interests, both public and private. On the other hand, as Paley recognizes, debates of prohibition of drugs and decriminalization of drugs tend to "obscure the militaristic nature of the war on drugs" and keep this phenomenon "firmly within the realm of ideas, and [avoids] a discussion of this war's legitimacy."

The third and last type of analysis on these so-called wars on drugs that I have identified is the one that guides the present text, one that explains the powerful forces and interests behind a conflict that mainly affects "the people" (*la gente/el pueblo/los pueblos*) and the most vulnerable groups in society. As *Drug War Capitalism* points out, it is important to put these conflicts "into a broader context of US and transnational interests in the hemisphere" and link "anti-drug policies to the territorial and social expansion of capitalism."

A key element of Paley's analysis is the one that identifies the US involvement in the militarization of anti–drug trafficking operations in the four countries she studies. The US-backed policy initiatives of Plan Colombia, the Mérida Initiative, and CARSI, according to her account, are the primary vehicles to advance drug war capitalism in the region. These initiatives, in her view, promote "the militarization of aid and the steering of anti-drug money toward fostering the creation of more welcoming investment policies and legal regulations. Though not often talked about in the context of the drug war, these policy changes often have little to nothing to do with illicit substances and everything to do with the transformation of the business environment."

The US-backed militarization of security strategies in the four countries—with the alleged key purposes of strengthening institutional reforms and the rule of law as well as of preventing violence—has coincided with a visible increase in the murder rate as well as with the militarization of organized crime or the creation or strengthening of countrywide structures of paramilitary control. In Paley's opinion, the militarization of crime groups can be very useful to the expansion of capitalism. And she correctly makes use of the word "paramilitarization" when referring to TCOs, since these criminal forces, at many times, seem to be "supported or tolerated by the state." In fact, the complicity between state actors and criminal groups has been present in most of the cases analyzed by the author.

The most important contribution of this book is its extraordinary explanation—utilizing different cases in the four countries of study— of how the state violence displaces urban and rural populations, leading to changes in land ownership and resource exploitation. Paley documents very well how several Indigenous communities in these four countries have had their lands taken away by war, and how these properties have been acquired by transnational corporations whose aim is to extract natural resources.

In general, we find in this text that internal conflicts and militarization have concentrated in "areas deemed important for energy projects or resource extraction." These phenomena have taken place in areas "where there are fierce social and land conflicts related to the imposition of mega projects" such as oil and natural gas exploration or exploitation, large-scale agriculture, hydroelectric projects, large-scale forestry, among others. And in this context, the real beneficiaries of drug wars in the Americas are, among others, large banks, local elites, and transnational oil and mining companies. These policies have also helped the United States to gain more leverage and achieve its strategic foreign policy objectives in the Americas and particularly in Colombia, Mexico, and Central America.

In Paley's view, connections between drug wars, the state, paramilitary violence, and natural resources are increasingly evident. In her account, paramilitaries or non-state armed actors "can serve to control dissent and conquer territory." And this also coincides with a cycle of accumulation and drug war capitalism, where "forced displacement ... is not a casual by product of the internal conflict." As part of this cycle, according to a report cited by Paley, "armed groups attack the civil population to strengthen territorial strongholds, expand territorial control, weaken the support of the opponent, and accumulate valuable assets (e.g., land or extraction of natural resources)." In such a context, as Marx notes, "the instruments of labor are the monopoly of the landowners (the monopoly of property in land is even the basis of the monopoly of capital) and the capitalists."[2]

The implementation of US-backed initiatives that further the militarization of security strategies in Colombia, Mexico, Central America, and the Caribbean have not achieved their alleged main aims. In fact, the amount of drug trafficking in these regions has not fallen. At the same time, as Paley explains, non-state armed actors have been empowered, thus "increasing extra-legal violence with no apparent effect on its stated goal of curbing drug production." Plan Colombia, for example, hasn't significantly reduced the amount of cocaine for sale in the United States, and homicide rates in the Andean country remain among the highest in the region. Regardless, Plan Colombia has been touted by authorities as a successful initiative. These sources would agree with Milton Friedman when he states that "one of the great mistakes is to judge policies and programs by their intentions rather than their results."[3] It seems that for them, positive results fall along the lines of what Paley suggests: an emerging series of metrics linked to security, an improved business environment, the transition to a US-style justice system, and the extension of police forces throughout the national territory.

Another important argument in *Drug War Capitalism* is the one suggesting that transnational oil and gas companies are among the biggest winners in this new context. For example, "immediately following Plan Colombia, the state oil company, Ecopetrol, was privatized, and new laws introduced to encourage foreign direct investment." At the same time, as Paley observes, "[s]pecial battalions of the army were trained to protect oil pipelines belonging to US companies. In the wake of Plan Colombia, foreign investment in the extractive industries soared and new trade agreements were signed." Something similar has been taking place in Mexico.

Energy reforms were recently passed in Mexico. In December 2013, the Congress approved constitutional changes to open up even more of Mexico's hydrocarbons industry to the participation of private transnational businesses. At the same time, Mexican states rich in hydrocarbons—such as Chihuahua, Coahuila, Nuevo León, Tamaulipas, San Luis Potosí, and Veracruz—have been militarized as part of the war on drugs. Some of these regions have shown high levels of forced displacement because of the severe drug-related violence. In this context, the government of Mexico intends to attract massive foreign investments to tap into the country's energy resources. Similarly, in Guatemala and Honduras national security seems to have been driven by the extractive industries in recent years.

Drug wars greatly transformed the economies of Colombia, Mexico, and Central America in the present era. However, this transformation has taken place at a large cost in terms of human lives. This cost can be considered a human tragedy, the tragedy of drug war capitalism.

In this tragic context, as Paley recognizes, "rural populations continue to be displaced from their lands and to fall victim to state and non-state violence." Overall, drug wars in the Americas have disproportionately impacted the poorest sectors of the population. This phenomenon contributes to the creation of increasingly stratified and unequal societies.

Paley does an incredible job explaining the complexities of the hemispheric dilemmas that have brought death and destruction, while benefiting corporate interests. She has done exhaustive field research in key places that exemplify the basic dynamics of drug wars in the Americas. *Drug War Capitalism* is a provocative, comprehensive, and very well documented analysis of the big picture of the war on drugs in this hemisphere. By evaluating specific violent events in four crucial countries—Colombia, Mexico, Guatemala, and Honduras—and supporting her assertions with interesting testimonies of numerous actors/victims/politicians and a variety of US government reports and other official documents, Paley tells a tale of modern post–Cold War capitalism, that is, a story of drug war capitalism.

This book is an antidote to the official discourse and confusing spot news reports on the drug war. As Bertrand Russell states in *Freedom in Society*: "Advocates of capitalism are very apt to appeal to the sacred principles of liberty, which are embodied in one maxim: The fortunate must not be restrained in the exercise of tyranny over the unfortunate."[4] *Drug War Capitalism* is an important attempt at revealing that tyranny at work.

CHAPTER I

DRUG WAR CAPITALISM

NOT long ago, I sat in the only restaurant in Santo Domingo—a nearly empty ranch house with three plastic tables, two fridges full of cold soft drinks and beer, and a rack of homemade chorizo hanging in the sun. Dogs slept in scraps of shade, and across the street an old man with his shirt slung over his shoulder sat silently and watched as every now and then a motorcycle went by, occasionally a large tractor-trailer. For these drivers, Santo Domingo is one more nondescript village on their route across Colombia's northern prairies. Beside the restaurant stands a curving stone monument in memory of the people killed by the Colombian Air Force in December 1998.

On December 12, 1998, an airborne chase led a number of army helicopters to this village of about 200 people, part of the municipality of Tame, in Arauca, Colombia. Local festivities were under way, but few ended up sleeping peacefully that night as flyovers, explosions, and gunfire kept people awake and fearful. Eventually the activity overhead stopped, but resumed around 5 a.m. As the noise picked up, locals began to assemble at the drugstore, right across the street from the restaurant where I would sit fifteen years later.

Maria Antonia Reyes Beltran lived in a palm-roofed house near the drugstore, and she remembers hearing the flyovers and trying to convince her elderly neighbors to evacuate, but they had previously been displaced and refused to budge. Reyes Beltran left her house and walked toward the meeting place. At 10:02 a.m., a WWII–era cluster bomb, made up of six fragmentation grenades, was dropped from a helicopter onto the road where community members were gathered. Seventeen people were killed as they huddled for protection in the drugstore. Twenty-seven others, including fifteen children, were injured. "It was almost ten, we were listening to the radio when the helicopter went over. The people who were on the edge of the highway were trying to signal us that something had been thrown from the helicopter, but we didn't know what it was. It was bright. It turns out that was the bomb that killed the people," she said in an interview conducted in the community's schoolhouse, less than 200 meters from the site of the bombing. "I was leaning against some boards; one of the pieces of shrapnel passed very close—it almost killed me. The people there were yelling, 'Help! Help!'"

As community members tried to evacuate the injured, above, the pilots of the Skymaster plane insisted that there were guerrillas among them, and so the helicopters continued to fire on the wounded.[1] "The helicopter kept shooting, way up the highway, it kept shooting. Many, many people were killed," Reyes Beltran told me. All of the survivors were displaced from Santo Domingo, taking shelter in a nearby school until the fifth of January, when they ventured back to the town and tried to start again.

Earlier on the morning of the bombing, two US citizens had met with members of the Colombian military inside the facilities of Occidental Petroleum's Caño Limón project, where they planned the attack. Barbaro José Orta and Charlie Denny were working for a private US security company called AirScan Inc, which Occidental had contracted to provide security from guerrilla attacks along the pipeline. Regardless of their mandate, the two men ended up leading a fleet of five Colombian military helicopters to Santo Domingo, over a hundred kilometers from Occidental's facilities. At 6:53 a.m., one of the two Americans got on the military radio from the Skymaster plane they were piloting, and suggested that guerrillas had infiltrated the population who were now gathering to take shelter from the bombing. He said, "I have a group of persons here, but they are all civilians, I cannot see any [...] all these people appear to be civilians here. They changed, they all changed clothes, that is the problem we have here, these guys have gone into the house and changed clothes."[2]

According to the court testimony of one of the Colombian crew members, the Skymaster belonged to Occidental Petroleum (Oxy). At that time, Oxy was funding the Colombian military to the tune of $750,000 in cash and in-kind, and "it supplied, directly or through contractors, troop transportation, planning facilities and fuel to Colombian military aircraft, including the helicopter crew accused of dropping the bomb."[3] Though supposedly restricted to doing pipeline surveillance, AirScan pilots and equipment were regularly used to help the Colombian Air Force hunt suspected guerrillas. "They frequently strayed from their missions to help us in operations against the guerrillas. The plane would go and check and verify [guerrilla] patrols and say, 'Hey, there are people here,'" one of the Colombians accused of participating in the massacre told the *LA Times* in 2002.[4] Following the bombings, ownership of the Skymaster aircrafts was transferred to the Colombian Air Force.[5]

After the bombings, the Colombian military claimed the dead were members of guerrilla forces—a story that didn't stick. Later, the military changed their story and said that it was in fact the guerrillas who had bombed Santo Domingo. Neither American on the Skymaster that day has faced charges or jail time in the United States. Some families of victims received reparations for their dead relatives, but people like Reyes Beltran, whose palm house later burned to the ground when an army helicopter dropped a flare, received nothing.

The Colombian government has never officially apologized to the community for the attack. Quite the opposite, in fact: over the past year, the Colombian Air Force began a new bombing campaign in the area. I interviewed nearly a dozen people from different areas of Santo Domingo, who came to the school cafeteria—an open room without walls or much other than cement tables and chairs—to tell their stories.

Daniel Zavala, a freckle-faced farmer with piercing green eyes and a traditional black-and-white straw hat, explained what happened to his neighbor in March 2013: "At my neighbor's house.... I'm not exaggerating, unfortunately he's not here.... But without word of a lie, a helicopter opened fire approximately fifty meters from his house; it literally rained lead. There were kids there—a family, he has a son who is around twelve years old and a daughter who is eight. It's incredible." As Zavala explained how flyovers traumatize children in the community, more and more community members arrived. Some suggested that I should visit one of the bombing sites, and community members discussed among themselves which one would be the most suitable. Finally, they decided to take me to an area that was bombed on December 7, 2013—a place called Lusitania.

I climbed on the back of a motorcycle, and three men and I went ten minutes down the highway, then turned onto a thin grassy trail, with rustic wood bridges and cows grazing on either side. After thirty minutes, we stopped so that they could show me the schoolhouse, a large palm hut without electricity or running water. We carried on for another twenty minutes until we arrived at Joel Armando Estrada's small house, which shelters seven children and five adults. When we pulled up, the boys were coloring and the younger kids were playing in the yard. Not a two-minute walk from the house into the jungle were two craters, each easily twenty meters wide and ten meters deep, evidence of the recent bombing. A large snake emerged from the bottom of one crater, which had since filled with water, and two boys took turns trying to kill it with a rock.

"It was four in the morning. We were sleeping when the planes came and bombed. All of my kids got nauseous because the explosions nearly made them burst, and the youngest one vomited," Armando Estrada told me, his hand on the shoulder of his youngest son. An hour and a half after the explosion, soldiers landed the helicopter, came into the house and went through everything. They asked Estrada where he had hidden guerrilla fighters—something the farmer, who cultivates bananas, yucca, and corn, said his family has never done. Miguel Otero, who lives with Estrada, told me that he was already awake when the bombing started, and that he looked out after the first one fell to see a sixty- to seventy-meter fireball less than 200 meters from the house. Moments later, a shower of shrapnel fell onto the roof and ricocheted off the house. Later, the children picked up hundreds of small round iron shells, and they showed me the fragments of the bombs they found in their yard. At least one of the shells penetrated the thin wall of the palm house, and many others lodged in trees near the family's home.

"You can imagine how we felt afterwards: totally psychologically ill. We've never lived through a situation like that, something so terrible," Otero said. "When the soldiers arrived, they were aggressive as usual, insulting us and asking us where the man was who was hiding inside the house. They arrived so angry, as if we were their targets. That's what it seemed like."

"Maybe they were chasing the guerrillas or other groups, but when we went to [the bombing site] we didn't see any traces of a dead human being, nothing, not even footprints of guerrillas or anything. We didn't see anything like that," said Otero, who sat across from me and fiddled with a piece of paper as he spoke. "We can't understand why they would bomb in this area where there's no one.... I don't know."

The possibility that oil exploration is going on in the lands surrounding Santo Domingo seems to others like the motivation behind the violence. "This is a policy of the government: to clear us off the territory that is ours, as *campesinos* and Indigenous peoples, because there are many Indigenous communities who have their lands taken away by war, by the terror that they instill in the communities to remove us from our territory so that they can come and extract natural resources," said Fernando Roa, a farmer who was elected vice president of Santo Domingo's communal action council. Roa and others who remain in the territory realize that staying is an act of resistance. "Our idea is to continue to live in our territory, and to struggle to defend our rights. We have the right to education, to health.... They only give us crumbs."

Conflicts and violence in Colombia, Mexico, and elsewhere often hold so much confusion, fear, and pain that it is difficult to step back and put events into an economic and political context. Hearing Roa utter these sentences while a breeze rustled through the school cafeteria reinforced, for me, the importance of critical research and writing on these conflicts. One motivation for this book is to bring these strains of analysis together in order to understand the violence in the context of struggles over territory, land, and resources. To learn of the ongoing humanitarian tragedy in Santo Domingo and hear Roa say that he and others believe the bombings are connected to oil was a crucial confirmation of how important it is to make these connections.

Through the devastating bombing in Santo Domingo in 1998 and the ongoing bombing campaigns, Colombia remains Washington's closest ally in the region. In the name of arming the state in its fight against drug cultivation and trafficking—as well as fighting leftist guerrillas—US aid to Colombia skyrocketed throughout the 2000s. But, as I shall explore in this book, rather than stopping the flow of drugs, funding the drug war has bolstered a war strategy that ensures transnational corporations access to resources through dispossession and terror. Through the Mérida Initiative and the Central America Regional Security Initiative, the United States sponsored the spread of Colombian-style war to Mexico and Central America. This book is not about infiltrating crime groups or trying to bring out the stories from inside the cartels; it isn't about reproducing the dominant narratives of the drug war or explaining which cartel does what where, since those tales change as quickly as the wind. Rather, it is about exposing the impacts of the drug war, a monumental task.

Drug War Capitalism emerges from a desire to consider other factors and motivations for the war on drugs, specifically the expansion of the capitalist system into new or previously inaccessible territories and social spaces. In addition to boosting US banks, propping up political campaigns, and feeding a profitable trade in arms, the imposition of drug war policies can benefit transnational oil and gas and mining companies, as well as other large corporations. There are other sectors that also enjoy benefits from the violence: the manufacturing and transportation industries, as well as a segment of the retail and commercial sector, specifically those represented by corporate players like Walmart, and real estate interests in parts of Mexico and the United States. The war on drugs is a long-term fix to capitalism's woes, combining terror with policymaking in a seasoned neoliberal mix, cracking open social worlds and territories once unavailable to globalized capitalism. This project is about re-thinking what is called the war on drugs: it isn't about prohibition or drug policy. Instead, it looks at how, in this war, terror is used against the populations in cities and rural areas, and how, parallel to this terror and resulting panic, policies that facilitate foreign direct investment and economic growth are implemented. This is drug war capitalism. Pillage, profit, and plunder have been mainstays of war since pre-colonial times, but there is little focus on the role of finance and economics in war. Mats Berdal and David M. Malone write that, in research and literature on the generation and maintenance of conflicts, there is little systematic attention paid to economic interests.[6] In the case of the war on drugs, a reading of the conflict that includes economic analysis has generally been reserved for speculation as to the profits of drug traffickers and reportage on cash laundering in major banks. But as Malone and Berdal state, in order to properly understand wars today, "The *role of the international private sector*, particularly that of extractive industries (petroleum, mining), is key."[7]

The driving impulse of this project is to create a more useful framework through which we can make sense of the drug war south of the US-Mexico border, where violence stems from state militarization and drug cartels, which I also refer to as paramilitary groups. One key element in understanding how drug wars strengthen irregular armed groups is that these groups may begin providing drug traffickers with protection, but later will work for whoever can pay them. At one moment in time they could be on the payroll of drug traffickers, at another, paid by elites looking for executors of extrajudicial repression. These elites could include politicians fighting among themselves for political power, or landowners wishing to move poor people off their lands. But as is documented in this book, structural factors are at play, by which irregular armed groups are allowed near total impunity to carry out extortion and acts of terror among populations when those acts tend toward benefiting transnational capitalism or US foreign policy.

In Mexico, the Zetas have led the path away from the dictionary definition of "cartel," from the old Italian *cartels*, or card, first used to refer to a coalition between Conservative and National parties in Germany in 1887. Later, cartel came to mean "an association of manufacturers or suppliers with the purpose of maintaining prices at a high level and restricting competition: *the Colombian drug cartels*."[8] Cartels do not exist solely to maintain high prices, though that doesn't stop the constant use of the word. In the case of Mexico, groups including the Zetas are known as cartels, though their purpose goes far beyond trafficking in drugs; they are also active in extortion (of businesses and migrants), kidnapping, massacres, controlling distributors of pirated goods, and so on. The Zetas are a paramilitary group, an armed organization officially outside of state command, financed at least in part by direct proceeds from narcotics trafficking, but with deep roots in state military structures.

The notion that there is a clear division between state forces and crime groups—that corruption and collaboration are the work of a few bad apples—is a hegemonic idea promoted by nation-states and the mainstream media. Undoing this binary means learning from the people whose lives have been directly affected by armed groups whose activity is carried out with impunity. Impunity is not the result of a weak or deficient state, but rather it is actively provided to the gamut of armed groups who commit crimes and acts of terror against citizens, migrants, and the poor. The provision of impunity to armed actors who are politically aligned with capitalism is part of a modern nation state's *raison d'etre*.

Mexican peace activist Javier Sicilia, whose son was murdered in 2011, warns against framing events in Mexico as cops versus cartels. "There is a war between the state and parallel states," he said in a 2014 interview in Mexico City. "Until we understand that organized crime is not made up of criminals, but rather that it is cells of a parallel state, with firepower, with the capacity to subjugate, and some with social bases, and if we don't see that this is a struggle for territory and for control of citizen life, we will not understand the problem." I asked Francisco Chavira, an activist and educator based in Reynosa, Tamaulipas, to explain how the narco-war interacts with the state in Mexico. "In my point of view, the true criminal, the true capo in Mexico is the president of the republic; the governors are the same in each of their state, and the *jefes de plaza* are the mayors," he said. "They all got where they are with financing from illicit sources. They protect each other; they are the same thing."

A key means through which globalized capitalism can penetrate new territories and social worlds is through the use of terror against the population. The *New Oxford American Dictionary*'s primary definition of terror is "extreme fear: the use of such fear to intimidate people, esp. for political reasons; terrorism." Mass killings and the public display of bodies is one example of a terror technique, practiced over centuries, by government and irregular forces, often in tandem with the imposition of political and economic regimes. Terror plays a specific role in ensuring control over the population. "In all its forms, terror was designed to shatter the human spirit. Whether in London at the birth of capitalism or in Haiti today, terror infects the collective imagination, generating an assortment of demons and monsters."[9] Whether it is bodies hung over busy thoroughfares or cut into pieces and dumped one on top of another on a highway, or explosions and massacres leaving dozens of civilians dead or injured, Mexico has seen an unprecedented array of bone-chilling episodes since former President Felipe Calderón launched the drug war in December 2006.[10]

Terror creates fertile ground for new forms of social control. It also impacts mobility—understood as peoples' ability to move freely on their own will—which is restricted by increasing border surveillance and police and military checkpoints, as well as by the fear generated through mass murders of bus passengers, shootouts on major roadways, and disappearances that occur while the victim is traveling. Reduced mobility is one of the first impacts that terror has on the affected population. Meanwhile, forced migration and involuntary displacement increase as the transition to a more repressive society claims victims and threatens survivors.

These drastic elements of repression and terror provide the basis for the continuation and intensification of capitalist expansion into Mexico and Central and Latin America. States and transnational capital take recourse in repression through terror in attempt to dispossess people from their communal lands and territories throughout the Americas and the world. As Uruguayan social theorist Raúl Zibechi notes, "It will be difficult for capitalism to survive if it fails to consolidate new forms of control and subjugation."[11] According to geographer David Harvey, the expansion of capitalism depends on accumulation through dispossession,[12] which can include forcible displacement, the privatization of public or communally held lands, the suppression of Indigenous forms of production and consumption, and the use of credit and debt in order to facilitate accumulation by dispossession, among others.[13] All of these things are occurring in Mexico today, as in other countries, and, as we shall see throughout this book, the war on drugs is contributing to the acceleration of many of these processes.

Deploying the army to fight an internal enemy, in this case drug traffickers, represents a crucial shift to allow a formally democratic state to justify soldiers attacking civilians on home soil by claiming those civilians are criminals.

History teaches us that so-called anti-drugs training and spending can be used for a variety of purposes. For his book on Colombia, Doug Stokes interviewed former US Special Forces trainer Stan Goff, who was unusually candid about what counter-narcotics training meant to him. "You were told, and the American public was being told, if they were told anything at all, that this was counter-narcotics training. The training I conducted was anything but that. It was pretty much updated Vietnam-style counter-insurgency doctrines. We were advised that this is what we would do, and we were further advised to *refer* to it as counter-narcotics training, should anyone ask. It was extremely clear to us that the counter-narcotics thing was an official cover story."[14] Republican senator John McCain came out and said as much himself in a 2002 speech: "To the President's credit, American policy has dispensed with the illusion that the Colombian government is fighting two separate wars, one against drug trafficking and another against domestic terrorists. The democratic government of Colombia has long insisted that it is the nexus of terrorists involved in the drug trade that threatens Colombian society. American policy now recognizes that reality, and abandons any fictional distinctions between counter-narcotic and counter-insurgency operations," he said.[15]

The creation of anti-drug police forces and army units and spending on the drug war must be understood within the context of global capitalism and global warfare. In this context, the acquisition of territory and resources, including increased control over social worlds and labor power, is a crucial motivating factor. Drug war discourses promoted by states and reported by mainstream media provide an efficient smokescreen, provoking moral panic in the population, which can also calcify and exaggerate divisions among communities (like between those who are and who are not involved in illicit activities), and impact relationships down to the level of neighborhoods, community groups, and *campesino* (peasant farmer) organizations. We know the quantity of drugs trafficked to the United States did not decrease significantly because of Plan Colombia. I argue though that this doesn't indicate a failure of the war, because the Plan Colombia model has more to do with improving the conditions for foreign direct investment and encouraging the expansion of capitalism than it does with stemming the flow of drugs.

When it comes to repression and terror in Mexico, the tactics employed by the state coercive apparatus go far beyond the Colombia experience, and are nourished by generations of US and other imperial warfare around the world.[16] In this context, I believe the experiences of US-backed counterinsurgency wars in Central America, and in Guatemala in particular, are of great importance in understanding what is happening in Mexico and the region today. Though rarely considered linked, these conflicts must be considered part of a repressive memory that has been activated in order to carry out the ongoing war on drugs in Mexico, Central America, and elsewhere. Some of the same repressive forces and the techniques used against populations in Central America in the 1980s are again being activated in the context of the drug war. This is a phenomenon that exists on a global level. As Laleh Khalili argues in her work on Palestine and counterinsurgency, "Officials and foot soldiers, technologies of control, and resources travel not only between colonies and metropoles but also between different colonies of the same colonial power and between different colonial metropoles, whereby bureaucrats and military elites actively study and borrow each other's techniques and advise one another on effective ruling practices."[17]

There are certain lines of continuity between the wars (including genocide) in Central America in the 1970s, '80s, and '90s and Mexico today. For example, grenades used by the Zetas in attacks in Mexico have been traced back to the 1980s, when they were sold to El Salvador's military by the United States.[18] Another thread connecting the thirty-six-year war in Guatemala to today is the Kaibiles, the country's elite special forces, whose members were responsible for horrific massacres then, and who today are active both as an elite government force and as members of criminal groups. It was a former Kaibil who was accused of directing the single most violent drug trafficking-related act in Guatemala. Hugo Gómez Vásquez was accused of supervising the massacre in Finca Los Cocos, Petén, in May 2011, when twenty seven farm workers were killed, allegedly as part of a land dispute between Otto Salguero, a local landowner, and the Zetas.[19] In addition to these concrete examples, many of the practices of terror used by armies such as Guatemala's have resurfaced in Mexico and Central America at the hands of criminal groups. In today's war, the "war on drugs," violence deployed against civilians—especially migrants and the poor—comes from official, uniformed troops, as well as from irregular forces, including drug cartels or paramilitary groups. And in Colombia, the model country for this type of warfare, it comes from the sky, as the air force continues to rain bombs on peasants from above.

Drug War Capitalism in Mexico

"This is what the beginning of neoliberalism felt like," said Raquel Gutiérrez when I interviewed her in 2012, reflecting on what it is like to try and understand the ongoing war in Mexico. Now a professor at the Autonomous University of Puebla, Gutiérrez was an underground militant in Bolivia in the mid-'80s when the first neoliberal policies took effect there, pauperizing the working class. It's been ten years since she's returned to Mexico. We're talking at the table in her downtown apartment. Raquel pauses and drags on a cigarette, as if trying to remember a language she's forgotten. It doesn't come. Then she asks me if I've read Naomi Klein's book *The Shock Doctrine*. I nod. Silence. "The thing is, in Mexico, the shocks didn't work," she says. It's not that there was a shortage of shocks, which Klein describes as ranging from natural disasters to economic crises that are exploited in order to deepen the neoliberal order. In *The Shock Doctrine*, Klein writes, "The most dramatic case to date came in 1994, the year after Yeltsin's coup, when Mexico's economy suffered a major meltdown known as the Tequila Crisis: the terms of the U.S. bailout demanded rapid-fire privatizations, and Forbes announced that the process had minted twenty-three new billionaires.... It also cracked Mexico open to unprecedented foreign ownership: in 1990, only one of Mexico's banks was foreign owned, but 'by 2000 twenty-four out of thirty were in foreign hands.'"[20] The impacts of these policies were felt especially harshly in rural areas. "These neoliberal policies ushered in a new era of nontraditional production of export fruits and vegetables, new forms of land control, realignment of labor relations under contract farming, and substantial out-migration by uncompetitive small-scale campesinos."[21]

The first wave of neoliberal economic policies was introduced in the form of structural adjustment programs. These programs came at the end of "the Mexican Miracle," a period of steady economic growth, import substitution industrialization, and high oil prices.

"From 1980 to 1991, Mexico received thirteen structural adjustment loans from the World Bank, more than any other country," wrote Tom Barry in his 1995 book *Zapata's Revenge.* "It also signed six agreements with the IMF, all of which brought increased pressure to liberalize trade and investment."[22] In the 1980s, sometimes called Mexico's "lost decade," oil prices collapsed along with the peso. "From over a thousand state enterprises in 1983, the Mexican state owned around two hundred by 1993.... In 1991, the Mexican program brought in more money to government coffers (US$9.4 billion) than all other sales of public companies in Latin America combined."[23] By 1988, the Mexican economy was already considered one of the most open to foreign investment in the world.[24] Many of the most important privatizations happened during the presidency of Carlos Salinas de Gortari, who was elected, in 1988, in what is widely believed to have been a fraudulent election. Mexico did go through a series of what Klein calls shocks, and some sectors (like banking and telephony) were thoroughly privatized. Still, at the outset of the drug war in Mexico, large corporations like the Comisión Federal de Electricidad (CFE) and Petroleos Mexicanos (Pemex)—the seventeenth-largest oil company in the world by oil reserves,[25] and by other counts the eighth-largest[26]—remained firmly in government hands; peasant and Indigenous communities continued to exercise communal title over lands rich in resources; a large middle class owned small businesses; and the richest Mexican families kept control over lucrative sectors of the economy. Mexican investors were favored in the privatizations that took place during Salinas's term, coming as they did before the North America Free Trade Agreement (NAFTA) was signed.[27] According to the US State Department, Mexico's ten richest families "are not the only obstacle[s] to improving competition in the Mexican economy."[28] Though weakened by constitutional amendments made by Salinas before NAFTA came into effect, communal landholder organizations, including *ejidos* and *comunidades índigenas*, have not been totally undone by neoliberal reforms. By the end of 1994, Mexico had signed on to the North America Free Trade Agreement, witnessed the Zapatista uprising, and undergone another major currency devaluation, but by the turn of the twenty-first century, Mexico's territory and economy still weren't fully open to foreign investors. In 2000, Vicente Fox of the National Action Party (PAN) was elected president, interrupting the Institutional Revolutionary Party's (PRI) seventy-one years of rule, and some say, returning democracy to Mexico.

But there is more than not-yet-privatized corporations that make Mexico interesting to transnational capital: take Mexico's strategic geographical location, for example. The Mexico-US border spans nearly 2,000 miles, a line that runs from Pacific to Atlantic, from Tijuana–San Diego to Juarez–El Paso and Brownsville–Matamoros. Along some stretches, the border is fenced, in other places the unforgiving desert polices it.[29] The US border with Mexico can and should be considered a valuable economic resource; low-cost labor on the south side of the border, within spitting distance of the United States, is a winning combination as transportation costs are also reduced. As such, Mexico is becoming an increasingly significant player in US and global manufacturing. For example, in the automobile sector, located along the border as well as in the country's interior, "Mexico is becoming the export hub for the Americas—not only North America but also South America," according to Nissan CEO Carlos Ghosn.[30]

One afternoon while driving through the border city of Nuevo Laredo, a local activist pointed out an overpass and mentioned that bodies had been hung over it more than once. I remembered the site from photos that appeared online, but there was one big difference seeing it in person: behind where the photograph was taken, a Sony factory dominates the block, with Japanese, US, and Mexican flags hoisted at the entrance. It seemed to me a crucial bit of context that Sony operates a factory literally a stone's throw from where human bodies have been publicly displayed. Knowing that the overpass isn't in some abandoned part of town, but rather is meters away from a bustling assembly plant, means knowing that the workers coming in and out of the factory at dawn, when bodies tend to be hung, would all have witnessed these gruesome scenes. As we shall see later on, while the violence in Mexico has generally not deeply impacted the owners of multinational corporations, it does impact the workers. These workers' decisions of whether or not to carry on working in hostile environments, where terror is used against residents, can impact the labor supply available to the assembly industry. According to a 2010 report by the Norwegian Refugee Council's Internal Displacement Monitoring Centre, in Juárez alone "estimates place the number of people who have fled their homes at around 230,000. Roughly half of those are thought to have crossed into the United States, which would leave about 115,000 people living as internally displaced people (IDPs)."[31] The fact that violence can impact the size of the labor pool in these areas means that it can also prevent labor organizing, which keeps wages depressed along the border—both important factors in determining the future of a vital sector of the US economy.

Then there are the natural resources. Mexico has only recently been opened up to modern mining. According to data from the Mexican government, Mexico produced about twenty-two tons of gold in 2001, and ten years later, it produced eighty-four tons, most of which was extracted by Canadian mining companies. Silver production doubled over the same period. According to Mexico's National Chamber of Mines, Mexico is the fourth destination worldwide for mining investment, after Canada, Australia, and the United States. Looked at in terms of the US government's more general foreign-policy goals, the condition of Mexico's large economy, driven by a handful of profitable, state-owned corporations, and the country's mineral-rich territory (much of which remains communally owned by peasant farmers) means there are attractive money-making opportunities to be had. William I. Robinson, author of *A Theory of Global Capitalism* among other books, explained the overarching goal of US foreign policy during an interview in 2010: "All the evidence shows us that what the US is doing is playing the lead role in organizing a new globalist capitalist system, a new epoch of global capitalism." According to Robinson, world capitalism was a system in which circuits of production existed first within and later between nations. Global capitalism, which is the current system, consists of transnational circuits of production and trade, in which manufacturing takes place across nations rather than within them. As an example, under world capitalism, clothes were sewn in Mexico from fabric made of Mexican-grown cotton, and under global capitalism, fabric is imported, clothing is partially assembled in Mexico and exported for completion in the US.

In his 1996 book *Promoting Polyarchy*, Robinson explains that "political and economic power tends to gravitate towards new groups linked to the global economy, either directly or indirectly through reorganized local state apparatuses which function as 'transmission belts' for transnational interests. In every region of the world, in both North and South, from Eastern Europe to Latin America, states, economies and political processes are becoming transnationalized and integrated under the guidance of this new elite."[32] Elsewhere, he notes that "'going global' allowed capital to shake off the constraints that nation-state capitalism had placed on accumulation and break free of the class compromises and concessions that had been imposed by working and popular classes and by national governments in the preceding epoch."[33] In Mexico, as we have seen, many of these compromises and concessions survived the imposition of NAFTA and the onset of neoliberalism into the twenty-first century.

In Mexico, something more than an economic shock was in order: a comprehensive strategy proven to increase foreign direct investment was needed. Among other things, this strategy had to ensure that local police and the army, and eventually the entire legal system, would operate according to US standards. A similar strategy had already been developed via Plan Colombia—a carefully planned, US-backed war on drugs. For example, over the past years in Mexico, the privatization of large state companies has taken place alongside attacks on the working population along the US-Mexico border and the displacement and murders of communal and small landholders. The drug war can be understood as forming the basis of a permanent shock in Mexico.

In December 2006, immediately after he was inaugurated, President Felipe Calderón launched a new phase of the war on drug cartels and organized crime in Mexico. It was a high point in social mobilization in Mexico City and throughout the country, as Calderón's inauguration took place amidst massive protests against election fraud, which brought over two million people, including left-wing candidate Andrés Manuel López Obrador, into the streets of the capital. Also that year, the Zapatistas carried out their Otra Campaña, consulting with Mexicans around the country from below and to the left. "There was also the Popular Revolutionary Army [EPR], there were movements like that in Atenco, which was repressed and which provoked important solidarity actions, and also between June and November 2006 in Oaxaca an important social movement against then governor Ulises Ruíz rose up," said Carlos Fazio, a professor at the Autonomous University of Mexico City (UACM). "In 2006 we could say that there were large mass protests by systemic and anti-systemic social forces, by people who wanted change."

Since 2006, social movements have not mobilized with such a vengeance, and the violence and terror in Mexico have instead taken center stage. The social costs of the drug war have been enormous: one of the few independent counts, carried out by Molly Molloy, a librarian at New Mexico State University, affirms that since December 2006, over 153,000 people have been murdered in Mexico.[34] At a March 2012 press conference, US Secretary of Defense Leon Panetta stated that the violence was tremendous, and that Mexican officials had told him there were 150,000 people dead because of drug violence.[35] The body count reported in the mainstream media is much lower, often referring to 60,000 dead as a result of drug war violence.[36] This is a misleading figure since it is known that less than 5 percent of all crimes in Mexico are investigated. As well, some bodies have been secretly disposed of in mass graves, while others are dissolved in chemicals; these bodies have not made it to the morgues to be counted. The number of murders increased sharply when US military aid came online—rising from 10,452 to over 25,000 in 2010 and over 27,000 in 2011.[37] Though the media fanfare about the war on drugs diminished when President Enrique Peña Nieto began his term in December 2012, reports show that in 2013, over 21,000 people were murdered in Mexico.[38]

In addition to the dead, one official count pegs the number of disappeared in Mexico at 42,300.[39] According to a survey carried out by the National Statistics Institute (INEGI), 105,682 kidnappings took place in 2012, and less than 2 percent of kidnappings were reported to officials that year.[40] Not included in these numbers are the kidnappings of migrants transiting through Mexico; from September 2008 to February 2009, Mexico's National Human Rights Commission (CNDH) recorded 9,758 such kidnappings.[41] Activists estimate the number of disappeared non-citizen migrants in Mexico since 2006 could be over 70,000.[42] In Mexico the majority of the dead are civilians, and their assassins are often members of state forces, but we are told over and over again that the dead in this war are criminals. We are told that the war on drugs is about in-fighting between the cartels that transport narcotics from Colombia through Central America and Mexico to the United States. Few analyses take a more in-depth look at how this violence interacts with capitalism, state power, and resource extraction. That is exactly what *Drug War Capitalism* proposes to do.

In Mexico, states along the US border, like Baja California Norte, Sinaloa, Chihuahua, Coahuila, Nuevo Leon, and Tamaulipas, have been hard hit by the war on drugs. Some non-border states like Veracruz, Guerrero, and Michoacán have also been affected by the violence, which has touched every state in the country to some extent. In nationwide polling in 2011 and 2010, over 60 percent of respondents polled by Mexico's national statistics agency felt that public security was worse or much worse than twelve months before, and a minority felt it was the same or better.[43]

The ratcheting up of conflict linked to what we are led to believe is inter-cartel violence and a state-led assault on drug trafficking goes beyond Mexico; violence is also on the rise in Central America, where insecurity reigns. Massacres linked to drug trafficking have shaken Guatemala in recent years, and in 2011, Honduras had the highest murder rate in the world.[44] The players responsible for the violence in parts of Mexico and Central America are not necessarily consistent, nor are their methods, which vary depending on the region and the environment. In Central America, unlike Mexico, the United States openly uses its own forces in the field, as evidenced by DEA activities in Honduras in the spring of 2012 and the deployment of US marines to Guatemala later that year. Seven military bases were designated throughout Colombia for use by US troops following Plan Colombia. Some say this could be part a plan to destabilize left-led countries in the region, like Venezuela, Bolivia, and Ecuador.

The overall picture is this: drugs, and particularly cocaine, are produced in Colombia (as well as Bolivia and Peru) and shipped north, often using small planes and go-fast boats. Trafficking organizations must cooperate with at least a segment of local authorities in each country they transit, paying bribes so that their product can cross borders and avoid impoundment. The state and state security forces are not a monolithic enterprise—while some politicians and judges are attempting to curb corruption, others are deeply involved in facilitating narcotrafficking, money laundering, and other sectors of the illicit economy. Similarly, in some cases units of the army or marines have faced off against police, who themselves are involved in drug trafficking. Major drug trafficking routes can only exist in places where sufficient cooperation with authorities has been achieved. When official cooperation ends or is interrupted, violence results. A 2012 paper found that in municipalities where Felipe Calderón's National Action Party defeated the PRI in 2007 and 2008 elections by a close margin, the probability of drug-related homicides increased by 8.4 percent. According to the study, "Analysis using information on the industrial organization of trafficking suggests that the violence reflects rival traffickers' attempts to wrest control of territories after crackdowns initiated by PAN mayors have weakened the incumbent traffickers."[45] Empirical evidence indicates that the election of the PAN Party in municipalities caused violence to increase, though the idea of a crackdown by PAN mayors reveals only one facet of the impacts of the anti-drugs policy in place since 2006. That said, we lack sufficient information to clearly understand the configuration of alternative trafficking networks operating with the support and complicity of the PAN, including on a local level. The interruption of drug trafficking does not signify cutting off the flow, rather, it leads to the diversion of routes elsewhere.

A similar logic applies to cultivation: in the 1990s crop eradication programs pushed coca growing for cocaine production from Bolivia and Peru into Colombia. The next generation of eradication programs in Colombia pushed coca growing back into Peru and Bolivia.[46] Through it all, the overall amount of cocaine produced was virtually unchanged. What this means is that both crop eradication and the interruption of drug trafficking effectively divert those practices into other regions. In addition to ensuring the continued supply of narcotics to the United States and other markets, the diversion of trafficking and production allows the militarization of the newly used regions, under the pretext of fighting the drug war.

Throughout the 1980s and until the mid-1990s, the dominant media and government narratives held that Colombian drug cartels, the top-down organizations with high-level government connections and high-profile leaders like Pablo Escobar, were responsible for much of the drug running. But even then, for those involved in the trade, it was apparent that the boogeyman figure of the cartel was being exaggerated for public consumption. Gustavo Salazar, who worked as an attorney to Medellín drug runners in Colombia, told journalist Ioan Grillo, "Cartels don't exist. What you have is a collection of drug traffickers. Sometimes, they work together, and sometimes they don't. American prosecutors just call them cartels to make it easier to make their cases. It is all part of the game."[47] Following the murder of Escobar in the mid-'90s, the organizations once portrayed as cartels were presented as having splintered into smaller groups that kept the cocaine flowing to the United States.

Mexico's oldest drug trafficking groups, formerly known as the "big four" (Juárez, Gulf, Sinaloa, and Tijuana) have splintered to varying degrees as a result of the drug war, resulting in what are estimated to be between sixty and eighty drug trafficking groups.[48] In addition, the Zetas, which splintered from the Gulf Cartel in 2010, are said to have established a presence through Mexico and Guatemala, often working in tandem with local and regional state security forces and government officials.[49] While the armed actors vary from place to place, it has long been established that the lines between the state and criminal groups are murky, and that each empowers the other. There are defecting soldiers and police, like those who formed the Zetas, and there's the phenomenon of double dipping—police receiving paychecks from criminal organizations and the state simultaneously. In some places, entire police corps has been known to double dip.[50] Sometimes those dressed up as police are actually soldiers or criminals, and military men are increasingly at the head of city police outfits, as was Colonel Julián Leyzaola Pérez previously in Tijuana and today in Juárez. There are also security corporations and private mercenaries, whose members are sometimes identifiable by their jackets, boots, and vehicles. And there are also community police, armed in defense of their (often Indigenous) communities through the blessing of local authorities, and self-defense groups, which are often more spontaneously formed groups in rural areas. Telling one from the other (from the other, from the other) in this war, and knowing who exactly is fighting whom, is difficult and dangerous.

The state role in drug trafficking and illegal activity runs deep and is complex. "It is known that it is not possible to move tons of cocaine, launder thousands of millions of dollars, maintain an organization with hundreds of armed individuals operating clandestinely, without a system of political and police protection, without growing alliances with the productive and financial apparatus," wrote Yolanda Figueroa, a journalist who wrote the seminal history of the Gulf Cartel in 1996.[51] Indeed, there is no reason to assume a clear division between state forces and cartels. Throughout this text I refer to what official discourse calls drug cartels using various terms, including paramilitary groups, organized crime groups, and cartels. The actions of so-called cartels can strengthen state control, and often consist of ex-special forces or state troops, and can thus be considered paramilitary groups. Another reason I don't always use the term "drug cartels" is that these groups in Mexico are responsible for carrying out actions that have little or nothing to do with drug trafficking, including attacks and extortion against civilians, migrants, journalists, and activists.

The term "war on drugs" is definitely problematic, and I debated using other terms for describing what's called the drug war, since as I argue throughout this book it is very clearly a war against people, waged with far wider interests than controlling substances. But in the end, I decided to stick with the familiar "drug war," so as to ensure the text is accessible and understandable for people who may only read a section at a time. The term "drug war" is the most visceral shorthand for what is taking place vis à vis US policies carried out in the name of stopping the flow of narcotics. In 2009, the *Wall Street Journal* ran a story headlined "White House Czar Calls for End to 'War on Drugs.'"

The story goes on to explain that the Obama administration has attempted to distance itself from the concept of the drug war. "Regardless of how you try to explain to people it's a 'war on drugs' or a 'war on a product,' people see a war as a war on them," said Gil Kerlikowske, who was then the US drug czar. "We're not at war with people in this country."[52] Indeed, people living through the impacts of the war on drugs in the US and elsewhere understand that it is a war on them and their communities. As for Kerlikowske's clarification that the US government is not at war with its own people, a maxim from reporter Claud Cockburn comes to mind: "Never believe anything until it's officially denied." For these reasons, and for accessibility and readability, I use the term war on drugs to describe these US-led policies, and drug war capitalism to underscore the connections between these policies and the economic interests of the powerful.

The Mérida Initiative, from Talk to Action

One Friday in September 2006, just after his election as president, Felipe Calderón and his wife invited Antonio Garza, then US ambassador to Mexico, and his wife over for dinner. At some point in the evening, Calderón told the ambassador that improving security would be a key part of his administration. When Garza recapped his evening to State Department bosses, he included Calderón's comment, to which, according to his own notes, the ambassador replied: "Gains on competitiveness, education, and employment could be quickly overshadowed by narcotics-related organized crime." To jump-start Mexico's economy, "foreigners and Mexicans alike had to be reassured that the rule of law would prevail."[53] What became the Mérida Initiative was first discussed between President George W. Bush and his homologue Felipe Calderón in Mérida, Yucatan, in the spring of 2007. The Mérida Initiative was crafted in secret negotiations, which took place the following summer. "These negotiations were not public, and Members of both the U.S. and Mexican Congresses reportedly have expressed frustration that they were not involved in the discussions."[54] The US State Department openly touts the success of Plan Colombia as an important factor in the creation of the Mérida Initiative, the Central America Regional Security Initiative and other similar plans. "We know from the work that the United States has supported in Colombia and now in Mexico that good leadership, proactive investments, and committed partnerships can turn the tide," Hillary Clinton told delegates to the Central America Security Conference in Guatemala City in 2011.

As soon as Felipe Calderón was sworn in as Mexico's president in December 2006, he announced that he would crack down on the drug trade. Less than a year later, Mexico announced the Mérida Initiative, a bilateral anti-narcotics initiative funded by the United States and Mexico. Critics immediately began calling the agreement Plan Mexico, after its predecessor, Plan Colombia, which ended in 2006. In 2007, the United States shifted its weight behind the war on drugs from Colombia to Mexico, Central America, and the Caribbean. The drug war in Mexico has some features that set it apart from Colombia, the most important of which is a shared physical border with the United States. A related dynamic of the drug war in Mexico, not present in Colombia, is the targeting of non-status migrants (mostly from Central America) as part of the conflict. The spike in attacks against and murders of migrants in Mexico has accompanied the creation of countrywide structures of paramilitary control, particularly by Los Zetas. The paramilitarization in Mexico differs from that in Colombia because of distinct historical, territorial, political, and economic roots of paramilitary and resistance forces. Paramilitaries have long existed throughout parts of Mexico with militant social movements, but the phenomenon has never been as widespread as it is today. Mexico's guerrilla movements have historically been much smaller and more dispersed than those in Colombia, in part because of land tenure, which has generally been more equitable in Mexico than in Colombia. On the economic front, Mexico's gross domestic product in 2010 was more than 3.5 times larger than Colombia's, and Mexico's economy is far more complex.[55] Despite the differences, there are important drug war precedents, first set in Colombia, now being applied in Mexico.

From a critical perspective, it is possible to understand the Mérida Initiative and the activity it has inspired within Mexico as consisting of three primary elements: legal and policy reforms, militarization, and paramilitarization. The formation and strengthening of armed groups by criminal organizations as a response to state militarization of trafficking routes is the third effect of the Mérida Initiative that can also prove beneficial to the expansion of capitalism.

The Mérida Initiative is the primary means through which drug war capitalism, as developed in Colombia and applied in Mexico, is enshrined bilaterally between the US and Mexico. As US and Mexican security cooperation (and spending) increased, violence spiked and violent incidents spread throughout Mexico, and the body count began to rise. According to Shannon O'Neill from the Council on Foreign Relations, "When the Mérida Initiative was signed in 2007, there were just over two thousand drug-related homicides annually; by 2012, the number escalated to more than twelve thousand. Violence also spread from roughly 50 municipalities in 2007 (mostly along the border and in Sinaloa) to some 240 municipalities throughout Mexico in 2011, including the once-safe industrial center of Monterrey and cities such as Acapulco, Nuevo Laredo, and Torreon."[56] Reports in local and US media generally fail to connect US investment in the drug war to the increased violence, even though it is a trend that is observed in Colombia, Mexico, and elsewhere. The link between US-backed militarization of the drug trade and the shifting geography of criminal activity (and therefore violence) is one that the US government itself has acknowledged. "Just as Plan Colombia helped push the focus of criminal activity and presence north to Mexico, so has the impact of the Mérida Initiative pushed the same activities into Central America itself," said William Brownfield, assistant secretary of the US Bureau of International Narcotics and Law Enforcement Affairs (INL), in March of 2013.[57] A lanky, blue-eyed Texan, Brownfield is a career diplomat who served as the US ambassador to Colombia immediately following the end of Plan Colombia (2007–2010).

The initial justification of the Mérida Initiative was the need to "confront the violent transnational gangs and organized crime syndicates that plague the entire region and directly undermine U.S. security interests" by dismantling criminal organizations; strengthening air, maritime, and border controls; reforming the justice system; and diminishing gang activity while decreasing demand for drugs.[58] In 2010, the Mérida Initiative was retooled to consist of four pillars, which remain as follows: Disrupt Organized Criminal Groups, Institutionalize Reforms to Sustain Rule of Law and Respect for Human Rights, Create a 21st Century Border, and Build Strong and Resilient Communities. But as will be argued throughout this book, the US-funded war on drugs, and all of its justifications, is not far afield from the US-led war on terror, with which the US government claims to be liberating women and increasing democracy. Canadian sociologist Jasmin Hristov puts this particularly well, explaining, "The efforts of the elite to eliminate any challenges to the status quo have found expression in various politicoeconomic models throughout history. The features common to all of them have been the highly unequal socioeconomic structure consisting of armed force, repressive laws, and anti-subversive ideology, packaged under different names—the War on Communism, the War on Drugs, the War on Terror."[59] The war on drugs maintains a specific location within the "war-on" triumvirate described by Hristov, since its backers can utilize discourses related to health in justifying its existence, something that each of us can relate to on a personal level. The language of the War on Terror is not useful in regards to Mexico, which shares a 2,000-mile border with the United States, and with over thirty million people in the US being of Mexican origin.[60] Raising the specter of cartel and gang members is the Western Hemisphere strategy of the United States for painting entire societies as bringers of harm to US citizens. In the words of the Stop the Injunctions Coalition in California, "Culturally and politically the lines between 'terrorist,' 'insurgent,' 'immigrant,' and 'gang member' have been aggressively blurred."[61]

Debates around the war on drugs tend to consist of two contrasting positions: one that posits the prohibition of drugs (the US federal government's position) and the other, a more liberal position, which advocates for their decriminalization. While this is an important debate, it tends to obscure the militaristic nature of the war on drugs, keeping the drug war firmly within the realm of ideas, and avoiding a discussion of the war's legitimacy. But there is an urgent need to deepen our understandings of this kind of war; we must put it into the broader context of US and transnational interests in the hemisphere, and connect anti-drug policies to the territorial and social expansion of capitalism. In the same way anti-war movements successfully linked the US occupation of Iraq to oil, we ought to be able to make connections between the US-backed war on drugs in Mexico, and that country's natural resources, workforce, and population, as well as its strategic geographical location. "With Mexico and then more generally, there's an international criminal economy, which overlaps with the international above-ground or so-called legal economy.... The US has been able to, through the drug trafficking, and the excuse of trying to control *narcotrafico*, [pour] hundreds of millions, now billions of dollars into Mexican security, and Mexican armed forces, and it is changing the whole nature of Mexican society. Mexican society is being militarized," Dr. Robinson told me during an interview in 2010.[62] "And again it's being done in the name of combating drug trafficking, but ... part of the face of this global capitalism is increasingly militarized societies in function of social control when inequalities and misery become just so intense that there's no other way but through military and coercive means to maintain social control."

Part of the system of social control imposed by the drug war includes extortions in certain parts of the country, which force the closure of mom-n-pop businesses and funnel consumers into big box stores. The violence deployed by the state and justified with claims of combating trafficking can lead to urban and rural populations being displaced, clearing territory for corporations to extract natural resources, and impacting land ownership and property values. The drug war creates a context where members of resistance movements and journalists can be assassinated or disappeared under the pretext that they were involved in the drug trade. It also acts as a mechanism through which the number of (primarily Central American) migrants traveling through Mexico to the United States can be controlled through harsh policing of their movements carried out by crime groups. Finally it creates institutional (legal and social) conditions that guarantee protection for foreign direct investment, creating the necessary conditions for capitalist expansion and flexible accumulation. In addition to the violence that disproportionately impacts poor and working people and migrants, drug war militarization favors some segments of the elite more than others, provoking in some places an elite struggle for the ability to maintain the control and territoriality necessary to continue to participate in capital accumulation. "What is taking place in Mexican territories is part of a global process that transcends territoriality.... It is an expression, without a doubt, of an inter-capitalist struggle ... and it will continue to be, for a very long time," according to a report published by a Mexican research collective in late 2011.[63]

The US-Mexico border has become one of the key elements in the drug war. Some of Mexico's most violent cities are located directly on the border, while on the US side, border cities remain among the safest (though some are also among the poorest) in the country. In one of the more critical English texts on the drug war, University of Texas at El Paso professor Howard Campbell used the term "Drug War Zone" to describe what he calls the cultural world of drug traffickers and anti-drug police. "This zone is especially prominent and physically observable on the US-Mexico border but the term also applies to any place or situation in which drug traffickers, drug users, and anti-drug narcs confront, avoid or attempt to subvert one another," he writes.[64] Campbell notes that he avoids the term "war on drugs" because it is used in a hypocritical and misleading way by the US government. While Campbell's concept of a Drug War Zone may be considered an improvement over the notion of a drug war, it leaves much to be desired for two reasons. First, because it ignores the role of armies and navies and other special non–"law enforcement" state organizations in the drug war, but second, and more importantly, because it leaves out the segment of the population that desperately needs to be made visible in the context of the drug war: civilians. These are the workers, families, campesinos, migrants, and youth who have been targeted by police, army, or paramilitary groups in the context of the drug war. In Guatemala and Honduras, entire villages have been labeled "narco-communities" as if to justify mass displacement.

Having traveled from Colombia, Honduras, Guatemala, and the US-Mexico border filing stories on the impacts of the drug war, I have found three primary hallmarks of this kind of war. First, in all of the regions touched by drug war violence, the pain, fear, and suffering resulting from militarization and paramilitarization are experienced in large part by poor and working people and migrants. It is clear that though they may have little to no involvement or contact with controlled substances, the violence and terror of the drug war are primarily against them. Second, one of the earliest, longest lasting, and most tangible impacts of the violence is a restriction on people's mobility, whether in moving around one's own neighborhood, traveling between cities, crossing the US border (in either direction), or migrating. Third, in each place where the violence stemming from the drug war has increased, free expression—individual and collective, through public activities, community and mainstream media, and otherwise—has been targeted. Even though these three factors together make up the most widely accessible and consistent narratives of the war on drugs for any reporter familiar with the situation on the ground, they are not the narratives that dominate accounts of the drug trade and the US-backed war. Instead of telling the stories of those affected by the drug war, newspapers, think tanks, and governments produce reports dominated by stories of drug cartels (criminals or criminal groups) at war with each other for control of trafficking routes and territory. I call this narrative the cartel wars discourse, which includes a few salient features, among them: an almost exclusive reliance on state and government sources for information, a guilty-until-proven-innocent and victims-were-involved-in-drug-trade-bias, and a foundational belief that cops involved in criminal activity are the exception not the rule, and that more policing improves security.[65]

Cartel wars discourse is the dominant and hegemonic narrative of the drug war, positing that state forces are out to break the cartels, and most if not all victims of violence are involved in the drug trade.

TV news reports in the United States bring the most horrendous acts of the war to the screens of millions of North Americans: fifty two people burned alive in a casino, hundreds of bodies discovered in unmarked graves, and so on. The victims are regularly portrayed as having been involved in criminal activity, or at least involved with somebody who was involved, a formulation that effectively criminalizes entire populations. In the mainstream media, common people are rarely given voice. Instead, the population-at-large is relegated to tweeting or blogging anonymously if they wish to have a say, though even that can be risky.[66] If you expose cartel members, according to the editor of one Reynosa paper, "They will abduct you; they will torture you for hours; they will kill you, and then dismember you. And your family will always be waiting for you to come home."[67] These acts against the media by members of crime groups are carried out with impunity, the perpetrators protected by a state that is unwilling or unable to investigate. Telling stories that fall outside of official lines can be deadly. To begin with, many sources fear talking, afraid that if they go on the record they will be tortured, disappeared, or killed. There are also major disincentives for journalists themselves. The press freedom organization Article 19 counts fifty journalists killed in Mexico between January 2007 and December 2013.[68] That's nearly double the number of journalists killed in the previous six years, during Vicente Fox's term.[69] Over the same time span, 726 acts of aggression and 213 threats against journalists and media organizations were reported. According to a report by the Committee to Protect Journalists (CPJ), in Mexico "Journalists across the country have told CPJ that they avoid coverage of crime and corruption in order to stay alive."[70]

In areas affected by the drug war, not only does the dominant media discourse win out, but it is incredibly dangerous for media workers to stray too far from it. An examination of media reports reveals that information on the drug cartels blamed for the violence and terror generally comes from a handful of official sources, namely from elements of the Mexican and US state coercive apparatus (police, army, prosecutors, anti-narcotics forces) as well as civilian arms of the government, the United Nations, and think tanks like the discredited Austin-based intelligence firm Stratfor.[71] That most reporting reflects the dominant discourse about the drug trade and the war on drugs is not a new phenomenon. In fact, the frequency with which the dominant narratives of the drug war are reproduced by the press could be considered one of the fundamental reasons for the longevity of the drug war discourse.[72] "Most information about narcotraffic is furnished by the *Miami Herald* and other U.S. newspapers that use the U.S. DEA (Drug Enforcement Agency [sic]) as their information source," wrote Colombian historian Germán Alfonso Palacio Castañeda in 1991. "Such media tend to follow the DEA's strategic orientation, which is empirically unacceptable."[73] It's been more than twenty years since Palacio wrote those words, and unfortunately, they still hold true today. For example, in early 2011, I met a photographer based in Monterrey, another city that plunged into drug war-related violence beginning around 2010. He didn't want to speak on the record, but having established anonymity, he didn't hold back. He told me that photographers regularly embed themselves with the army, waiting until soldiers visit the scene, as there is no other way to access certain areas safely. He explained how he once took photos of cadavers on a ranch not far out of the city, and how the victims looked like they had been holding automatic weapons, which he knew had been planted by soldiers. He and other photographers didn't question the set up or refuse to run the images they shot, out of fears for their safety.

Regardless of the risks, critiques of the drug wars in Mexico, Central America, Colombia, and South America are becoming more sophisticated as time reveals their lasting impacts. The links between drug war policies and an improving investment climate for transnational corporations are increasingly intelligible, especially as the outcomes from US engagement in Colombia, specifically between 2000 and 2006, are lauded, refined, and applied elsewhere. The first phase of Plan Colombia officially ended in 2006; the next year, the Mérida Initiative, or Plan Mexico, started. The Mérida Initiative would have been in the works early in former President Felipe Calderón's term (2006–2012), if not before. The Mérida Initiative was announced in fall 2007, and originally included Central America within it, but in 2010, the United States split off the Central America Regional Security Initiative (CARSI), which covers Belize, Costa Rica, El Salvador, Guatemala, Honduras, Nicaragua, and Panama. The US funded CARSI to the tune of $496 million between 2008 and 2013.[74] In April 2009, the Caribbean Basin Security Initiative (CBSI) was announced, and the Caribbean is increasingly the centerpiece of the drug war.[75] There is continuity in these US-backed aid packages. Though this book only deals with a handful of the countries affected by planned drug wars and drug war capitalism, the outcomes of these policies are similar wherever they are applied.

According to Gian Carlo Delgado Ramos and Silvina María Romano, Plan Colombia and the Mérida Initiative can be understood as two more examples of US interference in Latin America. In the name of protecting US national security, the United States pushes self-interested policies in target countries. This not only contributes to historical processes of despoliation, plundering, exploitation, and the transfer of wealth in Latin America, but also leads to the reorganization of internal power relations between civilian and military groups in the nations in which such programs are implemented.[76] Though the focus of this work is Mexico, Honduras, Guatemala, and Colombia, the drug war is under way around the globe. This is evidenced by the fact that in 2012, the US Drug Enforcement Administration worked in partnership with sixty-five countries.[77] In some areas, the drug war is latent, and in others (like the United States) its principle characteristic is criminalization and mass incarceration, particularly of young men of color. In December 2012, the government of Peru announced that it would be spending $300 million on fighting "terrorism and narcotrafficking" there.[78] Places like Afghanistan and Burma have also been testing grounds for drug war capitalism, and as this is being written, the State Department, together with the Woodrow Wilson Institute and others, are pushing to extend the drug war to Africa.[79] Mexico and Central America are today the regions that are experiencing the brunt of the explosive physical violence linked to the policies applied in the name of disrupting the flow of narcotics to the United States. These are the places where the war against controlled substances is serving as the basis for a deepening of previously existing militarization, as well as the sweetening of the terms of international trade and investment. Colombia is generally looked upon by pro–drug war hawks as a success story, even though little has changed in terms of the amount of coca produced there. But as we shall see, Colombia has become the sandbox for how non-state armed actors can serve to control dissent and conquer territory. Seen in this light, it becomes easier to understand how the drug war facilitates the continuation of a capitalist economic model predicated on security, in part by creating a public discourse that allows increased state militarization on the pretext of implementing security measures to protect civilians in the face of heinous acts carried out by criminal groups.

CHAPTER 2:

DEFINING THE DRUG WAR

IF there really was a war on drugs, it wouldn't make for very good media fodder: bullet-riddled packets of cocaine (or cigarettes, for that matter) don't bleed, and following the newspaper industry rhyme, they probably wouldn't lead. "War on drugs" is a misnomer, as war is defined as an armed conflict between at least two groups, and not between one group and a substance. As we shall see, in Mexico, Colombia, and elsewhere, the primary victims of the so-called war on drugs are poor people, migrants, and Indigenous and peasant farmers.

Since the Nixon administration declared that the United States was embarking on a "war on drugs" in 1969, the phrase has been part of the popular imagination.[1] Nixon's declaration of war was followed by the passage of the Comprehensive Drug Abuse Prevention and Control Act, which serves as the legal basis for US drug policy today.[2] Nixon's war was based on policies passed at the outset of the twentieth century, including the Harrison Act in 1914 and the Hague Convention for the control of opium sales in 1912. The Boggs Act, passed in 1951, put marijuana on the same rank as heroin and cocaine, and introduced the mandatory death penalty as punishment for selling it to a minor.[3] At the end of the nineteenth century, San Francisco banned opium smoking, and New York banned opium dens—laws that targeted primarily Chinese migrants.[4] Similarly, early attempts to control marijuana use and distribution in the United States were guided by an anti-Mexican sentiment. Legislation passed in 1969 was followed, on July 6, 1973, by the creation of the Drug Enforcement Administration (DEA), a new national anti-drugs force that would wage "an all-out global war on the drug menace," according to Nixon.[5] Beriah Empie and Lydia Anne M Bartholow use a Trojan horse analogy to describe the purpose of the war on drugs. "Despite the lack of evidence of a national narcotics issue, the war on drugs was the White House's Trojan horse for intensified federal involvement in policing. It allowed Nixon to deliver on his campaign rhetoric of being tough on crime while stifling organized political rebellion."[6]

The war on drugs kicked off on the heels of 1968, when worldwide protest and student movements shook the world, from Mexico City to Paris to San Francisco. It came at a critical moment of the United States war in Vietnam (by the fall of 1971, half of all US soldiers in Vietnam had tried heroin, and two were dying of heroin overdoses each month),[7] and at a time when youth were experimenting with legal and illegal drugs "to a degree unprecedented in American history."[8] The 1960s and '70s marked high points in anti-war and anti-imperialist activism, and existing anti-narcotics efforts were adapted to quash protest. "Strict anti-drug laws, punitive sentencing procedures and harsh enforcement made it possible to suppress and curb dissent," writes Julia Buxton in her book *The Political Economy of Narcotics.*[9]

It wasn't just the US that rolled out anti-drugs measures as a way to get protesters, hippies, and radicals off the streets. Buxton explains that anti-drug measures during that period "served to unite systems as diverse as the communist governments of China and the Eastern Bloc, the right-wing authoritarian military regimes in South America, Spain and Portugal and democratically elected governments in Australia, the USA and Scandinavia."[10]

The United States has focused its drug-control efforts internationally on supply reduction, which proposes that an attack on the supply of narcotics will reduce availability, causing prices to rise, and thus fewer people will use them. Take, for example, Operation Intercept, which was touted by the Nixon administration as aiming to stop the flow of marijuana from Mexico. Even this early in its existence, the war on drugs was interwoven with border control and controlling the migration of people from Mexico to the United States. According to Kate Doyle of the US National Security Archive, "Intercept was plotted in secret to produce an unprecedented slow-down of all plane, truck, car and foot traffic—legitimate or not—flowing from Mexico into the southern United States. In order to achieve their goals, the president's top enforcement advisors deployed thousands of extra Border, Customs and Immigration agents along the 2,000 mile line that separates the countries, from just north of Tijuana to Brownsville, Texas. Once in place, the agents were charged with stopping and inspecting anything that moved."[11] G. Gordon Liddy, a senior Nixon administration advisor who would later be convicted for his role in Watergate, wrote, "For diplomatic reasons the true purpose of the exercise was never revealed. Operation Intercept, with its massive economic and social disruption, could be sustained far longer by the United States than by Mexico. It was an exercise in international extortion, pure, simple, and effective, designed to bend Mexico to our will."[12]

Over the next decades, the DEA would carry out various experiments in drug interception and crop destruction in Mexico, which will be described later. Domestically, Ronald Reagan revived the war on drugs a decade later, in 1982, which kick-started crop eradication and interdiction in South America. In 1986, Reagan signed National Security Decision Directive 221; from then on drug trafficking was legally considered a threat to the national security of the United States.[13] That directive was updated in 1989 by George Bush Sr., and broadened the role of US troops in anti-narcotics activity in Latin America, allowing them to go on patrol instead of being restricted to their bases.[14] In an address following the invasion of Panama in 1989, Bush said: "The goals of the United States have been to safeguard the lives of Americans, to defend democracy in Panama, *to combat drug trafficking,* and to protect the integrity of the Panama Canal Treaty. Many attempts have been made to resolve this crisis through diplomacy and negotiations. All were rejected by the dictator of Panama, General Manuel A. Noriega, *an indicted drug trafficker.*"[15]

Under Reagan, a new wave of racialized mass incarceration began in the United States, one that continues today. "Between 1980 and 2005, the number of people in US prisons and jails on drug charges increased by 1,100 percent. By 2010 there were 2 million people in prisons and jails across the country," according to writer John Gibler.[16] "The use of prohibition for racialized social control is the genesis of the modern drug-prohibition era," he concludes. According to Michelle Alexander, a law professor and author of *The New Jim Crow,* "The racial dimension of mass incarceration is its most striking feature. No other country in the world imprisons so many of its racial or ethnic minorities. The United States imprisons a larger percentage of its black population than South Africa did at the height of apartheid. In Washington, D.C., our nation's capital, it is estimated that three out of four young black men (and nearly all those in the poorest neighborhoods) can expect to serve time in prison. Similar rates of incarceration can be found in black communities across America."[17] As of February 2014, 50.1 percent of all federal inmates in the United States were imprisoned on drug charges.[18]

The number of prisoners in the United States soared along with increased budgets for the drug war. So have the number of drug users.

The DEA admits as much, noting in a 2008 report that "in 1960, only four million Americans had ever tried drugs. Currently, that number has risen to over 74 million."[19] Meanwhile, the DEA enjoys a budget of over $2 billion (up from $75 million when it was created) and employs over 5,000 agents (compared with its 1,470 agents in 1973).[20]

Drug users are sentenced to prison on the pretext of protecting communities from the impact of drug use. But in his groundbreaking work on drug abuse, Dr. Carl Hart emphasizes that drug addiction is not in fact what is devastating communities, as we are often led to believe. "The problem was poverty, drug policy, lack of jobs—a wide range of things. And drugs were just one sort of component that didn't contribute as much as we had said they have," he said in an interview in January 2014. "One of the things that shocked me when I first started to understand what was going on, when I discovered that 80 to 90 percent of the people who actually use drugs like crack cocaine, heroin, methamphetamine, marijuana—80 to 90 percent of those people were not addicted. I thought, 'Wait a second. I thought that once you use these drugs, everyone becomes addicted, and that's why we had these problems.' That was one thing that I found out. Another thing that I found out is that if you provide alternatives to people—jobs, other sort of alternatives—they don't overindulge in drugs like this."[21]

Experiments in ending prohibition are taking place around the world: from legalized marijuana in Colorado and Washington states in the United States, to full decriminalization of narcotics in Portugal, and supervised safe injection sites, including one in my long-time home of Vancouver, Canada. In 2014, Uruguay became the first country in the world to legalize the production, sale, and use of marijuana, in an open challenge to the United Nations' international drug control conventions. Time and again evidence shows that addiction is a health issue, and that criminalization of drug users and people dependent on drugs exaggerates social and personal harms. There is virtually no compelling proof that the war on drugs has worked to cure addiction or meaningfully reduce the supply of narcotics over the medium or long term. A comprehensive study by *The Lancet* found that crop eradication did little to reduce the supply of cocaine in the United States, that expensive interdiction campaigns only provide a temporary reduction in supply, and there was "some evidence but diminishing returns from imprisonment beyond specific levels."[22]

Rather than actually dealing with controlling illegal substances, the war on drugs is a concept invented and promoted by the US government, and a motto that has also been adopted by other states to serve their interests, both domestically and abroad. According to drug historian Paul Gootenberg, "Although its genealogy has not been rigorously researched, the contemporary metaphoric idea of a 'war on drugs' followed: a universal progressive reformist version before World War II; a socially rooted, hard-nosed Cold War ideology version of the 1950s through 1970s (akin to containment); melding into the Reaganesque total victory 'Star Wars' drug war fantasy of the 1980s and beyond."[23] As mentioned, the Obama administration has made an effort to move away from the terminology of the war on drugs, and Gil Kerlikowske, the former director of the White House's National Drug Policy, disavowed the term in his first interview on the subject. Though discourse has shifted, and the Holder memo modifies mandatory minimums in certain drug cases, little has yet concretely changed in terms of US federal policy.[24]

When it comes to the drug war and militarization domestically, it is worth pointing out that it was Colombian drug cartels that served as a pretext for the 1981 modification of the US Posse Comitatus Act, which forbade the military from participating in domestic policing. Amendments to the Act "allow [the Department of Defense] to support civilian law enforcement agencies and the Coast Guard. Although not explicitly stated, congressional intent was clear: the military needed to support law enforcement officers in combating drug smuggling."[25]

Outside of the fifty states it is clear that the drug war is the means by which states are waging a war against poor people, workers, migrants, and others. The drug war model inside the United States provides a mechanism of social control through criminalization and mass incarceration, which targets communities of color. In Mexico, Central and South America, the drug war model relies on the use of terror in order to impose social control.[26]

Empire and the Drug Trade

Leaving aside the concept of the drug war for a moment, even the word "drug" on its own poses challenges. In his book *Forces of Habit,* David Courtwright uses the word "drugs" "as a convenient and neutral term of reference for a long list of psychoactive substances, licit or illicit, mild or potent, deployed for medical and non-medical purposes."[27] Courtwright goes on to write about what he calls the big three (alcohol, tobacco, and caffeine) and the little three (opium, cannabis, and coca). Trade in the first three was an essential plank in the European colonial project—by 1885 taxation on booze, tobacco, and tea made up half of the revenues of the British government.[28] "Historians of commodities know that key stimulants—exotic spices, coffee, tobacco, chocolate—played defining roles in consumption and class styles in the construction of European capitalism," writes Gootenberg.[29]

Courtwright sums up the connections between narcotics and the colonial project succinctly. "The elites most responsible for promoting drug cultivation and use were European. They could not have over-spread the world so rapidly, nor brought it so completely under their dominion, without the large-scale production of alcohol and the cultivation of drug and sugar crops, the latter commonly used in, or made into, potent drinks. With these psychoactive products they paid their bills, bribed and corrupted their native opponents, pacified their workers and soldiers, and stocked their plantations with field hands."[30] In the Americas, the introduction of sugar by the Spanish went hand in hand with the enslavement of millions of African people throughout Central and South America and the Caribbean. The colonization of North America was made possible in part through the introduction of alcohol into Indigenous communities. Today, coffee covers 44 percent of arable cropland in Latin America.[31] And tobacco smoking spread from Hispaniola through European traders, eventually gaining a foot-hold as a cash crop in colonized lands around the world. But it is not to these substances, so vital in the creation and maintenance of empire, to which our minds turn when we hear of drugs, and especially not in the context of a war against them.

Instead, within the state framework of the drug war, the public is made to fear the by-products of what Cartwright calls the little three: opium, cannabis, and coca. Each of these substances was used for a long time by Indigenous peoples around the world. Opium was used for curing illness in Europe and North Africa before Arab traders introduced it to China more than two millennia ago. Marijuana, a hearty crop that produced not only cannabis but also strong hemp fiber, was long used in India and Asia. Indigenous folks throughout the Andean region ingested coca leaf to quell hunger and boost energy and strength.

Coca, opium, and cannabis have, to different extents, played key roles in state and elite formation, like their licit cousins. In the Andean highlands, Spanish colonizers commercialized coca plantations in order for mine workers to have access to the stimulant.[32] The opium wars in China were key to British colonialism, and English and American colonialists defended their right to make money off the trade. "I do not pretend to justify the prosecution of the opium trade in a moral and philanthropic point of view, but as a merchant I insist that it has been a fair, honorable and legitimate trade; and to say the worst of it, liable to no further or weightier objections than is the importation of wines, Brandies & spirits in to the U. States, England, &c," wrote Warren Delano II, who was the grandfather of FDR, and whose firm, Russell and Company, had a stake in the opium trade (smuggling opium into China) in the nineteenth century.[33]

The role of governments and particularly the US government in determining what constitutes illicit markets and illegal drugs is a crucial element of their war on drugs. "States monopolize the power to criminalize: laws precede and define criminality. Through their law-making and law-enforcing authority, states set the rules of the game even if they cannot entirely control the play," writes scholar Peter Andres.[34] The ease with which substances can be prohibited by a state is the ease with which they can be made legal as well, a point not lost on drug policy reformers or students of history. "For instance, alcohol smuggling networks linking the United States to suppliers in Europe, Canada, Mexico, and the Caribbean created a formidable policing challenge during the Prohibition Era—and were eliminated with the stroke of a pen with the repeal of the Volstead Act in 1933."[35]

It is also important to keep in mind the historical context of narcotics cultivation itself, as this too has been determined to a great extent by North American and European interests. The isolation of morphine, heroin, and codeine from opium was achieved by European chemists in the nineteenth century, and commercialized by pharmaceutical companies that still exist today. The first cocaine labs to transform coca leaves into concentrate were set up by German scientists, the process invented to prevent the leaves from rotting in transport to colonial centers. The US and German governments both played integral roles, together with the government of Peru, in the promotion of coca and cocaine exports. "In the 1890s, US commercial attachés in Lima honed contacts with local cocaine makers.... And helped Peruvians to upgrade their shipping and leaf-drying techniques."[36] By 1902, 2,400 kilos of cocaine were produced in the Andean region, and Merck, a German pharmaceutical company, controlled a quarter of the market.[37] Around that same time, an estimated 600–1,000 tons of coca was being imported into the United States, mostly for use as an ingredient in Coca-Cola.[38] It was Bayer that first marketed heroin as a cough suppressant, and later, Smith, Kline & French of Philadelphia promoted amphetamines for the treatment of the common cold.[39] At that time there were no legal controls over the trade and marketing of pharmaceuticals, or over the claims the pharmaceutical industry made about emerging wonder drugs like cocaine.[40] It wasn't until the twentieth century that the international community got together, at the urging of the United States, to create a global regime of prohibition.

Foreign Occupation and Drugs

Processes of modern colonization that reach back to the period when Nixon first declared a war on drugs have shaped the geography of drug production and trafficking. It was in that period that new marijuana plantations in Mexico were sown by US smugglers. Don Henry Ford, a blue-eyed smuggler-turned-organic-farmer in Texas, told me about pushing seeds on Mexican farmers in the Sierra Madre, the northern mountain range splitting Chihuahua from Sonora, Sinaloa, and Durango: "I was one of the guys that did it, see, I used to go down to Sinaloa you know, and show 'em the money. I'd say look, ya know, here's some seeds, why don't you plant these instead, this is what we want."

Ford and I met in a small ranching town in Texas not far from San Antonio. He picked me up from the Greyhound station in a pick-up truck littered with hay, and we drove over to a classic Texas BBQ joint, where we talked over meat, pickles, and coleslaw. "It was like look, if y'all grow this shit for me instead of this other kind, I can sell this better. We were the ones that created the demand.... It's like, I'll pay you a shitload of money, $100 a pound or whatever, you know."

Though there were lone wolves like Don Henry Ford, who eventually ended up serving prison time for smuggling, the Mexican Army was historically the primary organization dedicated to marijuana trafficking. "The case based data collected by the author over a 7-year period unequivocally point to the army as the primary transporter of marijuana shipments to the border," writes scholar Patrick O'Day, who relied on data he gathered through his own observations when he encountered an unwillingness on the part of authorities and police on the US side of the border to speak openly with him about drug trafficking.[41] "The lack of reporting and misreporting of relevant facts, the disappearance of incident reports, and the extreme paranoia of law enforcement personnel interviewed for the purpose of shedding light on this politically sensitive topic became so noteworthy during the course of the author's research that the obstruction itself has become part of the findings," he wrote.[42]

Eventually, also because of a push from the United States, mass marijuana production made its way south toward Colombia. Washington ran interdiction programs in Mexico in the 1970s, in Sinaloa, Guerrero, and elsewhere,[43] and in 1976 began aerial spraying of poppy crops in Chihuahua, Durango, and Sinaloa as part of Operation Trizo.[44] Twenty-two thousand hectares of land had been sprayed by the end of 1977. According to the DEA, "The large numbers of arrests that resulted from Operation Trizo caused an economic crisis in the poppy-growing regions of Mexico. In order to reduce the social upheaval, the Mexican government formally asked the DEA to stop participating in the surveillance flights."[45]

In Mexico, in the 1980s, the US launched Operation Condor, a new program of aerial pot plantation spraying. Operation Condor and Operation Trizo, together with the intercept programs, pioneered the supply side, cat-and-mouse-style drug control tactics used up until today. In their book *Drug War Mexico,* Peter Watt and Roberto Zepeda argue that these US programs made heroin and marijuana prices spike and encouraged the "cartelization" of the drug trade. "For the producers and traffickers with the best political contacts, the largest networks, and sufficient resources, and for those who had adapted to survive the initial years of this new phase of anti-drug policy, this sharp and sudden rise in the price of their exports was both rewarding and tantalizing," they write.

There was international fallout from early US crop spraying programs as well. "Some Mexican traffickers apparently made a fatal mistake—they harvested poisoned marijuana and sent it to El Norte. Lab tests by the US government found Mexican ganja with signs of paraquat," writes Ioan Grillo in his book *El Narco.*[46] Paraquat, a toxic chemical used as a herbicide, also poisons and kills humans and animals if ingested. Grillo continues: "The bad publicity pushed dealers to look for a new source of weed for millions of hungry hippies. It didn't take long to find a country with the land, laborers, and lawlessness to fill the gap—Colombia. Farmers had been growing weed in Colombia's Sierra Nevada since the early 1970s. As Mexico cracked down, the Colombians stepped up, creating a boom in their own marijuana industry known by local historians as the Bonanza Marimbera."[47] In a clear link between colonization and the introduction of narcotics production, coca plantations arrived in Putumayo, a southern province bordering Ecuador, which is inhabited by the Cofán people, as well as the oil industry. "The main coca crops began to appear in the 1970s, with the colonization of territory linked to petroleum interests. Many work contracts in the petroleum sector were temporary, and workers sought alternative sources of income, including coca cultivation."[48]

The Magdalena Medio region, a geographically strategic area replete with oil deposits and pipelines, gold, lead, marble, quartz, forests containing rare and valuable wood, important water sources, and rich agricultural areas, was previously home to Shell, Texaco, and Frontino Goldmines (now Medoro Resources), and now to drug traffickers. Resource-rich areas of Colombia, like the Magdalena Medio, where multinational corporations distorted local economies and the populations had little access to state services were prime territory for drug traffickers. "The presence of the state in the area has not provided for equitable development, which benefits local populations who have lived there since the distant past, or those who have arrived there searching subsistence, rather it has favored the interests of large companies with foreign capital, which introduce an exclusive development model of social, political, and economic domination. Many of these characteristics led to these lands being coveted by the big powers in drug trafficking, who made important investments in land there, aggravating all of the conflicts."[49]

These examples provide some insight into how the geography of narcotics in the Western Hemisphere has taken shape over the last 150 years. Though it's difficult to say exactly how much land is used for drug cultivation, the Bureau of International Narcotics and Law Enforcement Affairs—part of the US State Department—claims that in 2011, 12,000 hectares were sown with opium and roughly the same amount of cannabis. As economist Peter Reuter notes, "No detail has ever been published on the methodology of these estimates, beyond the fact that they are generated from estimates of growing area, crop per acre, and refining yield per ton of raw product; the information sources, even the technology used to produce them (for area estimates) are classified."[50]

What is clear, however, is that free trade agreements and neoliberal restructuring have defined the shape of the drug market today. A study of over 2,200 rural municipalities in Mexico from 1990 to 2010 found that lower prices for maize, which fell following the implementation of NAFTA, increased the cultivation of opium and cannabis. "This increase was accompanied by differentially lower rural wages, suggesting that households planted more drug crops in response to the decreased income generating potential of maize farming," write the study authors.[51] Mexico scholars Watt and Zepeda argue that the North America Free Trade Agreement (NAFTA) "provided both the infrastructure and the labor pool to facilitate smuggling," further developing the idea of a narcotics industry intertwined with neoliberal transformation. For example, highways built to bring agricultural exports to US markets also serve drug traffickers, and increasing inequality makes more people willing to risk working in the illicit economy.

This book takes the long view on the drug war, positing that the United States and its allies control the demand and create the conditions for the production, flow, and demand of illegal narcotics.

It is in large part US policy that creates the criminal networks that traffic drugs, and US policy that generates extreme violence. Take, for example, the murder of Mexican drug runner Miguel Treviño Morales, alias Z-40. As a member of the Zetas, Treviño Morales was said to have killed thousands, and was himself murdered in 2013. To get a handle on his death, which the media flaunted as a blow against the Zetas and a victory for the Mexican government, I interviewed Sean Dunagan, a former DEA intelligence analyst in Mexico and Guatemala, and a member of Law Enforcement Against Prohibition. "The one thing that really stands out, that really isn't reported, is that we created Miguel Treviño," Dunagan told me. "I mean he is entirely a product of American drug policy. Without our current drug policy he wouldn't exist. He might have been a carjacker who probably would be sitting in a Mexican jail right now. Our policy of prohibition is what creates people like that. It incentivizes violence to a tremendous degree, so we shouldn't be surprised when someone rises to the top and commits 2,000 murders to get there, because in the scheme that we've created and forced on the Mexican government, that's necessarily going to happen.... If we want people like him to stop terrorizing Mexico we need to stop our policies. He's just a logical product of what we've done."

But the impacts of US policy obviously go beyond individual players and their connections to drug-smuggling empires. The violence connected to the war on drugs is moved depending on where the United States pumps anti-drug money, which is to say the explosive violence in narcotics-producing or transshipment countries is often directly linked with external pressures and the provision of resources to local security forces. American officials have admitted as much, noting that anti-drugs programs in Colombia pushed the problem into Mexico, and from there into Central America and the Caribbean, and so on. As we will see in Mexico, Central America, and Colombia, the shifting geography of the drug war fosters state and non-state militarization, and can deepen the ability of transnational corporations to exploit labor and natural resources.

In countries where US-backed anti-drug programs go—Colombia, Mexico, and the Caribbean, for example—drug flows often increase, as does violence. In the words of Peter Dale Scott, writing about Colombia in 2003, "Drug trafficking thrives in times of conflict; and by now it is obvious that US military interventions in drug areas have been, and will be, accompanied by significantly increased drug flows into [the United States]. The new [increases in trafficking] are more because of US efforts than despite them."[52] Scott connects the police and army roles in facilitating the transport of narcotics, something that intensifies, as does violence, as their numbers and resources are boosted in the name of controlling illicit substances. To make the connection domestically, the periods with the most recorded homicides in the US between 1900 and 1990 were during Prohibition (1915–1930) and the period after Nixon declared the war on drugs.[53]

Today, the United States Northern Command has jurisdiction over the United States, Mexico, Canada, and part of the Caribbean, while the Southern Command is the US military's primary organization in Central and South America. For the Southern Command, transnational organized crime is the number one regional security issue, and particularly cocaine trafficking. But despite the billions of dollars the US has poured into combating drug trafficking, the threat continues to rise; "according to US Customs and Border Protection, there was a 483% increase in cocaine washing up on Florida's shores in 2013 compared to 2012."[54] Rather than acknowledging that the drug war has designs other than stopping the flow of narcotics, we are meant to believe that the enemy is becoming increasingly sophisticated. "Mr. Chairman, gone are the days of the 'cocaine cowboys.' Instead, we and our partners are confronted with cocaine corporations that have franchises all over the world, including 1,200 American cities, as well as criminal enterprises like the violent transnational gang Mara Salvatrucha, or MS-13, that specialize in extortion and human trafficking," said US general John F. Kelly, the commander of SouthCom, in the 2014 posture statement before the House Armed Services Committee.[55]

If we cannot see how the drug war serves as a tool for expanding capitalism, we will be left imagining this imperial strategy as a futile whack-a-mole game, where feisty criminals consistently outrun a series of multibillion-dollar military operations. In this scenario, drug traffickers are run out of the Caribbean into Mexico, out of Colombia into Venezuela,[56] and from the Pacific Ocean to the Atlantic. But we have seen how marijuana, opium, and cocaine production not only responds to US markets, but has been historically shaped and created by US demand. Now it is time to delve into just how the drug war serves to reconfigure trafficking routes, and as it does so, brings further militarization and violence to said regions.

CHAPTER 3:

A LOOK SOUTH TO COLOMBIA

TALL and clean cut with a serious look and a small scar on his cheek, thirty-seven-year-old Fabian Laverde has been an activist for more than half his life. We met in the bottom floor of a collective house in a hip neighborhood in central Bogotá, finding a quiet room to talk while younger organizers met to plan a protest in the living room. A tent was pitched near the table, indicating that here too had become an informal safe house for someone displaced because of Colombia's conflict. Laverde, who is the director of the Social Corporation for Community Support and Learning (COSPACC), gave the immediate impression of a rigid professional, and someone who doesn't talk much. By the time I visited Colombia I had nearly finished the first draft of the book, and I explained to him and one of his colleagues the gist of the project. I asked what he thought of the war on drugs, and I was pleased to find out that my impression of Laverde as a man of few words was wrong. "There's a discourse about attacking production and that whole story related to coca, but really what they try to attack is the social movement," he said, clearing his throat gently. "If you look at the map of conflicts in Colombia, you'll find that the highest concentrations of uniformed public forces are in the zones where the social movements resist the most. So you'll find that there is a large military concentration in Casanare, that there's a large military concentration in Arauca, in Catatumbo, in Cauca, and if you look at it from the other side you'll see that the social movements become stronger and try and resist in an organized manner in these regions."

Laverde turned the US supply-side discourse on its head, arguing that his experience of the war on drugs is nothing like what's publicly stated. "Beyond the fact of the militarization under the discourse of the war on drugs, and saying that Colombia is a country that produces cocaine, and if Colombia didn't produce cocaine the US wouldn't experience the scourge of consumption, it also has to do with the fact that in most of these regions there are important concentrations of natural resources, especially for mining and energy."

As an example of an area where transnational oil companies—in this case British Petroleum (BP), Petrobras, and others—are at the center of the conflict, Laverde cites the Casanare region, where COSPACC works. "It was possible to see that, in Casanare specifically, as transnational investment—especially in the oil industry—grew, the military apparatus strengthened, represented by the 16th Brigade of the Colombian Army," he told me. "As those two large sectors—multinational capital and the military apparatus—were strengthened, paramilitarism also strengthened in the region.... If you take a map of Casanare and divide it into its nineteen municipalities, and you start to put some kind of symbol for assassinations, in this case false positives [civilian victims dressed up by soldiers to appear as if they were guerrilla members] or forced disappearances that took place in each municipality, we will find that Agua Azul was the epicenter ... Agua Azul and Yopal. Agua Azul is the second largest city in Casanare, and Yopal is the capital. But if we look it all over carefully, all of the cases occurred very close to where the oil installations are, which belonged to the British Petroleum Company, BP."

Casanare doesn't have a history of coca cultivation, but it is considered an important transshipment point for the chemicals needed for cocaine production, as well as for cocaine itself. It has also been a focus of Revolutionary Armed Forces of Colombia (FARC) activity, and the National Liberation Army (ELN) and various local paramilitary organizations have also been active there. In Casanare, as elsewhere in Colombia, resources from Plan Colombia were used to go after the guerrillas, and it was civilians who paid the highest price. Laverde explained that he documented the case of a municipality called Recetor, a town that had little state presence and ongoing guerrilla activity, until the Peasant Self-Defense of Casanare (ACC) paramilitary group entered the area. Between December 2002 and March 2003, after the ACC's arrival, at least thirty-three people were disappeared. Survivors and family members who did not vacate the area were arrested en masse by soldiers, police, and members of the secret service, and accused of being guerrillas before they were eventually released without charge. In 2011, Recetor's city council reported that 1,232 people—95 percent of the population—were displaced.[1] But as is so often the case in Colombia, the displacement of civilians in the conflict did not mean that their lands and villages sat abandoned. Rather, one year after terror was visited on the population, Brazilian oil giant Petrobras opened offices in tiny Recetor in order to coordinate oil exploration. "This company was in charge of the Homero 1 oil well, located in the community of El Vegón, where it is believed in the coming years there will be new seismic testing for oil reserves; all of this in exchange for victims, who are added to the list of the thousands of disappeared in Casanare and Colombia,"reads Laverde's report.[2] The same phenomenon took place with startling regularity in various areas, as entire communities were driven out of their homes only to return years later to find that their land had been planted with palm oil trees or was being explored for minerals.

In Colombia, the connections between Plan Colombia, state, paramilitary, and guerrilla violence, and natural resources vary greatly from one region to another, but organizers, activists, and those who are directly impacted regularly insist upon their connection. In addition to state security forces' collusion with narcotrafficking groups, the country has powerful paramilitary structures that support not only the drug trade but also the repression of insurgent groups and social movements. Colombia also has multiple, long-running guerrilla insurgencies, a factor that differentiates it from any other country in the hemisphere. Thus, in addition to fighting narcotics, an important part of United States policy in Colombia is combating leftist insurgencies and (in terms of official discourse) terrorism.

In 1997, the Revolutionary Armed Forces of Colombia (FARC) was added to the US State Department's Foreign Terrorist Organization list, and with increasing frequency after September 11, 2001, the FARC were labeled narcoterrorists by US security agencies. The focus on the FARC implies that it was guerrillas who were the primary conduits for cocaine heading north, but that has little basis in reality: in 2001, the Colombian government estimated that paramilitaries controlled 40 percent of the drug trade, while the FARC controlled just 2.5 percent.[3] Indeed, in a television interview in the early 1990s, United Self-Defense Forces of Colombia (AUC) leader Carlos Castaño admitted that 70 percent of his paramilitary organization's funds came from drugs.[4] In 2003, the government and AUC entered into negotiations aimed at dismantling the organization and reintegrating its members into society, and by 2006 criminal bands (*bandas criminales*, or Bacrim) emerged. These supposedly apolitical groups are presented as ideology-free, neither left nor right wing, but as we shall see, the reality is that they are often made up of former paramilitaries who did not demobilize in the early 2000s.

Through this whole period, the Colombian army played a role in drug trafficking, working closely with paramilitary groups, even as it received more and more funding from the United States. In many areas, local and state governments were at the behest of paramilitary and drug-trafficking groups, as were the police and secret police. The US and Colombian governments have continued experimenting with various methods of controlling the flow of narcotics, while also exercising social, economic, and political control in Colombia.

The overlap between anti-narcotics and counterinsurgency, as well as the connection between drug trafficking and paramilitarism, is explained well by William O. Walker III: "Since South American drug traffickers have carefully established routes for narcotics through Central America and the Caribbean, often with the help of conservative or reactionary elements that the White House has also relied upon, it is no surprise that there exists a connection between security operations, coming under the broad rubric of low-intensity conflict, and drug control."[5] Fourteen years after the initial imposition of Plan Colombia, understanding who the players were in the drugs game and how their activities were linked to the state is worthwhile, but it seems urgent that we go beyond an exclusive focus on drug trafficking to look at the roles that the expansion of capitalism, the acquisition of lands through dispossession, and the extractive economy have played in Colombia's drug war.

Plan Colombia and the Drug War

Plan Colombia consisted of US legislation and funding for Colombia, based on an economic development strategy first advanced by Colombian president Andrés Pastraña in 1999. Pastraña's vision of a Marshall Plan for Colombia was taken up by US policy makers and crafted into Plan Colombia, which consisted of a military strategy, a legal strategy, and a humanitarian strategy. Non-US diplomats claimed that the first draft of Plan Colombia was written in English, and later translated to Spanish.[6] While Colombia and the United States had maintained close military links since the late 1940s, Plan Colombia, which began in earnest in 2000, represented a much closer relationship than had previously existed.[7]

The military component was focused on intelligence gathering, disrupting drug trafficking routes, the training of Colombian police and prosecutors, and eradication programs that included aerial spraying of coca crops. It included the transfer of equipment including radars, heavy artillery, and at least seventy-two helicopters to the Colombian armed forces.[8] Plan Colombia was justified as a means to destroy the country's burgeoning cocaine trade and to decimate the FARC and other rebel groups. The Colombian military received $4.9 billion worth of US State Department and Defense Department assistance between 2000 and 2008, the majority of which was provided under the rubric of Plan Colombia.[9] In addition, the CIA is responsible for a covert action program in Colombia that has a "multibillion-dollar black budget" first approved by George W. Bush in the early 2000s and continued by Obama.[10] Significantly, special battalions of the Colombian army were trained to protect oil pipelines belonging to US companies.

The "humanitarian" component of Plan Colombia was designed to encourage farmers to grow legal crops instead of coca and opium, and along with the military component of Plan Colombia, the program of aerial spraying proved to be the most dramatic, and the most devastating for the country's rural poor. Plan Colombia's legal component helped to spearhead the transformation of the Colombian judiciary as well as spur economic reforms. Immediately following Plan Colombia, the state oil company, Ecopetrol, was partially privatized, and new laws were introduced to encourage foreign direct investment. Throughout the 2000s, the mainstream media made it appear that the country was in the throes of a battle that pitted right-wing paramilitaries against left-wing guerrillas, with the state, backed by the US, stepping in to eliminate and demobilize irregular armed groups through force as well as through demobilization programs. This sketch of the conflicts, however, leaves out the role of the Colombian army as well as that of US troops and mercenaries as protagonists with their own agenda, which as we shall see is tied directly to the protection of corporate and commercial interests. According to one study, anti-narcotics and military assistance given to Colombia was regularly diverted to paramilitary organizations, strengthening them.[11] Overall levels of violence in Colombia increased markedly with the launch of Plan Colombia, and in 2002, its second year, there were 673,919 victims of the war—largely Colombia's poor and working majority—the highest recorded number for any year in the past decades (tellingly, homicides in Mexico peaked in 2010, two years after the Mérida Initiative began).[12]

One example of the brutality suffered by Colombia's working poor is the aerial spraying of coca crops as a form of chemical warfare; peasants and their crops—illicit and otherwise—were poisoned from above with toxic compounds. I asked Sonia López, an activist with the Joel Sierra Human Rights Foundation in Saravena, Colombia, what Plan Colombia meant for people in Arauca, a state bordering Venezuela. "It was a dirty trick to boost the war against the people. The supposed war on drugs generated a food crisis throughout the country," she said. "Many people had to leave, because what they had was a little piece of land where they had plantains, and it was fumigated, and it ended up desolate." She explained that though many people were forced into urban centers by fumigations, they have never been counted among the country's displaced, as crop spraying was not considered a cause of displacement. But the results of these crop-dustings fit neatly within the aims of the counterinsurgency war and the drive to displace small farmers from their lands. "Those who were not removed *a plomo* [by lead, which is to say, bullets] were removed by fumigations, and today they're begging in social programs, in Families in Action, in Forest Protector Families, in all of these programs that seek to put people to sleep and make them forget what the real struggles are that we have to carry out.... In addition to the fumigations, [Plan Colombia] strengthened the entire military apparatus," she told me. "Fumigation from the skies, and on land the soldiers killed, raped, and displaced." Monsanto manufactures Glysophate, the primary chemical used in fumigation, which "damages the human digestive system, the central nervous system, the lungs and the blood's red corpuscles. Another constituent causes cancer in animals and damage to the liver and kidneys of humans," according to a report on Colombian crop spraying that appeared in the *London Observer* in 2001.[13]

Plan Colombia officially ended in 2006, but there has been strong continuity between the policies of President Álvaro Uribe, whose two terms spanned Plan Colombia, and those of President Juan Manuel Santos, who was Uribe's defense minister.[14] Over time and thanks to a brave press corps, details of the army's role in mass murders, disappearances, and various scandals have emerged. In 2005, five years into Plan Colombia, there were an estimated 800 US military personnel and 600 private military contractors in Colombia, working with an army mired in increasingly serious controversies. [15]

During Uribe's presidency, while the country received an unprecedented amount of US aid, the army was known to carry out joint patrols with right-wing paramilitary groups, and was found to have perpetrated the false positives scandal, in which soldiers captured and murdered civilians, later dressing them up as guerrilla combatants, in order to claim progress in the war. According to a 2009 report by the United Nations Human Rights Council, Colombian soldiers were preying on local people as a form of career advancement: "With a view to obtaining privileges, recognition or special leave, soldiers detain innocent people without any valid reason and then execute them. Their bodies appear the day following their disappearance tens of kilometers away and are identified as members of illegal armed groups killed in combat. These are mainly vulnerable people—street dwellers, adolescents from poor areas of big cities, drug addicts and beggars—who are dressed in a uniform and executed. In some cases, for example in Soacha, young people are tricked with promises of work and transferred to a place where they are finally executed."[16] In the case of Soacha, twenty-two young men were offered jobs, only to end up dead at the hands of soldiers. The same gruesome practice was repeated thousands of times, in other regions of the country; some claim it carries on today.

Colombia and the United States enjoyed extremely close relations, while the Colombian army committed atrocities and paramilitary groups bought enough politicians to control Congress. Links between these paramilitary groups and members of Colombia's Congress (a scandal known as *parapolítica*) became so prevalent that it to led to the investigation of 126 members of Congress, forty-one of whom were formally charged.[17] Regardless of the ongoing repression of opposition movements and illegalities in Congress and otherwise, Uribe was the closest US ally in the region and lauded as a partner and a true democrat. In Colombia, he was referred to as a "Teflon" president, as it appeared that none of the serious allegations made against him could stick, no matter what the proof.

In the years following Plan Colombia, foreign investment in the extractive industries soared and new trade agreements were signed, including the US-Colombia and the Canada-Colombia free trade agreements. The success of Plan Colombia in achieving US foreign policy goals—though not in meeting anti-narcotics targets—marked an important point in the evolution of decades of US experiments using anti-drugs policy to impact society, politics, and the economy in Colombia. It's worth reviewing the factors that led the US and Colombia to make a pact and spend billions of dollars to supposedly fight drug trafficking.

More than twenty years after his murder, drug kingpin Pablo Escobar remains a household name. Leader of the Medellín Cartel, he was the US's prime drug boogeyman through the 1980s and until his murder in 1993. His story reads like an early version of Mexico's Joaquin

"El Chapo" Guzmán: Escobar was the undisputed king of the drug world, a criminal wanted worldwide, his name listed among *Fortune* magazine's richest people in the late 1980s. After the elimination of Escobar in 1993, the Cali Cartel would be credited with controlling the business, until it was attacked in a way that encouraged the formation of smaller clandestine groups devoted to the production and trafficking of narcotics. The US-backed assault against Escobar and its operations against the Colombian traffickers, particularly through the DEA's Operation Snowcap in 1987, were what would end up putting Mexican traffickers on the map.[18]

"What happened was not the lesser of two evils: it was the greater. Our success with Medellín and Cali essentially set the Mexicans up in business, at a time when they were already cash-rich thanks to the budding meth trade in Southern California," according to Tony Loya, the former DEA agent who ran Operation Snowcap.[19] Paramilitarization took place in two waves in Colombia, first as state-created and elite-supported groups formed in the 1960s and '70s, later as elite-created, state-supported groups through the 1980s and '90s.[20] In the 1960s, various guerrilla groups were formed in Colombia, and legislation was passed allowing for the creation of so-called self-defense groups. "In the framework of the struggle against the guerrilla groups, the State fostered the creation of said 'self-defense groups' among the civilian population, and their main aims were to assist the security forces in counterinsurgency operations and to defend themselves from the guerrilla groups. The State granted them permits to bear and possess weapons, as well as logistic support."[21] By the mid-1980s it was no longer possible for the state to deny that these groups had turned to supporting organized criminal activity. Officials and lawmakers promised that these death squads would be repressed by the state, and they resisted the "paramilitary" label, insisting it was misused.[22] During this time, increasingly organized rural and urban groups were rising up for land re-distribution and the right to live in dignity, and not coincidentally, it was paramilitary forces, whose activities the state tolerated, that carried out repression against these organizations. Between 1988 and 1994, there were over 67,000 politically motivated assassinations in Colombia—or 23.4 per day.[23] "In an earlier period, repressive social control was administered abruptly by the Colombian armed forces, with institutional support from a Constitutionally mandated state of siege. Now, extra-official armed groups do the army's job, though they seemingly have no organic links to the army."[24]

The second wave of paramilitarization in Colombia took root as the cocaine industry began to reap previously unforeseen profits for local drug runners, an elite new group whose irregular forces were backed by the state. The panorama of the armed conflict began to change dramatically for Escobar and for all of Colombia in 1989. In August of that year, leading presidential candidate Luis Carlos Galán was shot to death as he and his entourage ascended a wooden platform to address 10,000 of his supporters outside of Bogotá. Galán, a progressive, had been in favor of an extradition treaty with the United States, and was vocal about drug money eroding democracy. His killing marked a pivotal moment in Colombia. "The 1989 assassination of Luis Carlos Galán, senator and primary Liberal Party candidate for the Colombian Presidency, made is clear that the Colombian-US war on narcotraffic had transformed the capitalist cocaine business into a mechanism of US control," wrote Palacio Castañeda in 1991.

A few months after Galán was killed, a bomb exploded on Avianca Flight 203, killing all 107 passengers onboard. This attack was blamed on Pablo Escobar, and as there were US citizens on the flight, it provided the basis for then-president George Bush to argue that the United States take a more active role in the drug war. After that, the United States ratcheted up its fight against drug trafficking organizations, in the form of increased funding and manpower. Already "the war on drugs was being used to counter social turmoil in Colombia."[25] By the early 1990s, it was clear that in Colombia, drug trafficking was "a political device used by governments, particularly though not solely the United States, to justify repressive disciplinary social control operations."[26] The creation of Special Vigilance and Private Security Services (CONVIVIR) groups, which was encouraged by then-governor of Antioquia state Álvaro Uribe in the mid-1990s, laid the basis for the emergence of the United Self-Defense Forces of Colombia, the country's largest and most articulated paramilitary group.[27] In the mid-90s, before tapping a formula later dubbed Plan Colombia, the United States applied narcotics-related sanctions against Colombia. The Council of American Enterprises—an American business consortium in Colombia—reported that in 1996 its member companies lost $875 million in sales because of the sanctions.[28] That same year, the State Department reported that the decertification decision required the Overseas Private Investment Corporation and the Export-Import Bank to freeze about $1.5 billion in investment credits and loans. This included a $280 million loss in Colombia's oil industry alone.[29]

Anti-drugs efforts that went against economic growth and the interests of US and transnational investors were destined to fail over the long term. Plan Colombia emerged in 1999 after the failure of the sanctions program. Even through the US government has spent over $8 billion on Plan Colombia and related initiatives, the flow of drugs to the United States has not been meaningfully reduced.[30] A US Government Accountability Office (GAO) report on Plan Colombia published in 2008 found that it failed to meet its targets for reducing drug production, and that the "estimated flow of cocaine towards the United States from South America rose over the period" from 2000 to 2006.[31] The GAO also found that, in 2006, coca cultivation was up 15 percent from 2000, the year Plan Colombia began.[32] Regardless of a donation of over seventy helicopters, police training, and other military aid, "Colombia remains one of the world's largest producers and exporters of cocaine, as well as a source country for heroin and marijuana," according to a State Department report released in 2012.[33] These statistics are what have led many commentators to declare Plan Colombia and the US-led war on drugs a failure, but, as we shall see, there are other ways in which US anti-drugs assistance to Colombia are considered a roaring success.

Colombia's Paramilitary Problem

Though the anti-drugs component of Plan Colombia was an unabashed failure, the counterinsurgency segment, which some estimate to have cost upwards of half a billion dollars, reduced FARC numbers by half. Then there was the ongoing process of paramilitarization in the country, which was essentially funded by the war on drugs. It forced Indigenous, Afro-Colombian and peasant communities, who for generations had defended their collective rights and/or title to their lands, off their territories and opened these lands up for corporate plunder.[34] In his excellent book *Colombia: A Brutal History,* English journalist Geoffrey Leslie Simons provides an example of how, in the early 2000s, paramilitary activity provided cover for oil giant BP after it took a 15 percent stake in a company called Ocensa, which built an 800 km pipeline from the Cusiana-Cupiagua oil fields to the port of Coveñas. "The construction of the new pipeline destroyed hundreds of water sources and caused landslides that ruined local farmers. To protect the pipeline an exclusion zone was created around it—denying the farmers more of their land. [Lawyer Marta Hinestroza] began to hear the complaints of many farmers, but it proved impossible to represent them effectively in the courts. Four of her colleagues—ombudsmen in neighboring municipalities—were assassinated by the paramilitaries. Then Hinestroza began to receive death threats. A short time later, the paramilitaries arrived at the home of her aunt, dragged her out, tied her hands behind her back, made her kneel down, and then in front of the villagers shot her in the back of the head. Hinestroza resigned but continued to represent her clients. BP has offered £180,000 to 17 families affected by the ODC pipeline, but offers of less than £100 per person to other claimants who have been rejected: some 1,600 people are holding out for claims worth a total of around £20 million."[35]

In rural areas, the presence of armed actors representing state, guerrilla, narco, or other interests severely impacted people's daily lives. "Peasants and rural inhabitants have been deliberately terrorized by these uniformed, armed groups of men," wrote María Victoria Uribe about the army, paramilitaries, and guerrillas.[36] Violence in Colombia, as manifested during La Violencia of the 1950s and the war between uniformed armed factions today, has taken the form of acts of terror against the population, including mass killings and the public display of mutilated and tortured bodies. "In these massacres, perpetrators carry out a series of semantic operations, permeated with enormous metaphorical force, that dehumanize the victims and their bodies. These technologies of terror seek to expel rural inhabitants from their homes in order to consolidate territorial control."[37] Of all of the armed actors, it is the paramilitaries, operating with complicity and support from the army, that are the most effective at carrying out displacement, and it is they who are responsible for the lion's share of attacks.[38] By 2014, the total number of people displaced in Colombia was estimated at 5,368,138, and the total number of victims of the conflict over the past fifty years reached 6,073,437.[39] In a 2014 piece about memory, which criticizes Colombia's national cinema institute for not distributing the trailer of a film about the war in Colombia, Colombian-Mexican writer Camilo Olarte writes, "The blood of fiction is fine. It's acceptable. What's real, no. And this isn't fiction: 220,000 assassinations, 81.5 percent of them civilians, almost all *campesinos*; 25,007 disappeared, more than double the dictatorships of the Southern Cone; 1,754 victims of sexual violence; 6,421 children recruited by armed groups; 27,023 kidnappings associated with the armed conflict between 1970 and 2010; 10,189 people mutilated by antipersonnel mines, almost the same number as Afghanistan, 8.3 million hectares dispossessed and abandoned."[40]

In Colombia, in addition to fortifying the national army, paramilitarization has been beneficial to transnational corporations wishing to dissuade labor organizing. "As part of the protracted US-supported counterinsurgency campaign, paramilitary-state violence continues to systematically target civil groups, such as trade unions organizations, which are considered a threat to the political and economic 'stability' conducive to the neo-liberal development of Colombia. This has made Colombia very attractive to foreign investment as poor working conditions and low wages keep profit margins high.[41]" According to a 2010 report by the United Nations Special Rapporteur for Human Rights, "Recent developments in Colombia [indicate] the deteriorating situation of human rights defenders in recent months, in particular the killings, harassment and intimidation of civil society activists, trade-union leaders and lawyers representing victims."[42] The well-documented cases of Chiquita Brands, mining company Drummond, and BP have shown the links between paramilitary groups and US and transnational corporations.[43]

Making the link directly between payments from multinationals to paramilitaries and the violence and massacres that displaced thousands is dangerous and complicated. To learn more about the relationship between displacement caused by state and paramilitary violence and the operations of transnational corporations I met with Francisco Ramírez Cuellar, a spirited Colombian lawyer and former president of Colombia's National Mineworkers' Union (Sintraminercol). Today, Ramírez is the head of the Funtraenergetica, the United Federation of Miners, Energy, Metallurgical, Chemical and Allied Industries union, and maintains a practice in Bogotá. Ten years ago, he co-wrote a book about paramilitary activity and corporate gain, which was translated into English as *The Profits of Extermination*.

After a typical meal of sancocho and fish, during which a clever thief pretending to sell football memorabilia stole his cell phone, Ramírez and I sat down in a Bogotá cafe, where his voice boomed above the busy coffeeshop talk. I asked him what has changed since he wrote the book. "We intuited the use of paramilitary groups by corporations, but we couldn't openly say it because we didn't have convincing evidence. Well it turns out that it wasn't just true, but that it was a permanent practice of, according to my calculations, 96 to 98 percent of the companies that are operating in this country.... In fact, after investigating in detail, we found that the paramilitaries created something called the North Bloc, and we calculate that 80 percent of the money to create the paramilitary North Bloc was provided by mining and oil companies, who produce coal and exploit gas and oil in the whole northern and Caribbean zone of Colombia."

Since then Ramírez's investigations have uncovered evidence of individual cases of collaboration between paramilitaries and energy sector corporations, including Drummond, Glencore, BHP Billiton, Xstrata, Anglo American, Perenco, British Petroleum, Pacific Rubiales, as well as Chiquita, Dole, and Del Monte, which have large, land-intensive operations for the production of African palm for biofuels. "In our calculations, the operations of these companies over the last twenty-five years has produced 2.5 million forcibly displaced people in the zones they operate in. In our initial calculations 60,000 people have been killed, 11 percent or 10 percent of those 60,000 were workers affiliated to unions," said Ramírez, who survived eight assassination attempts and two bombings between 1993 and 2007. He told me about a handful of cases in which oil companies collaborated in the formation of paramilitary groups, which he said were often financed using money obtained through drug trafficking.

An illustration from the banana industry is particularly compelling: "I'll give you an example from the eastern plains of the country, from the Guaviare and Guainía departments. That area is today entirely planted with African palm, through front companies belonging mainly to Chiquita but also to Dole and Del Monte. What did Chiquita do? They moved in the paramilitaries they created and financed through narcotrafficking, which did as they pleased in the Urabá region, and that's why there was the famous Mapiripán massacre."

Though some of the facts of what took place in Mapiripán remain cloudy, much has emerged about what has become one of the country's most emblematic paramilitary massacres. Between July 15 and July 22 of 1997, over one hundred members of the Autodefensas Unidas de Colombia (AUC) paramilitary group took over the small town in the department of Guaviare. The paramilitaries arrived at an airport under military control and were transported to Mapiripán in army vehicles. Beginning July 15, paramilitaries killed at least forty-nine people, torturing and dismembering them before throwing their bodies into the Guaviare River. According to a statement by Mapiripán's municipal judge, "Every day, about 7:30 p.m., these individuals, through mandatory orders, had the electric generator turned off, and every night, through cracks in the wall, I watched kidnapped people go by, with their hands tied behind their backs and gagged, to be cruelly murdered in the slaughterhouse of Mapiripán. Every night we heard screams of people who were being tortured and murdered, asking for help."[44] The army didn't respond to calls for help from villagers until July 22. According to the Inter-American Commission on Human Rights, "The incursion of the paramilitary in Mapiripán was an act that had been meticulously planned several months before June 1997, carried out with logistic preparatory work and with the collaboration, acquiescence, and omissions by members of the Army. Participation of agents of the State in the massacre was not limited to facilitating entry of the AUC into the region, as the authorities knew of the attack against the civilian population in Mapiripán and they did not take the necessary steps to protect the members of the community."[45] A second massacre took place in the rural hamlet of La Cooperativa, as the paramilitaries evacuated Mapiripán. At the time, AUC leader Carlos Castaño claimed that his men carried out the massacre in order to destroy a stronghold of FARC insurgency that controlled the entire cycle of drug production and trafficking.[46] But the events that followed seem to confirm Ramírez's version, whereby companies dealing in palm oil are the major beneficiaries of the slaughter.

Four to five years after the massacres, Ramírez told me, "the companies came in to buy [land] and the farmers were obliged to sell. Those who were still alive. The rest ran away such that they were never indemnified, and through frontmen they ended up selling an entire region ... and then the planting of African palm began." In Guaviare, as elsewhere in Colombia, African palm was planted on lands belonging to displaced people once their lands were abandoned. According to a report about land grabs in the Chocó region, prepared by Colombia's Inter-Ecclesiastic Justice and Peace Commission, "Paramilitaries, with the complicity and negligence of the 17th Brigade and Urabá Police, assassinate, disappear, torture and displace local inhabitants, while claiming to fight the guerrilla. Businessmen associated with these criminal structures appropriate the territories that traditionally belong to the Afro-descendant communities; authorities at the service of the businessmen try to legalize this fraudulent land-grab; and the national government supports more than 95 percent of the illegal investment. This leads to oil palm agribusiness being implemented on the ruins of the communities' homes, cemeteries and communal areas."[47]

It is well established that Chiquita had long been paying off illegal armed groups. In March of 2007, representatives of Chiquita Brands International pleaded guilty in a Washington, D.C., court to making payments to the Autodefensas Unidas de Colombia (AUC) paramilitaries.[48] Chiquita found representation for the case in high places: Eric Holder, who went on to become the US attorney general, led negotiations between the company and the US Department of Justice.[49] According to the Associated Press, "In 2001, Chiquita was identified in invoices and other documents as the recipient of a shipment from Nicaragua of 3,000 AK-47 assault rifles and 5 million rounds of ammunition. The shipment was actually intended for the AUC."[50] According to the 2007 indictment, "From in or about 1997 through on or about February 4, 2004, defendant Chiquita made over 100 payments to the AUC totaling over $1.7 million."[51] Over half of those payments were made after the AUC was designated a terrorist organization by the United States in 2001. It was poor and working-class Colombians who paid the highest price for the company's payments to paramilitary and guerrilla groups: Chiquita funded the AUC during a period of seven years when over 4,000 people, mostly civilians in Urabá, were murdered by the paramilitaries, and another 60,000 were displaced.[52]

Chiquita sold off its Colombian assets in 2004 to Invesmar, a British Virgin Islands–based holding company that owns Banacol, a Colombian company that continues to supply Chiquita with bananas.[53] Displaced people returning to Curvaradó in Colombia's north are again being threatened, and fear being displaced again by paramilitaries at the service of Banacol.[54] In addition to payments received from Chiquita, it is documented that the AUC helped finance its operations by running cocaine out of the Port of Turbo using Chiquita boats. "Éver Veloza García, former commander of the paramilitary Turbo Front in Northern Urabá, explained how paramilitaries evaded the control points of security agencies by tying narcotic shipments to the hulls of banana vessels at high sea. Indeed, authorities have seized over one and a half tons of cocaine, valued at USD 33 million, from Chiquita ships."[55]

Transnational mining companies benefit time and time again from the regime of fear imposed by the drug war and paramilitarization in Colombia. Coal was discovered in Guajira state in the early 1980s, and Carbocol, the state-owned mining company, was sold to Exxon, which later resold to some of the world's biggest mining companies: Australia's BHP Billiton, South Africa's Anglo American, and Switzerland's Glencore (today Glencore-Xstrata). "These mining corporations then accelerated their exploitation of Colombian natural resources. Settlements of the Wayuu people and Afro-Colombians were cleared to give the companies easy access to the land. On 9–10 August 2001 the village of Tabaco was destroyed, displacing 350 families from their homes. Two hundred police and soldiers fought the helpless villagers as Intercor bulldozers smashed down their houses, and forcible ejection was being backed up by the usual panoply of terror. The nickel mine Cerro Matoso, another Billiton operation, was in an area where the paramilitaries held the people in a grip of fear."[56] Today, the Cerrejón mine, which expanded onto lands cleared by paramilitary activity, produces thirty two million tons of coal per year, and is the largest open pit coal mine in the world.[57]

Social control via military and paramilitary operations in the coal region is ongoing. "The climate of regional tension, especially that surrounding the mining projects in Cesar and the Guajira, is smothering, as there is a constant armed control that attempts to discipline the population, restricting, for example, the use of roads adjacent to the coal deposits," reads a 2011 report by the Social Observatory of Transnational Megaprojects and Human Rights.[58] The Guajira was historically a region with coca production, and anti-narcotics as well as counterinsurgency efforts, and Cesar more recently has also entered the list of states with coca production.[59]

Displacement caused by paramilitarization and cemented by state military presence has also occurred in relation to precious metals mining. In the mid-1990s, state forces arrived in the south of Bolívar state, which has long been home to small-scale mining activities, surrounding communities and preventing the free movement of residents. "Simultaneously, there was a strong advance by paramilitary forces in the period from 1996–2001, which initially generated two mass exoduses of the population from the countryside to municipal centers. Then, in 2006, various areas exploited by small miners were militarized, and construction began on various military bases."[60] South African company Anglo Gold Ashanti has active operations in the area, where small-scale miners have been killed in what they say are attempts to displace them from their lands. According to a 2010 press release by the Federation of Small-scale Miners of the South of Bolivar (FEDEAGROMISBOL), "These assassinations are part of a long string of acts of aggression against the people of the south of Bolivar, such as the assassination of Alejandro Uribe Chacón on September 19, 2006, and others that we consider to be actions which are part of a strategy to force us to leave our territories, as part of a larger more macabre alliance between the national government and the gold mining multinationals, such as Anglo Gold Ashanti, and palm companies such as Grupo Dabon, who are trying to take control of the natural resources in the south of Bolivar."[61] Anglo Gold, which holds nearly 800,000 hectares in mining concessions in Colombia, "tends to have their technicians accompanied by military personnel in areas with mineral potential, including in the exploration phase."[62] Or, as Ramírez boldly put it, "part of exploration is the creation of the paramilitary group."

Though they no longer make headlines, violence and displacement continue to be hallmarks of Colombian society. According to the United Nations, "While there has been a drop in the rate of new displacements, an estimated 100,000 people were displaced internally in 2010, representing a net increase of 35 percent compared to 2009, according to the Government."[63] The number of displaced measured by Colombian NGO CODHES the following year is more than double the 2010 number, at 259,146 persons.[64] In 2010 and 2011, at least 271 queer people were murdered, illustrating a pattern of violence against LGBTI people that is also evident in Mexico and Central America.[65] Between 2005 and 2010, 265 trade unionists were murdered, many by the same paramilitary groups spawned to fight guerrillas and protect narcotics traffickers.[66] And between 2008 and 2012, 142 human rights activists were killed and six disappeared.[67] Interestingly, as paramilitary murders began to drop off, killings by police rose: "Between the first and second halves of 2010, extrajudicial killings attributed to Law Enforcement grew by 68.18%. That equates to a daily rate more than double that of the previous Government. UNHCHR confirmed that this practice continued in 2011."[68]

In terms of merchandise that enters and exits the country, Buenaventura is Colombia's most important port city. It is also a place where forced displacement is still the norm, and a tragic example of how the phenomenon of paramilitary-initiated displacement is not confined to rural areas. Between 1999 and 2013, more than 6,000 people were murdered in the municipality of 359,753 people. Over that period, tens of thousands of people were displaced. In a shocking example of what is happening there, over the span of just fourteen days in late 2012, more than 4,000 people were forcibly uprooted.

According to the 2005 census, 88.5 percent of people living in Buenaventura identified as Afro-Colombian or of mixed African heritage. Their ancestors were forced to leave Africa between 1536 and 1540 in order to exploit the resources of the Pacific Coast region. In addition, more than 40,000 people moved to the city after being displaced from their homes in rural Colombia.

Violence in Buenaventura exploded in 1999, when two blocs of the AUC entered the city supposedly to rid it of guerrillas; various massacres were carried out as the population was accused of collaborating with the guerrillas. Following the official demobilization of the AUC blocs in 2004 and 2005, the FARC re-entered the municipality, and a new wave of paramilitaries was not far behind. The violence returned with a vengeance. As government forces weakened the FARC's ranks, other paramilitary groups entered the city, and today the government claims the ongoing violence is related to struggles between criminal bands trying maintain control over various areas in the city. The names of these groups change regularly: for example, in only two years, the Verdaderos Urabeños became the Campesinos del Pacifico, which became Los Gaitanistas, which became Los Chocoanos, which became La Empresa, leading to mass confusion in addition to terror. According to reports, paramilitary groups tend to be led by *paisas* (light-skinned Colombians from other regions, particularly from the state of Antioquia), while the foot soldiers are local Afro-Colombian youth. These groups have access to drug money, as the port facilitates an important outflow of cocaine (an estimated 250 tons per year).[69]

Fumigations and other activities under Plan Colombia pushed cocaine production out of Caquetá and Putumayo beginning in 2002, transforming Buenaventura and the Pacific region into cocaine producers and increasingly important transshipment points.[70] The city is heavily militarized, though soldiers and police collaborate with criminal groups and generally aggravate the violence. "It's as if we have a little Haiti within Colombia. It feels like another country," police officer Lt. Nikolai Viviescas told the *New York Times* in 2007.[71] Movement between neighborhoods, controlled by different paramilitary groups, is tightly restricted, and for a civilian to step foot into enemy territory is to risk death. Reports of people being murdered in broad daylight, killed by chainsaws, picked to death by screwdrivers, cut into pieces and dumped in the sea, and other barbaric, terror-inducing techniques swirl below the surface in private conversation and unpublished reports, but in general people are afraid to speak about what is happening. A list of clandestine mass graves is in circulation, but authorities have made no effort to excavate them. Extortion is the norm, and levels of violence are so intense that some residents are unable to go to the market for food. In some parts of Buenaventura, leaving is the only chance of survival.

The interests of the port, according to the Archdiocese of Cali, supersede the rights of the population. "The interests of the port dynamic and of transnational capital have gobbled up the Black and Indigenous Buenaventura, the majority of the residents are excluded, marginalized from the social, economic and political life of the port."[72]

In June 2013, Buenaventura was declared the capital of the Pacific Alliance, a US- and Canada-backed trade bloc made up of Colombia, Mexico, Peru, and Chile. The link between the terror exacted against Afro-Colombians and the rising profile of Buenaventura as an expanding neoliberal port is undeniable. Local observers note that in areas where the new container port and airport are being constructed, where highway corridors are being built, where the convention center is under construction, and where other mega projects are planned, forced displacement, threats, expropriations, torture, and killing of residents have increased.

Throughout the country, displacements have a disproportionate effect on Indigenous people and Afro-Colombians: nearly a quarter of the displaced population is Afro-Colombian, and an estimated 7 percent is Indigenous.[73] According to the National Indigenous Organization of Colombia (ONIC), sixty-four of Colombia's 102 Indigenous groups are at risk of extinction, and Indigenous peoples have been and continue to be disproportionately impacted by the armed conflict in Colombia.[74] The situation of Indigenous people has become so dire that human rights groups warn of genocide.

Plan Colombia's Measure of Successes

For all of the damage wrought and the money spent in Colombia, Plan Colombia failed to meaningfully reduce the amount of cocaine flowing from South America to the United States, and homicide rates in the Andean nation remain among the highest in South America.[75] Colombian and US authorities continue to hail Plan Colombia as a successful initiative, despite the program's goals not being met. Instead of forcing a change of strategy, Plan Colombia's failure was minimized in favor of an emerging series of metrics linked to security and an improved business environment. In a response to the GAO report on the failure of Plan Colombia to meet drug reduction targets, the State Department argued that other impacts of the plan should be emphasized, including Colombia's transition to a US-style justice system and the extension of Colombian police forces throughout the national territory. "In many ways, Colombian programs and US support have evolved from our original, more narrow focus into a comprehensive strategy that can now serve as a model to inform efforts in other challenged or failing states," wrote Bradford Higgins, the assistant secretary for resource management and CFO of the US State Department.[76] Higgins's assessment was echoed by another official review of the program.

"U.S. support for Plan Colombia has significantly strengthened Colombia's security environment, which may eventually make counter drug programs, such as alternative agricultural development, more effective," said Jess T. Ford, director of international affairs and trade, as part of her testimony before the Subcommittee on Domestic Policy, Committee on Oversight and Government Reform.[77] "Support for legal institutions, such as courts, attorneys general, and law enforcement organizations, in drug source and transit countries is not only an important part of the U.S. counter narcotic strategy but also advance State's strategic objectives relating to democracy and governance,"she said. [78]

Changes to the legal system implemented between 2005 and 2007 took away defense attorneys' right to access state assistance for investigations and to access the information garnered by prosecutors in advance of their appearance before the courts. "The accusatory criminal system was a cheap copy of the gringo system," said Gloria Silva, a lawyer with the Committee in Solidarity with Political Prisoners, an NGO founded in 1973. While her bodyguard looked on, Silva told me the reforms resulted in a regression in terms of access to justice, amounting to a privatization: the defense is now required to pay for its own investigations and legal assistance, where it wasn't previously. Like the reforms introduced in Mexico, there are no juries in Colombia's new legal system, meaning power is concentrated with judges. "The victims of state crimes in this country are poor people who don't have the chance to access independent experts who can represent them, and who could permit them to demonstrate a situation different from that presented by state prosecutors," she said. Alongside US-sponsored legal reforms, prison sentences have become increasingly harsh in Colombia.

In addition to the reforms of the justice system, the 2005 passage of two laws, 962 and 963, was crucial to ensuring investor security in Colombia. Law 962 simplified the investment process in Colombia, and Law 963 allows investors to sign "legal stability contracts" with the Colombian government, which ensure that "the laws applicable to the investment at the time the investment is entered into will remain in effect for a period between three and twenty years, depending on the type and amount of the investment."[79]

Foreign direct investment (FDI), the measure by which spending by transnational corporations in host countries is measured, has increased steadily since the early years of Plan Colombia. "Colombia's economic takeoff after 2003 did not happen by chance," boasted US-AID in 2008. During Plan Colombia, fifty-two areas of Colombia's economic system were targeted for reform, and "USAID provided technical assistance to the [government of Colombia] to help it design and implement policies ranging from fiscal reform to financial sector strengthening to improving the environment for small businesses, and many others."[80] At the outset of Plan Colombia, total FDI was calculated at $2.4 billion.[81] By 2011, Colombia's FDI stood at $14.4 billion, the fastest growth in FDI in Latin America.[82] This has not only been a boom for US and transnational companies, but there is also a growing Colombian elite whose fortunes are pegged to the new legal and financial regime there. "The total number of Colombian millionaires is forecast to grow by 36%, to reach over 48,600 in 2017 ... WealthInsight expects there will be strong growth in wealth held by Colombian multimillionaires; their wealth is projected to increase 28% to reach US$89 billion by 2017 ... The number of multimillionaires, however, will grow faster."[83]

In 2002, over 40 percent of Colombia's budget was going to paying foreign debt, and a third was being spent on state security forces like the police and army. "Even then, the IMF and the World Bank were pressing for further reductions in state spending on health and education."[84] Halfway through Plan Colombia, in January of 2003, the International Monetary Fund approved a $2.1 billion loan to Colombia, and a wave of austerity measures were applied, including the restructuring of the pension program, cuts to the public sector workforce, and the privatization of a major bank (BANCAFE).[85] According to the Committee for the Abolition of Third World Debt, "Although not directly related to Plan Colombia, the IMF's Colombia loan fits in to Plan Colombia as part of the larger strategy to revive the Colombian economy."[86] In 2002, 300 state companies were privatized or shut down, impacting over 150,000 workers.[87] In the final year of Plan Colombia, the government privatized 30 percent of the electrical grid and sold off the national gas company and part of Ecopetrol, the state oil company. "The most important Uribe energy reform was the creation of the Agencia Nacional de Hidrocarburos (ANH, the National Hydrocarbons Agency) and the introduction of new ways to attract private and foreign investors to explore and exploit the country's underground energy resources."[88] At this time the government introduced new mechanisms to allow for coordination between the army and extractive industries companies. Though not initially made explicit, it was eventually revealed that Plan Colombia was considered a precursor to the signing of a free trade agreement between Colombia and the United States. According to a report prepared by the Colombian government, "promoting conditions for employment generation and social stability" and expanding "tariff preferences in compensation for the negative effects of the drug trade and to favor a free trade agreement that will broaden employment opportunities" were among the objectives of Plan Colombia.[89] The Canada-Colombia Free Trade Agreement was brought into force in 2011, followed by the US-Colombia agreement in 2012.

Oil & Gas in Colombia

Oil and gas make up an increasingly important portion of Colombia's inward FDI, up from around one-tenth in the mid-90s to almost one-third by 2010, when it reached $4.3 billion.[90] Colombia's oil has long been in the sights of the US government, as "the current U.S. Interest in Colombia began one year after Occidental Oil discovered the billion-barrel Caño Limon oilfield in 1983. It led to the national security decision directives of 1986 and 1989 that authorized a U.S. military presence."[91] Ecopetrol, short for Empresa Colombiana de Petróleos, was formed in 1951 when a concession belonging to Ohio's Standard Oil expired and wasn't renewed. Ecopetrol took over the concession, though foreign companies like Mobil, Texaco, and Chevron were still allowed to operate in the country.[92] In 2010, Ecopetrol was the largest corporation in Colombia, controlling 100 percent of Colombian refining, 55 percent of oil production, 60 percent of gas production, and 79 percent of existing pipelines (equivalent to 8,815 kilometers of pipeline).

The steps toward the company's partial privatization are familiar to anyone who has studied the oil industry. First, there were cuts, which rendered the company unable to perform properly. "On 29 November 2002 Ecopetrol, Colombia's state oil company, announced that it wanted to cut benefits for the roughly 50 percent of its workers who belonged to a trade union.... Already the company had started court action to alter the working conditions agreed with the union—to hive off oil-well maintenance, to cut pension benefits for new workers, to cut health care costs and to be able to sack union members more easily."[93] Five years later, in 2007, Ecopetrol was partially privatized, and is now a mixed corporation, 89.9 percent of which is owned by the Colombian state, and 10.1 percent owned by shareholders (Ecopetrol is listed on the Colombia Stock Exchange [BVC] and the New York Stock Exchange). In 2010, Ecopetrol promised to invest $60 billion in exploration, infrastructure, transportation, refining, production, marketing, and acquisitions over the following five years. That same year, construction work began on a new, $3.5 billion pipeline from Ariguaney in the department of Meta to the port of Coveñas in Sucre.[94] These developments transformed Colombia into "one of the world's fastest growing and most important energy development stories," according to Luke Burgess, an energy sector commentator, who in 2010 dubbed Colombia "The World's Hottest Oil Frontier." He went on to note that the billions of dollars that Ecopetrol and the state plan to invest in oil and gas infrastructure and exploration means investors have "huge opportunities for easy profits."[95]

Not only did oil companies in Colombia get a boost from paramilitary groups and the opening up of Colombia's oil sector, the US government also threw down to ensure their assets were protected: "Violent attacks on Colombian energy installations, prior to and within the context of the post–11 September global anti-terrorism campaigns, have provided US lawmakers and members of the executive branch with legitimating arguments for increasing military aid to Colombia and expanding significantly and without precedent, the US mission there beyond counter-narcotics to include counter-insurgency and counter-terrorism."[96]

At some junctures, the connection between Plan Colombia and the protection of the oil industry was particularly evident. Part of Plan Colombia was dedicated to carrying out counterinsurgency in order to protect from bombing the Caño Limón-Coveñas pipeline, which was operated at that time by Ecopetrol (Colombia), Oxy (US), and Repsol (Spain). By 2005, US Special Forces had "provided training and equipment to about 1,600 Colombian Army soldiers" tasked with guarding the pipeline.[97] The US Narcotics Affairs Sections of the US Embassy in Bogotá administered the aviation component of the US-led militarization of the pipeline.[98]

The economic incentives for investing in the extractive industries in Colombia come with an added bonus: in 2010, the government of Colombia promised that the military would train a battalion of soldiers to assist companies in obtaining and transporting seismic testing results in parts of the country where there may be operational risks.[99] This marked the first time that the Colombian army provided troops for companies in the exploration phase, as previously the army's role was restricted to protecting oil and gas production and transportation in the exploitation phase. The Colombian government announced that by 2015, it would install a military radar base in Meta (an oil-producing region) and build domestic drones for the surveillance of oil pipelines and other military interests.[100]

The unfolding of Plan Colombia in Putumayo, a vast region encompassing Colombia's southern jungles, which shares a border with Ecuador, shows concretely how anti-drugs initiatives have impacted the economic and social landscape since the plan launched in 2000. "In December 2000, U.S.-trained counter narcotics battalions, U.S.-supplied Blackhawk helicopters and U.S.-piloted spray planes descended on Putumayo department to conduct Plan Colombia's initial aerial fumigation campaign," wrote journalist Gary Leech in 2004.[101] "But while Plan Colombia has failed to affect the price, purity and availability of cocaine in U.S. cities, its militarization of Putumayo has contributed significantly to increased oil exploration by multinational companies in this resource-rich region." In 2006, there were 4,500 soldiers guarding oil facilities in Putumayo, as well as two extra brigades and one special brigade, trained by the US Army.

One of the key points about the conflict in Colombia is that civilians are not murdered and displaced as a consequence of the war, nor are they "collateral damage"—instead, the displacement of civilians, the threats to activists and community organizers, the forced disappearances, and the terror are integral to the conflict.[102] "Forced displacement in Colombia is not a casual by-product of the internal conflict. Armed groups attack the civil population to strengthen territorial strongholds, expand territorial control, weaken the support of the opponent, and accumulate valuable assets (e.g., land or extraction of natural resources). Forcing out population as a war strategy aims at impeding collective action, damaging social networks, and intimidating and controlling the civilian population."[103] By moving people off the lands, new territories are opened up for these so-called frontier investments. When people are forced off their land and are living in camps and slums, it becomes much more difficult for them to effective-ly organize to control their territories.

Part of the oil drilling in Putumayo is taking place on the land of the Cofán people, some of whom have been displaced as part of a concerted strategy to make their lands available for mega projects. According to the Colombian government's Sistema de Información Indígena de Colombia (Indigenous Information System of Colombia, SIIC), "The fumigation of their territory as part of a military plan to weaken the stability of the guerrillas and battles between the FARC and paramilitaries caused a migration of the Cofán to Ecuador."[104] However, there have been challenges to the government's assertion that the displacement of the Cofán from their oil-rich lands was a re-sult of military battles. "This displacement is not only the result of armed actions by the various factions fighting in the area; it must also be seen as the outcome of a strategy for expropriating lands that are part of the Cofán's ancestral territory."[105]

Among the prime beneficiaries of the conflict in Putumayo are Canadian oil companies: Grand Tierra Energy Incorporated, a Calgary-based firm, produces approximately 14,000 net barrels per day in Putumayo, and controls over 750,000 net acres of territory there. Calgary's Petrobank has fourteen exploration blocks, covering a total of 1.6 million acres. Calgary's Parex Resources Incorporated, formerly Petro Andina, is also active in Putumayo and in the plains region. But the most important oil company in Colombia today is To-ronto-based Pacific Rubiales.[106]

In December of 2009, Pacific Rubiales became the first foreign company listed on the Colombian Stock Exchange. Today, Pacific Ru-biales is the second most important oil company in Colombia, after Ecopetrol. It is an early mover in the latest phase of oil and gas explo-ration and production in the country. In a newspaper interview, CEO Ronald Pantin explained why his company was in Colombia: "The stars aligned. It was a combination of Uribe's politics, the new hydro-carbon laws, the national security policies and very promising geolo-gy."[107] But it wasn't stars aligning. Colombia's oil boom is the result of a deliberate set of policies and practices applied over the previous years, some of which, like the training of Colombian military brigades by US troops specifically to guard pipelines, were part of Plan Colom-bia. The 600 Colombian troops that were stationed at a military base inside the Rubiales oilfields illustrate a national security policy that Pantin probably appreciates.

When Pantin mentioned the "new hydrocarbon laws" in Colombia, he was referring to laws rewritten with Canadian assistance. In a project funded by the Canadian International Development Agency, the Calgary-based Canadian Energy Research Institute worked with Colombia in 2001 and 2002 to "streamline the country's mining and petroleum regulations."[108] This initiative can be understood as part of a multinational effort to improve investment conditions in Colombia. As mentioned, the passage of legislation to encourage investment was part of Plan Colombia. This legislation increased legal security for corporations seeking long-term guarantees from the Colombian state.[109] At the end of Plan Colombia, corporations enjoyed a new legal regime as well as increased security provided by the Colombian state.

From Drug War to Open Occupation

The drug war policies backed by the United States in Colombia did little more, in terms of the flow of narcotics, than create the perception that the drug trade was suffering as a result of a military strategy against trafficking. The same policies failed to create a safer environment for rural populations, who continue to be displaced from their lands and to be targets of state and non-state violence. In 2008, Uribe signaled to the United States that Colombia would be interested in hosting what is euphemistically called a Cooperative Security Location, which the United States said it would be interested in pursuing if Ecuador didn't renew their agreement to use the Manta base (it didn't).[110] In 2009, the United States and Colombia signed an agreement to allow US troops to access seven military bases in the South American country for ten years, with the possibility of renewal.[111] The agreement, which Colombian officials tacked on to Plan Colombia so that it did not go before Congress, was declared unconstitutional and struck down months after it was signed. That didn't stop US troops from moving in or the Pentagon from beginning construction on the new bases.[112] People I interviewed in Arauca and Meta attested to the fact that US military personnel are present in bases in their regions, though there is no official confirmation of how many US soldiers are present in Colombia.

What has changed is official and media discourse regarding the war in Colombia: today, the general message is that paramilitary groups and drug cartels have demobilized and been disbanded. These irregular forces have today been rebranded as criminal bands (the Bacrim), which are presented as apolitical criminal groups without links to the state apparatus, and as such can be persecuted by police under the rule of law. According to international organizations active in Colombia, since the end of negotiations with the AUC in 2005, much of the Colombian government has acted as though paramilitaries no longer exist. They quote the attorney general's office as stating that "criminal organizations that emerged after the demobilization of the AUC, developed as a new form of paramilitarism, considered to be the third generation of paramilitary groups in Colombia and whose initial purpose was maintaining control of the lands that had been abandoned by the AUC. Paramilitaries have not been dismantled and their crimes go unpunished."[113] Attempting to rebrand paramilitaries as narcotraffickers without links to the government or state security forces is particularly interesting because it represents a shift in Colombia to a Mexican-style discourse around organized crime, which depoliticizes the reactionary actions of these groups and creates discursive distance between them and state actors.

I asked Fabian Laverde, with whom I opened this chapter, about the difference between paramilitary groups and Bacrim. "It is exactly the same thing," he said. "If you look at who are the commanders of the Bacrim, as they call them, they are effectively the same commanders who were in the paramilitary blocs." Today, the lay of the land looks similar to how it did throughout Plan Colombia, but instead of big-name regional paramilitary blocs, there are smaller, localized groups able to work with perhaps even less media scrutiny. "The lands that they take or that they're after, or the leaders that they murder, don't even benefit the commander of the Bacrim, rather it benefits a third party, who was the same person who robbed the peasants of their lands twenty years ago using the armed power of the paramilitaries with the complicity of the state, and now those who are impeding the recuperation of those lands are the famous Bacrim," said Laverde. His analysis was one that I heard repeated over again by people I met in Colombia: the emergence of the Bacrim was a public relations tactic to conceal the state's ongoing connection with armed groups.

There can be no doubt that Plan Colombia was a failure when it came to stopping the flow of drugs, and increasing how safe many Colombians—especially but not exclusively rural Colombians—felt in their homes. What it did achieve, however, was increased security for investors, both on the ground in regions where the state previously did not exercise control, and legally, through entrenching protection of investments and the ratification of free trade agreements between

Colombia and the US and Canada. Colombia's economic boost following Plan Colombia has to do with financial and legal reforms instituted as part of the "anti-narcotics" program, but it also goes hand in hand with the repressive social order and militarization imposed during (and after) the initiative. Armed groups cleared territories around the country of the people who lived there, and then corporations arrived to occupy and exploit them. Unions were weakened, and Indigenous and popular movements were left reeling from the violence leveled against their members.

What did the US government learn from Plan Colombia? First, that the war on drugs can be used as a mechanism to promote business-friendly policies, and second, that paramilitarism strengthened by prohibition can assist in the maintenance of control over territories and populations.

A refined version of the comprehensive, US-backed drug war strategy is what has been applied in Mexico, Central America, and elsewhere, beginning in 2007. Seen through this lens, the war on drugs appears to be a bloody fix to the US economic woes. Today, the United States and Colombia fund and promote security-related trainings by Colombians throughout the hemisphere. For the US State Department, "Colombia is also a significant contributor to Central America's security sector and is becoming a partner in addressing citizen security in the region."[114]

General Kelly, commander of US SouthCom, notes that "with Colombia increasingly taking on the role of security exporter, we are facilitating the deployment of Colombian-led training teams and subject matter experts and attendance of Central American personnel to law enforcement and military academies in Colombia as part of the U.S.-Colombia Action Plan on Regional Security Cooperation. This is a clear example of a sizeable return on our relatively modest investment and sustained engagement."[115]

It is with this in mind that we can begin to explore the impacts of the Mérida Initiative and CARSI in Mexico and Central America. The economic results achieved with Plan Colombia, combined with its proximity to the United States, made Mexico a natural next place to roll out the drug war. Making the links between US anti-drug policy and the expansion of capitalism in Mexico is difficult because the impacts of these policies are continuously being implemented and felt, and we don't (yet) have the benefit of hindsight. We do know, however, that Colombia is considered a model for Mexico's anti-drug war, and we can see what the results have been there in terms of the anti-drug strategy serving to increase Colombia's integration into global capitalism. Today in Mexico we're presented with a confusing, jumbled picture, but that is all the more reason to attempt to analyze events taking place there with a view to the broader context.

CHAPTER 4:

MEXICO'S DRUG WAR REFORMS

IN 2010 and 2011, grenades exploded at city hall buildings in Reynosa, Matamoros, Nuevo Laredo, and Ciudad Victoria, all located in the Mexican border state of Tamaulipas. Organized crime was blamed for the explosions—in particular, members of the Zetas or the Gulf Cartel. I visited the region in early 2011, at a loss for what could be driving criminal groups to fight against local governments that are, for all intents and purposes, under cartel control. I went to the region against the counsel of various journalists, who said it was too dangerous. Most of my sources refused to go on the record, and the stories they told in hushed tones were enough to give any reporter the chills. It wasn't until I met Francisco Chavira Martínez that things began to become clear. The first time we met, he suggested we eat together at the back of a Reynosa restaurant that caters to well-heeled locals. Waiters dressed like penguins bowed in and out; the rest of the tables were occupied mostly by older men. Chavira, who runs a private university with campuses throughout Tamaulipas, spoke loudly between bites, not seeming to mind the fact that others could hear him.

After a bit of small talk and a couple of sips of coffee, I asked about the bombs. Local governments "use car thieves to steal the cars of anyone who opposes them; house thieves who will rob your house to frighten you; narcotraffickers, who they use as a way to create fear in the people, so that you don't participate, so that you don't raise your voice or go against the government; they even send their own to throw grenades at city halls," Chavira explained.[1] Silence. Maybe Chavira noticed the quizzical look on my face. He quickly explained what it was he meant. "Why?" he asked himself, pausing for a moment. "So that the people are scared and don't go to City Hall to make demands; they won't go and demand that public accounts be transparent, or [ask] what the money is being spent on." Some months after our interview, Chavira, a candidate for the left-leaning Democratic

Revolutionary Party (PRD), was arrested on trumped-up charges and held in jail until after the elections, in what he referred to as a "legalized kidnapping" by the state.

Members of the Mexican government have used many means to defend their position in society, from explosions to extortion and threats. The methods Chavira describes above can help us understand the extent of this, and go a little ways toward illustrating the complicity between state actors and criminal groups. But the politics of the drug war isn't just about bombs and bad guys. Alongside the violence, there are legal and policy reforms embedded in Plan Mexico that have everything to do with creating a more hospitable business environment as well as entrenching the US-backed rule of law framework.

The stated focus of the Mérida Initiative is fourfold: dismantle criminal organizations; strengthen air, maritime, and border controls; reform the justice system; and diminish gang activity while decreasing demand for drugs.[2] The Mérida Initiative, or Plan Mexico, is the overarching policy and legislative framework that establishes drug war capitalism in Mexico. It takes a page directly from Plan Colombia in terms of enshrining support for disrupting narcotics trafficking while transforming Mexico in three key ways: introducing a new legal system and promoting structural reforms, increasing levels of militarization, and, as a by-product of the latter, encouraging the formation and multiplication of paramilitary groups.

As with Plan Colombia, the Mérida Initiative is not strictly a military agreement. It has four "pillars": disrupt organized criminal groups, institutionalize reforms to sustain rule of law and respect for human rights, create a 21st century border, and build strong and resilient communities. According to the US Government Accountability Office, "The Mérida Initiative is an assistance package with diverse program components that is being implemented by a wide range of U.S. agencies under the leadership and management of the State Department."[3]

The first component of the Mérida Initiative is officially known as "Assistance to Enhance the Rule of Law and Strengthen Civilian Institutions."[4] Tied to—or simultaneous with—anti-drug funding, laws are adjusted, and reforms are brought in that encourage privatization and increased foreign direct investment. According to the US government, this will "Build Strong and Resilient Communities," and "Strengthen Institutions."[5] An alternative analysis of this component of drug war funding could instead carry a title that represents the spirit of these adjustments: in the case of Mexico these policies could be called "NAFTA-plus" as they are a form of deepening institutional changes formalized in the Canada-US-Mexico (North American) Free Trade Agreement, signed in 1994. In addition, this component fulfills an important part of counterinsurgency, as it attempts to convince and capture the hearts and minds of Mexicans.

The second component of the Mérida Initiative is officially called "Law Enforcement and Security Assistance."[6] This consists of state-funded militarization of police and of borders, as well as increased police and military powers, training, and weaponry. This represents agreements made in a legal manner between cooperating governments, though implementation can be on the margin of legality in host states.[7] The US government tells us that this is designed to "Disrupt Organized Criminal Groups" and "Build a 21st Century Border,"[8] but in actual fact it looks a lot like counterinsurgency. Back in 2010, Hillary Clinton, then US secretary of state, compared the situation in Mexico to an insurgency. "It's looking more and more like Colombia looked 20 years ago," she told delegates at a Council on Foreign Relations event. Drug cartels "are showing more and more indices of insurgencies," she went on.[9] In 2009, the head of the US Joint Chiefs of Staff stated that he backed the use of counterinsurgency in Mexico.[10]

Counterinsurgency can be understood not only as a form of warfare but also as a kind of war with outcomes that may differ from those of traditional combat. "Victory in the context of counterinsurgent warfare is measured not by the number of enemies vanquished but by the increase in trust and sympathy among native peoples that would wean them away from the insurgents' influence," writes Vicente L. Rafael, a professor of history at the University of Washington.[11] Keep Rafael's description of victory in mind, and then take a look at how John D. Feeley, principal deputy assistant secretary of the Bureau of Western Hemisphere Affairs at the US State Department describes the US's National Drug Control Strategy as it is applied in Mexico. He describes the core of the strategy as enhancing citizen security and strengthening the rule of law, "while empowering average citizens to collaborate with police, prosecutors, and judges, as well as teachers, community activists, non-governmental organizations (NGOs), and human rights advocates."[12] Seen from an alternative perspective, the law enforcement segment of the Mérida Initiative can be understood as the application of counterinsurgency war within a formally democratic framework. It also serves as a program to limit human mobility while encouraging the flow of goods and services.

The two components described above are both formally acknowledged by proponents of anti-drug policy. The policy component and the policing component reinforce one another: as public companies are privatized and state revenues fall, more force will be required on the part of the state in order to maintain social order. Take Pemex, the state oil company, for example. Before reforms in December 2013, 99 percent of the state-owned oil company's profits went to paying taxes, representing the largest revenue source in Mexico's national budget.[13] It remains to be seen how the reforms to Pemex will affect the country's revenue stream and budget. If the taxation of private oil companies fails to fill state coffers in the future, it could result in the application of the harshest austerity measures yet in Mexico, which may in turn trigger mass social protest.

To this end, the capacity of security forces to make massive arrests and jail dissidents is being increased through Mérida Initiative programs. As more people are arrested by larger and more aggressive police forces, the expedited justice system offered by the United States model could prove useful in processing them. The increased prison capacity, also funded by the US through the Mérida Initiative, will doubtless be useful in detaining them. Looked at from this perspective, the Mérida Initiative appears to be a long-term strategy to enforce austerity and globalized capitalism while militarizing Mexico.

The third and final component of the Mérida Initiative is a generally unacknowledged yet known effect of the application of the drug war: the emergence of new forms of social control that stem from the reorganization of narcotics flows and crime groups provoked by the militarized disruption of existing trafficking networks. In the dominant discourse of the drug war, this phenomenon is described using cartel war discourse. However, from a critical perspective it can be understood as something closer to a form of paramilitarization. This part of the drug war is the most nebulous and difficult to describe. Journalists are encouraged to use a frame around cartels warring with each other to explain this phenomenon, but a closer look shows that paramilitarization is a known effect of militarizing drug trafficking. As we saw in the example of Colombia, paramilitarization can serve the interests of investors and transnational corporations seeking to prevent unionization or community mobilization.

The Mérida Initiative served as catalyst for a sharp increase in domestic police and military spending in Mexico. Before the Mérida Initiative, the US was giving Mexico in the neighborhood of $60–70 million a year.[14] The drug war changed that, and fast. US security spending in Mexico in 2010 was over $500 million, compared with $434 for Colombia, before falling off to $160 million or less (compared to over $250 million in following years for Colombia).[15] World Bank data shows Mexico's military spending as a proportion of gross domestic product (GDP) has risen 0.4 to 0.6 percent over recent years, between 2012 and 2013 Mexico increased military spending "by 5.1 per cent, despite weaker economic growth."[16] "It should be noted that Mexico has devoted considerable monies of its own to combat drug-related crime in the country, increasing the defense budget from just $2 billion in 2006 to $9.3 billion in 2009. This investment has been used to mobilize thousands of troops and federal police, underwrite interdiction of drug shipments, implement institutional reform, and enhance inter- and intra-agency cooperation and intelligence sharing," reads a report by the US army–linked RAND Corporation.[17] It is worth pointing out that military spending does not include the full spending on policing. Calderón's offensive "was backed by the U.S. under the Mérida Initiative and included deployment of 96,000 army troops, together with thousands of marines and the appointment of dozens of military officers as police chiefs in towns and cities."[18]

Total US funding appropriations for the Mérida Initiative in Mexico between 2008 and the end of 2014 totaled $2.35 billion. Congress requested $115 million for the Mérida Initiative in 2015.[19] It was estimated in 2012 that for every dollar that the United States spent on the Mérida Initiative, Mexico spent thirteen.[20] Central America Regional Security Initiative funds began flowing to Central America in 2008, by the end of 2014 totaled approximately $806.3 million, with an additional $130 million requested by Congress for 2015.[21] By mid-2013, the US had disbursed $27,151,000 for the Caribbean Basin Security Initiative, a fraction of the over $157 million allocated.[22]

The US government did not provide any cash to the Mexican government as part of the Mérida Initiative, instead spending the earmarked dollars on US-made equipment and various private contracting firms. Additionally, non-Mérida counter-drug assistance was provided by the US Department of Defense, totaling $208.6 million between 2009–2012.[23] Through newspaper reports generally focus on the police and military aspects of the drug war (the violence), recent testimony by the US point man for anti-drugs policy in the Americas, William Brownfield, highlights how the US government's motives in funding the Mérida Initiative go beyond security: "In every society, citizen security underpins economic stability and allows trade, investment, energy development, and education exchanges to flourish. The partnership forged between the United States and the Government of Mexico over the past six years under the Mérida Initiative exemplifies how strengthening citizen security supports these broader objectives."[24] The objectives outlined by Brownfield could be more important than they first appear. According to economist Dr. Paul Collier, "Conflicts are far more likely to be caused by economic opportunities than by grievance. If economic agendas are driving conflict, then it is likely that some groups are benefiting from conflict and that these groups therefore have some interest in initiating and sustaining it."[25] Collier is referring to civil wars, but the same applies to Mexico. The drug war in Mexico can hardly be called a civil war, due to the extent of international involvement in the conflict (the same can also be said of other so-called civil wars, like those in Guatemala and El Salvador, for example). The scale of the killing has pushed the conflict far beyond the frame of being a dirty war. In some senses, it is a war with no proper name. Regardless, Collier's point about economic opportunities holds true for Mexico.

In the case of the drug war in Colombia, Central America, Mexico, and elsewhere, it is clear that dominant factions in the state apparatus stand to benefit. State military power, policing, and the prison system are strengthened through increased aid and cooperation with the world's military superpower. Another beneficiary of drug war policies generally is the transnational corporate sector. It experiences improved conditions for investment thanks to reforms as well as an increasingly militarized and repressive social context that allows a freer hand to pursue destructive and/or controversial mega projects.

Criminal groups, the ones moving the drugs, are the third category of beneficiaries. These are the war profiteers the mainstream media and governments focus on. According to a 2010 report by the UN Office on Drugs and Crime, 85 percent of gross proceeds in the $35 billion cocaine market stayed in the United States. Of that amount, 15 percent went to US wholesalers and mid-level dealers, and 70 percent went to street-level dealers who sold to US consumers. Compare this to the $4.6 billion (13 percent) that stayed with traffickers moving the product between the Andean region and the US, or with the mere 1 percent that stayed with Andean producers.[26] These statistics help us understand that drug traffickers in Mexico are accessing amounts of money that are, all told, relatively small. A similar division of profits in the narcotics trade exists worldwide. According to the Global Commission on Drug Policy, "drug prohibition has fueled a global illegal trade estimated by the UNODC to be in the hundreds of billions. According to 2005 data, production was valued at $13 billion, the wholesale industry priced at $94 billion and retail estimated to be worth $332 billion."[27]

Though it is the military aspect of the Mérida Initiative that gets the lion's share of funding and media attention, it is worth examining policy aspects that constitute the first component of the Mérida Initiative. Of the $400 million the United States promised to spend on Mexico's security, $73.5 million was devoted to funding judicial reform, institution building, and rule of law. The rule of law, judicial and institution building or policy component of the Mérida Initiative is of crucial importance. It brings together security and economy in what is perhaps one of the greatest innovations of Plan Colombia: the militarization of aid and the steering of anti-drug money toward fostering the creation of more welcoming investment policies and legal regulations. Though not often talked about in the context of the drug war, these policy changes often have little or nothing to do with illicit substances and everything to do with the transformation of the business environment.

The policy part of the Mérida Initiative is carried out and coordinated by USAID, with participation by the Department of Justice, the Department of Homeland Security, the Department of Defense, the State Department, and the Office of National Drug Control Policy.[28] USAID's general focus is on "furthering America's foreign policy interests in expanding democracy and free markets while also extending a helping hand to people struggling to make a better life, recover from a disaster or striving to live in a free and democratic country."[29] The agency, together with the US State Department, requested nearly $50 billion from the federal government in 2014.[30] "U.S. policy toward the Western Hemisphere seeks to seize and expand opportunities for inclusive economic growth, transforming the region's emerging middle class into dynamic new markets for U.S. exports and creating jobs at home," according to the US State Department.[31] The US government plans to spend about $205.5 million in Mexico in 2014, a significant reduction from the previous year, but still the third highest amount in the hemisphere, after Colombia at $323 million and Haiti at $300 million (together these three countries make up over half of total US government spending in the Western Hemisphere).[32]

After seven years of destabilization and terror linked to the drug war, Mexico is undergoing a series of reforms and signing on to new agreements that deepen the North American Free Trade Agreement, which took effect in 1994. As the Mérida Initiative continued into 2014, the US government proposed to use it increasingly to focus on political and legislative reforms that are under way. "In Mexico, Mérida Initiative assistance will continue to transition to increased capacity-building activities geared towards strengthening Mexican institutional reforms, rule of law, and violence prevention in partnership with the Peña Nieto administration."[33] There's no shortage of ways for the US to get involved in policy changes in Mexico, as there has been a slate of reforms since Peña Nieto was elected in July of 2012, including energy reform, financial reform, tax reform, labor reform, political reform, education reform, and telecommunications reform. "If all of this unfolds successfully, Peña Nieto will have moved Mexico forward more than anyone since NAFTA was passed, putting Mexico on the path to economic and democratic modernity," James R. Jones, co-chair of Manatt Jones Global Strategies, told journalist Eva Hershaw in late 2013.[34]

In addition to the reforms, Mexico is party to the Trans-Pacific Partnership, a secretive trade agreement between twelve nations: Australia, Brunei, Canada, Chile, Japan, Malaysia, Mexico, New Zealand, Peru, Singapore, the United States, and Vietnam. According to the Office of the US Trade Representative, "This agreement will advance U.S. economic interests with some of the fastest-growing economies in the world; expand U.S. exports, which are critical to the creation and retention of jobs in the United States; and serve as a potential platform for economic integration across the Asia-Pacific region."

The US and Mexican economies are deeply linked, and the robustness and protection of both countries' economies is an oft-cited justification for the drug war. According to *Strategic Forum*, a US military journal, "In recent years, almost 85 percent of Mexico's exports have gone to the United States, making Mexican economic success dependent on the balance between trade and security. U.S. economic success is also dependent on this balance. Continued prosperity depends on reliable homeland defense and security, which can only be achieved through greater coordination and information sharing among military partners as well as the law enforcement and interagency community. President Calderón promised to improve security, thereby enhancing prosperity for the Mexican people."[35] Though at the beginning of his term Peña Nieto made links between violence and economic growth, it is an increasingly rare refrain for high-level politicians in Mexico and the United States, who are attempting to shift the discourse toward the purely economic. "Preventing violence and promoting economic and social development are part of a vicious cycle," President Enrique Peña Nieto told *Time* magazine after his election. "Without better economic opportunity you can't have better public security, and vice versa."[36]

Not all of the policy reform work is taking place using Mérida Initiative funds. Nonetheless there is coordination between Mérida programs and USAID's competitiveness programs, which aim to create a policy environment that is more favorable to transnational capital.[37] One of USAID's program goals is to see that the "Government of Mexico becomes more effective in curbing monopolies and eliminating anticompetitive practices."[38] According to a call for proposals issued in January 2012, "USAID is working with Mexican partners to improve economic governance and increase private sector competitiveness."[39] The agency's focus is on advocating for a new regulatory regime and additional privatization, efficiency, and foreign direct investment in the transportation, financial, energy, and telecommunications sectors.[40] "USAID is supporting Mexican-led initiatives to improve the country's competitiveness by working with Mexican federal, state, and local government entities, nongovernmental organizations, and the private sector to improve Mexico's business-enabling environment and build sustainable support for continued policy reforms and systemic changes."[41] USAID funds the Red Mexicana de Competencia y Regulación (Mexican Network on Competition and Regulation, RMCR) and the Centro de Investigación para el Desarrollo, A.C. (Center for Research for Development, CIDAC), whose policy proposals for Mexico's economy look like they are drawn directly from a US State Department wish list.[42] CIDAC promotes the advantages of increased foreign direct investment and more aggressive privatization programs. In addition, USAID subcontracts work to private firms, which are tasked with carrying out various programs designed to improve the investment climate in Mexico. This is significant because many of the firms subcontracted by USAID are military contractors who have participated in reconstruction efforts in post-war zones. These firms are the same ones that were tasked with helping implement reforms once the US and its allies invaded and occupied Iraq. In Mexico, the destruction isn't wrought by US bomb attacks, but nevertheless the country has been deeply damaged by the drug war. Here, reconstruction and reforms are implemented alongside ongoing terror and violence.

In 2009 USAID awarded Abt Associates $17.8 million to carry out the Mexico Competitiveness Program, which is made up of four parts: building sustainable environmental governance, increasing private sector competitiveness, making precursor markets more competitive, and increasing investment in and use of clean energy.[43] Abt subcontracted out the private sector competitiveness section of the program to Casals & Associates. According to Casals & Associates, this segment of the program has the following goals:

- Increasing government transparency and accountability
- Promoting competition within government through policy reforms and regulatory changes
- Improving government communication
- Promoting nongovernmental organization networks and public-private partnerships to strengthen the role of civil society [44]

Casals & Associates and Abt Associates both have direct ties to the US military; Casals & Associates belongs to DynCorp, a defense contractor that, according to its website, has "recruited, trained, and deployed more than 6,000 highly-qualified civilian peacekeepers and police trainers to 11 countries, including Haiti, Bosnia, Afghanistan, and Iraq, for the Department of State," while Abt got its start "transferring defense-related technology and systems to civilian application."[45]

Both of these military-linked corporations are today at work in Mexico promoting policy reforms designed to improve the experience for transnational corporations and investors seeking to do business in Mexico. Their programs are unfolding at the same time as the country undergoes militarization and paramilitarization because of the drug war.

Another USAID-funded program in Mexico is being carried out by Evensen Dodge International, a global capital markets firm that helps Mexican states raise money by arranging for the issuance of bonds and loans that make resources available to invest in public private partnerships.[46] According to the US State Department, "Evensen Dodge International, a financial company, is working with U.S. Embassy Mexico and the Government of Mexico to carry out reforms to the legal framework of pension funds at the federal level. [Fernando J. Gama of Evensen Dodge] said that these reforms are enabling Mexican states to finance renewable energy systems."[47] If there is any doubt about the benevolence of USAID and foreign assistance programs, it was quelled in 2001 by US Secretary of State Colin Powell, when, in a rare admission, he spoke to the true role of US development aid: "Just as surely as our diplomats and military, American NGOs are out there serving and sacrificing on the front lines of freedom.... [NGOs] are such a force multiplier for us, such an important part of our combat team."[48]

Peña Nieto's Reforms?

Days before President Enrique Peña Nieto's inauguration, the *New York Times* reported that "he has promised to rewrite the tax laws, open the state-owned oil sector to private investment and rein in Mexico's powerful monopolies."[49] Peña Nieto's promises align almost perfectly with USAID-coordinated economic and financial proposals for Mexico.

Before assuming office, Peña Nieto's PRI party joined with Calderón's PAN to pass a labor reform law that introduced hourly wages (about 70¢ per hour) instead of daily minimums, and lessened the legal requirements on corporate contributions to the social security program. This strike against the already precarious Mexican working class was Calderón's parting shot and helped usher in a new era of reforms under the PRI. When he took office on December 1, 2012, Peña Nieto launched the "Pact for Mexico," a coalition of the country's three largest political parties that has introduced education, financial, tax, political, and energy reforms.[50] By and large, the reforms being implemented in Mexico are based on the model of austerity and structural adjustment. The promotion of structural reforms in Mexico is enshrined in the Mérida Initiative and provides a crucial example of how drug war capitalism works to transform national economies to benefit the corporate sector.

In early 2014, I visited Alejandro Hope at his office in Polanco, one of Mexico City's swankiest suburbs. He's an analyst who has worked with a variety of Mexican and US think tanks—including the Mexican Institute for Competitiveness (IMCO) and the Wilson Center—and I asked him what he thought of Peña Nieto's first year. "There's a lot of wishful thinking and propaganda. Peña Nieto's first year was not a good one," he said. Hope pointed out that the education reform, the telecommunications reform, and the political reform are still only partially realized, stalled at the level of implementation and state acceptance. "If the energy reform hadn't have been passed in mid-December, Peña Nieto's first year would have been declared a failure."

Regardless, it's worth a look at some of the reform initiatives that have been pushed through under Peña Nieto's leadership. On December 11, 2012, ten days after he took power, the Mexican government changed two articles of the constitution, resulting in what they said was an education reform. "What was approved isn't an education reform, rather a labor and administrative reform in disguise," wrote columnist Luis Hernández Navarro in *La Jornada*.[51] Hernández maintains the legislation opens the pathway to the privatization of the education system. The changes introduce standardized testing and increased labor precarity for Mexican teachers, and require English classes for Mexican students. The reform was heavily contested; two months of marches and blockades by teachers, especially Indigenous teachers from impoverished rural areas in the southern states of Oaxaca and Chiapas, showed street-level resistance against it. Tents were erected, and a protest camp, which lasted for months at the Monument to the Revolution in Mexico City, was built. For months, teachers refused to return to classes until their demands—for multilingual education (Spanish and Indigenous languages, not English) and no standardized testing—were met.

The stakes are high when it comes to Mexico's education system, and the US corporate sector in particular has a lot riding on innovation and education in Mexico. "With Mexico able to provide US companies with young, skilled and cheap labor, and with the US able to play a potentially crucial role in the transfer of technology and know-how to its southern neighbor, there is clearly plenty of room for the two administrations to push ahead with further economic integration," according to a recent article in the *Financial Times*. General Electric has an important center for research and design in Querétaro, which is fast becoming the country's most important aerospace cluster. Engineers, 115,000 of whom graduate in Mexico each year, are particularly sought after, as they can be hired in Mexico for less than $1,000 a month. This is a crucial element in Mexico's ability to attract foreign direct investment in advanced manufacturing, like the automobile and airplane industries. According to data from Mexico's Secretary of the Economy, the number of aerospace companies in Mexico rose from 61 to 249 between 2005 and 2011, and 85 percent of aerospace exports are to the United States. Aerospace exports more than doubled to $4.3 billion over the same time period.[52] By 2011, the automotive industry represented 6 percent of FDI in Mexico and 23 percent of Mexico's exports. In a speech given the same day Enrique Peña Nieto assumed his role as president of Mexico, the US ambassador to Mexico had this to say: "Increasing competitiveness has enabled Mexico to take a larger share of U.S. imports—about 13 percent this year. This trend is being driven by the rising cost of labor in China and the impact of high-energy prices on transportation. There are compelling reasons to believe that it is not just a short-term phenomenon. While Mexico has been the second-largest destination of U.S. exports for some time, some economists now predict that Mexico will overtake China to become the largest source of imports into the U.S. by 2018."[53]

There has been pressure from international finance institutions to change the education system in Mexico; in a December 2012 press release announcing the renewal of a $73 billion credit line for Mexico, the IMF called for reforms to the education system, among other things.[54] Peña Nieto has already earned the admiration of the International Monetary Fund, whose leaders said they were "very impressed with President Pena Nieto's structural reform agenda."[55]

The strategy, at least according to economic elites, is working. On May 8, 2013, Mexico's Finance Ministry (SHCP) presented to Congress a 927-page financial reform, consisting of thirteen decrees and amending thirty-four federal laws. Changes to the financial system are necessary not only to encourage foreign direct investment, but also to allow for the beginnings of shifting the tax base away from state-run petroleum company Pemex, which in turn was part of clearing the path to privatization. The same day the reform was published, Fitch Ratings raised Mexico's credit rating to BBB+, citing "greater than anticipated commitment of the new administration and Congress to pass structural reforms."[56] Finance Minister Luis Videgaray explained that the reform aims to increase competition in the banking sector and create incentives for lending.[57] Videgaray twice pointed to Chile, long the Latin American poster child of neoliberalism, as a model for Mexico's financial system. "Regardless of the reforms, the performance of the Mexican economy over the last three decades has not been satisfactory," read a report released prior to the reforms by the Mexican Central Bank.[58] In a March 2012 presentation, a Bank of Mexico representative correctly said that the pending reform agenda for the country's central bank would improve the ease with which companies can do business in Mexico, remove "legal obstacles," prevent labor flexibility, "strengthen the rule of law," and consolidate macroeconomic policies.[59] "A poor track record of paying back loans, limited consequences for non-payment and a challenging legal environment for collections also dull lending in Mexico," reported the *Wall Street Journal*,[60] so among the key objectives of the reform bill, is "improving trial procedures seeking faster resolution of controversies and granting enhanced rights to lenders through the courts, which are likely to expedite collections."[61]

The financial reform, far from extending credit to poor and rural Mexicans and farmers who own land collectively (who do not have fee simple title), encourages the extension of credit in the form of credit cards. It creates the legal framework for the government to facilitate repossession of property belonging to debtors, something not previously contemplated in Mexico. Citibank and Banco Bilbao Vizcaya Argentaria are the biggest players, and HSBC, Santander, and Banorte round off the banks that essentially control the sector in Mexico. Experts say the financial reforms introduced on May 8, 2013, as part of the Pact for Mexico will primarily benefit these big banks. "The financialisation will take place through an increased penetration in small and medium sized communities, including poor and rural areas, that could finally mean an even deeper process of indebtedness of a good part of the population of Mexico," said Dr. Luis Ignacio Román Morales, a professor and researcher in the department of Economics, Administration, and Finances at the Western Institute of Technology and Higher Education (ITESO) in Guadalajara, Mexico. "For the banks and financial institutions in general, it will become much easier to collect from the debtor. That's very serious on a number of levels."[62]

Ejidos are also under threat from the financial reform.[63] The system of ejidos is similar to the calpulli system of the Aztecs' rule of Mexico, in which part of the lands was farmed by single families and other parts were used collectively. Ejido land was formerly only collectively owned by groups of farmers and passed on through the generations. Since pre-NAFTA reforms in 1992, parceled lots of ejido land can be converted to fee simple land. Under the 2013 financial reform, these lands could be collected for debts in the countryside, further devastating the rural land base. "In other words, we could go back to having banks as major land owners," said Román Morales. For the first time, banks could also seize goods and real estate for non-payment, as well as take over small businesses.

Isabel Cruz Hernández, director of Mexican Association of Credit Unions in the Social Sector (AMUCSS) and president of the Latin American and Caribbean Forum on Rural Finances, points out the financial reform will not assist the millions of Mexican farmers who have resisted converting their lands to fee simple title. "Those who receive credit are those who have material guarantees, but 80 percent of our farmers have social property, which is to say, they're part of ejidos and they can't use their land as collateral for a loan—that is forbidden by the constitution," she told me. "This reform will never benefit [farmers with less than five hectares or using ejidal land], never ever, and there is no movement within the financial reform to ensure that rural and agricultural credit can be activated for food production."

The IMF loan renewal granted for Mexico in late 2012 noted "a broad structural reform agenda would be needed to unleash Mexico's growth potential." Mexico's finance minister has admitted that the financial reform is necessary to other reforms pushed ahead in Mexico by the Pact for Mexico, which was supported by all of the major political parties.[64] "What some countries are doing, and this is the case of Mexico, we are trying to push a structural reform agenda that differentiates our economy from other economies in the world," said Mexico's vice finance minister, Fernando Aportela Rodríguez.[65]

As if to confirm Washington's glee at Peña Nieto's reforms, in February 2014 *Time* magazine featured him on the cover. In the photo, Peña Nieto's head is slanted slightly upwards; he looks smug, confident, and handsome. Across his chest, bold white letters scream "Saving Mexico." Below them: "How Enrique Peña Nieto's sweeping reforms have changed the narrative in his narco-stained nation." Critics pointed out that the *Time* piece read like a paid advertisement. Journalist Daniel Hernández wrote, "Weirdly, though, I don't know of anyone who is calling this 'Mexico's Moment,' other than people who stand to directly benefit from the construction of an *impression* of an economic boom in Mexico, a boom which actually has not manifested, and has certainly not 'trickled down' to the average Mexican."[66]

The *Time* cover showed the new heights the US media would go to put a positive spin on Mexico. Beginning in 2012 and accelerating with the return of the PRI, there was a public relations push to rebrand the country as an economic Aztec Tiger undergoing a new Mexican Miracle. This kind of reporting focuses on dubious assertions that Mexico has an expanding middle class, and ignores ongoing state and paramilitary violence. According to a 2012 position piece by Vianovo, a branding and PR company, to change Mexico's brand, a good story "should highlight that Mexico's stable GDP growth and burgeoning middle class represent a true economic miracle in spite of these challenges. It should emphasize that the violence is contained within certain geographies, and that most of the country isn't affected. You wouldn't postpone a trip to New York City because of violence in St. Louis, right?"[67]

"In India, people ask you about China, and, in China, people ask you about India: Which country will become the more dominant economic power in the 21st century? I now have the answer: Mexico," wrote Thomas Friedman in the *New York Times*.[68] Friedman, a journalist and columnist known for his strong neoliberal position, went on to extol Mexico's competitiveness and suggest the United States should divert its war spending in Afghanistan to Mexico. "Better integration of Mexico's manufacturing and innovation prowess into America's is a win-win. It makes U.S. companies more profitable and competitive, so they can expand at home and abroad, and it gives Mexicans a reason to stay home and reduces violence. We do $1.5 billion a day in trade with Mexico, and have been spending $300 million a day in Afghanistan. Not smart."

Extractives

Without a drug war, Mexico would have continued to implement neoliberal reforms, but there is little doubt that the fear, distraction, and terror created by the war, as well as the special funding provided through it, helped speed up the reform process. It also shifted the balance of power, as many Mexicans, disgusted by the perception that the drug war was the PAN's doing, went back to voting PRI, whose election shifted public relations discourse—the economy became the central issue and talk of security challenges and the drug war were kept off the agenda. "It is a mistake to limit our bilateral relationship to drugs and security concerns," wrote Enrique Peña Nieto in a *Washington Post* editorial the month before he assumed office.[69] "In NAFTA we have a solid foundation to further integrate our economies through greater investments in finance, infrastructure, manufacturing and energy. Together, we must build a more competitive and productive region." On Obama's first visit to Mexico during Peña Nieto's term, the *New York Times* reported that the presidents would focus on "competitiveness [sic], education and innovation, along with border infrastructure, commerce, migration and citizen security among other subjects of shared interest."[70] In Mexico City, Obama pumped the immigration reform that was about to go before the Senate, where the Immigration

Reform Bill was transformed into an effort that would see the United States spend another $46 billion on militarizing the US-Mexico border.[71] It has since stalled and appears unlikely to be adopted in 2014.

Today, governments prefer the term "competitiveness" when talking about privatization and regulatory reforms designed to benefit the corporate sector. Previously, competitiveness was known as austerity, a term that has fallen out of favor among the economic elite due to the growing awareness of the harsh consequences austerity has on the public.[72]

Pemex, the state-owned oil company, was founded in 1938 when President Lazaro Cárdenas announced that the oil industry in Mexico, until then largely controlled by US companies, would be expropriated. The company is now the crown jewel of the privatization effort.[73] Many prominent Mexicans, including Peña Nieto, advocated its privatization,[74] and some, like the head of the Mexican Stock Exchange, have proposed using as their model Colombia's oil sector reform.[75] According to the *Financial Times*, "An opening of Mexico's highly protected oil sector, which is dominated by state behemoth Pemex, could provide untold opportunities for US oil companies as well as the sort of technology-transfer Mexico desperately needs."[76] Much of 2013 was dedicated to preparing the political ground for the constitutional reforms required to open the oil sector to private investment. In a 2013 talk at a Council of the Americas event, Emilio Lozoya, head of Pemex, suggested that foreign companies will be allowed to begin extracting shale oil and shale gas in Mexico once new legislation is adopted. "Pemex is not making as many deals as it could, because like any other company it has a limited capacity for investment. Regardless of this, legislation does not permit other players to develop what Pemex leaves on the table because of a lack of investment capacity. Not only are the hydrocarbons not extracted and cheaper energy not generated, neither is the employment generated. Thus, exploring the possibility of more private sector participation would benefit the country, and this is part of the energy reform that President Enrique Peña will launch this year," said Lozoya.

An initial energy reform passed by Calderón in 2008 didn't modify the constitution but it allowed for an increase in service contacts between Pemex and private companies. Lozoya, whose father was energy secretary under former Mexican president Salinas, underscored that Peña Nieto is not in favor of outright privatization, but he hinted that opening up Pemex to increased Mexican investment would be a positive step forward. Until reforms in December 2013, the Mexican Constitution stipulated that hydrocarbons are the patrimony of all Mexicans, which means foreign corporations operated on fixed contracts instead of earning based on the amount of oil extracted.

Following the December 2013 constitutional changes, limitations on foreign participation in Mexico were lifted. Prior to the energy reform, Mexico had one of the world's most closed oil sectors—more so than even Venezuela's, which was partially nationalized under Hugo Chávez. "There's no comparison in Latin America; the only regime that continues to be markedly closed is Kuwait, and possibly North Korea," said Dr. Miriam Grunstein, who teaches at the Centre for Economic Research and Teaching (CIDE) in Mexico City. "Chávez's Venezuela was more open than Pemex was up until two months ago," she said as we spoke on a warm Mexico City afternoon in late January, 2014. To further open up Mexico's extensive oil and gas fields to foreign companies required constitutional changes to Articles 25, 26, and 27, which would allow companies other than Pemex to draw their proceeds directly from the oil or gas removed from the ground. These reforms, passed in December 2013, were justified on the grounds of job creation (there were promises of up to 2.5 million new jobs in Mexico by 2025 if the reform was passed),[77] competitiveness, and the promise of providing cheaper gas and electricity to Mexicans.

Grunstein described the results of the Energy Reform as surprising, and said that oil-industry experts didn't think that such a radical reform would be possible in Mexico. "This reform, without a doubt, changes Mexico's energy sector 180 degrees. For the first time, we will have private participation from the oil well to the private vehicle, or as they say in the US, from the well to the wheel. The change is total, and it will change not only the energy sector, but rather the entire economic order of the country." The fact that the state-owned oil company's profits go into the federal budget, representing about 40 percent of the state's total income and 70 percent of the total national budget, is generally skirted in the media. The longer-term consequences of privatizing Pemex, and removing the corresponding revenue stream from the budget, would be akin to implementing a severe austerity program, creating a massive shock for the country's working poor. In addition to the loss of profits, collecting what would be relatively high taxes for companies to operate in Mexico could pose a problem. "The government of Mexico has historically not been a good tax collector.... It is highly questionable whether it can, or whether there is a fatal level of corruption," said Grunstein. "If Mexico doesn't manage to maintain its share of tax revenues, there will be a coup d'état" sometime in the next fifteen years, she predicted. In Venezuela, private participation in the state oil company was permitted in 1993, and in 1998, Hugo Chávez Frias, an openly socialist candidate, won the presidency. Should Mexico similarly mismanage oil revenues and move sharply to the left, the militarization and the expansion of the prison system in Mexico, which has taken place in lockstep with the drug war, could eventually be used in controlling dissent.

In addition to the opening up of Pemex, the Federal Electricity Commission (CFE) was gutted as part of the energy reform. The CFE held a monopoly over electricity generation and distribution in Mexico since 1937, and historically operated at a loss while providing many in Mexico with subsidized electricity. There were protests against dams and high tariffs in some areas, but the extreme tensions that exist in private energy markets were largely avoided (for example, the 2012 protests and massacre in Totonicapán, Guatemala, which were partly motivated by higher energy prices). The CFE's monopoly was swiftly undone with the December 2013 reforms. "The CFE will undergo a very important change, and I actually think it will be weakened more rapidly than Pemex, in the sense that there will be a competitive market for [electricity] generation, and the possibility of bilateral contracts directly with industrial users," said Grunstein. For mining and other energy-intensive industries to be able to harness their own energy source will surely be a boon to investment. It could also create lucrative side businesses for transnational corporations, which—to encourage investment—other jurisdictions (like British Columbia, Canada) allow to sell surplus energy generated from state-subsidized dams back to the government buyer at market rates.

The Mexican government has actively promoted mining investment, and today the sector is 70 percent foreign owned.[78] Mining projects have been among the most conflictive sites of recent capitalist expansion in Mexico, and the majority of gold and silver production in the country takes place in states with the highest rates of violence (Sonora, Chihuahua, Zacatecas, Guerrero, and Durango). "Mining production in Mexico has been skyrocketing, up 50% in 2010, and more than double in the ten years ending in 2010 what three centuries of mining by the Spaniards produced. Today, eight out of the top 11 gold producers in the country are Canadian, and gold production was up 118% between 2007 and 2012."[79] In a move contrary to many of the policies passed by previous governments, taxes imposed on the mining industry, including a 7.5 percent royalty tax, were introduced as part of the tax reform, to the dissatisfaction of many foreign mining companies.[80] However, "forgotten in the flood of criticism is that as much as 60% of the royalty amount will be tax deductible."[81] Anti-mining activists estimate there are fifty active mining conflicts in Mexico, and as investment in the sector continues to grow, the pro-mining/anti-mining divide is bound to become more polarized.

As we have seen, over the seven years since the war on drugs started in Mexico, a series of reforms have been passed that go a long way toward improving the country's macroeconomic indicators. In February 2014, Mexico's credit rating was again increased, this time to AAA, based on the energy and taxation reforms. The large financial institutions are pleased with Mexico's performance, and Mexico's economy is expected to grow faster because of the reforms.[82] But it has long been established that stronger macroeconomic performance does not translate to better quality of life, especially for the poor. Over the first six years of the war on drugs, the number of Mexicans living at or below the poverty line increased from 42.9 percent to 52.3 percent, according to the World Bank.[83] Austerity measures, decreasing labor standards and increasing precarity, and the increased cost of buying basic goods are forms of deepening structural violence against the poor majority.

Legal Reforms

We must also consider the judicial and rule of law aspects of the Mérida Initiative. In February 2012, the United States government announced a new training program for 8,500 prosecutors and investigators in Mexico.[84] By 2016, all of Mexico is expected to be using a US-style legal system, a complicated transition funded by the Mérida Initiative.[85] At one point, current Attorney General Jesús Murillo Karam claimed that drug trafficking had broadsided Mexico, as if it was a boogeyman that sneaked up on unassuming politicians and police in the dark of night. "We Mexicans had a justice system, an investigative system, and a policing system made for a country where the most serious crime was cattle rustling, which is to say, cows were stolen. And then all of a sudden, before we realized it, we were seated in a terrain where narcotrafficking, organized crime, the organization of crime had already surpassed all of the institutions," he said.[86] His words not only betray the Mexican state's level of involvement in the drug trade historically, but they imply that Mexico was a country without massacres, dispossession, and femicides before the drug war started, which is simply false.

Mexican officials used the specter of narcotrafficking to shift blame away from structural impunity and police abuses, the drug war has provided them with a chance to push for reformation of the justice system. "Mexico is doing things that go much beyond fighting drugs. Yes we're fighting organized crime and organized delinquency, which is one aspect of drug trafficking, but the truth is that the struggle in Mexico is a struggle for the transformation of its security and justice institutions," stated Alejandro Poiré Romero, who served as secretary of the interior during part of Felipe Calderón's administration.[87]

Many human rights groups herald the transition to oral trials and an accusatory justice system as a positive step, and progressive groups have provided trainings promoting the new legal system. But the reforms also have their detractors: "Just as within globalized commerce [the United States] wants a world where everywhere there is a McDonald's, an Applebee's, a Home Depot, a Walmart, a Sam's [Club]; they also want a world where tribunals are the same everywhere as they are in the United States, so that whatever legal issues they have can be dealt with perfectly well by a legal firm from the United States, which can operate in the US, in Puerto Rico, in Argentina, in Chile, and so on," said Oscar Castrejón Rivas, the president of the College of Lawyers in Chihuahua City, during an interview in late 2011.[88] Chihuahua was one of the first states to adopt the new legal code, beginning in 2007, and Management Systems International (MSI), which was contracted by USAID to promote and carry out legal reforms in Mexico, maintains the state has what is "considered to be the most advanced, progressive criminal justice Code in Latin America." Using US taxpayer money, MSI sent politicians from Chihuahua to Chile and Argentina to study their justice systems, since decades earlier, in the 1990s—funded by USAID, the World Bank, the United Nations, and the Inter-American Development Bank—both South American countries transitioned toward an accusatorial system.

When I spoke to Castrejón Rivas just over a year later, he told me that "in the opinion of the community of people in Chihuahua and the lawyer's forum, what has happened has been a counter-reform, something very different than what Washington and USAID promised." Incarceration rates increased, and "basically, the presumption of innocence has been cancelled." There is no doubt that the Mexican justice system is racked with irregularities, and advocacy groups—some of which are US funded—are clamoring for reform. But the statistics are generally lost amid the barrage of publicity claiming the USAID-imposed model will clean up Mexico's justice system.

It is also important to note that at the same time as the US-backed reforms to the legal system are being carried out, the penetration of Mexico's judiciary by criminal groups is on the rise. "In many cases, judges, court officials and legal professionals are unable to act freely or fully independently because they are faced with threats, intimidation, harassment and other forms of undue pressure," according to a 2011 report by the UN's special rapporteur on the independence of judges and lawyers.[89] "The impetus behind rule of law projects has often been the belief that markets require predictable legal structures to protect property rights, facilitate foreign direct investments, and contract enforcement—that is, to establish U.S. law as the 'lingua franca for business and politics.'"[90] In addition to USAID, the Quebec Bar Association, the US Federal Judicial Affairs Council, the National Judicial Institute, the National Democratic Institute, and the Federal Judicial Affairs Council have all been involved in promoting such legal reforms in Mexico. The economic bases for the reforms have been established by the Mexico Competitiveness Institute, which "identifies the creation of an objective and reliable justice system as Mexico's top priority to improve competitiveness and to attract both foreign and domestic investment," according to a statement by USAID chief Roger Garner.[91] "Our Mérida programs in Mexico are designed to support those Mexican institutions as they fundamentally change their entire justice system and train an estimated 1 million people in new, more transparent and accountable ways of administering justice." Garner didn't mention that the Mexican Competitiveness Institute receives funding from the Mexican Council of Businessmen and USAID, and does consulting work for the US Embassy and the World Bank. His comments reflect the classic US echo chamber, though which US-funded civil society groups reinforce the State Department's policy prescriptions.

The push to change Mexico's legal system could impact Mexican legal traditions, which, according to law professor Deborah M. Weissman, include "ongoing attention to indigenous rights, constitutionally designed cooperative land use, corporative models of labor relations, and legal pluralism."[92] In turn, these changes could negatively impact popular resistance to mega-projects with foreign beneficiaries. The US rule of law program in Mexico falls in lockstep with counterinsurgency efforts. "If you look at the allocation of rule of law money, it's for surveillance, it's for activating, whatever the heck that means, new prisons in Mexico, it's for training Mexicans with regard to the adversarial and oral trial systems, yet they do not introduce the jury system," Weissman told me. "You have a rule of law program in what is essentially a plan to militarize the drug war. You see that everywhere."

Take this telling example of the connections between US police training and US-backed reform from 1960s Venezuela: "In the first place, the Venezuelan legal system had to be changed. Venezuelan law required the arrest of a police officer who killed a suspect, this, according to the *Los Angeles Times* reporter, frequently meant three months in jail while awaiting trial. But 'under American tutelage, a policeman who killed a terrorist would be examined in one day by a civilian board of lawyers, and would be quickly restored to duty.'"[93]

The use of torture to obtain confessions is a common tactic used by Mexican police and soldiers, and the practice shows no signs of waning. In 2008, Felipe Calderón modified the constitution to introduce *arraigo*, a legal provision allowing the lengthy detention of suspects on the pretext that it allows authorities more time to gather evidence against them. This increases the possibility that torture be used against individuals or groups detained by the state. According to Mexican human rights groups, "This measure is clearly a form of arbitrary detention contrary to the obligations of human rights that Mexico has acquired, and violates, among others, the right to personal liberty, legality, presumption of innocence, due process and the right to an effective remedy."[94]

Arraigo can be applied without any formal charges being laid, and the accused are held incommunicado for a period of up to forty days (which can be extended to eighty days with a warrant). In a 2011 report, the Inter-American Commission on Human Rights noted that it "received complaints having to do with the use of arraigo to hold individuals in private homes, hotels, and military facilities without respect for judicial guarantees, indicating that those being held in this manner have been subjected to torture for the purpose of obtaining confessions."[95]

Who Benefits?

Some of the most important companies in the world will gain from financial and legal reforms in Mexico. The country is the world's largest exporter of flat screen TVs and fridge-freezer units, and the manufacturing sector includes investment from firms including Toshiba, Hitachi, Mitsubishi, Pioneer, Ericsson, Sony, Sanyo, Panasonic, Xerox, Siemens, Foxconn, and Motorola, among others. Recent announcements indicate that new investment in auto and aerospace manufacturing in central Mexico will continue.

"Mexico fell into a deep recession in 2009 when American demand for Mexican-made imports collapsed. But the recovery under President Felipe Calderón has been notable, with growth expected to reach almost 4 percent this year, roughly twice that of the United States," according to an article published in the *New York Times* in 2012.[96] In 2008, before the financial crisis spread to Mexico, FDI reached $23.2 billion, and fell the next year to $11.4 billion.[97] FDI has since rebounded: to $19.43 billion in 2011, and by 2013, to over $35 billion, primarily in manufacturing (73.8 percent), mining (7.9 percent), and commercial services (4.9 percent).[98|99]

An important and underreported aspect of the Mérida Initiative is the building of new border crossings and expansion of existing ones, both key demands of the US commercial sectors. "Financially, investment in border crossings and infrastructure has not matched the exponential increase in trade crossing the border each year," reads a December 2012 memo from the Council on Foreign Relations.[100] This infrastructure is necessary for the *maquila* (assembly) industry in Mexico, as well as to ensure efficient and regular supply of fruits, vegetables, and other food products to the United States. There are huge subsidies for US and other corporations that operate along the US-Mexico border, and so the US requires Mexico's cooperation on these crossings. With regards to port and border posts, "the U.S. Government funded the development of licensing officer training; provided end-use/end-user and risk analysis training and enforcement training; developed an internal compliance program for private industry; and provided targeted donations of radiological and chemical detection and identification equipment in collaboration with the U.S. Department of Energy's Megaports program and the Mérida Initiative."[101]

Possibly the highest profile beneficiaries of the drug war are large banks. As mentioned previously, the United Nations Office on Drugs and Crime reported in 2010 that 85 percent of the gross profits from the $35 billion US cocaine market are generated in the United States.[102] This is where the big banks in the United States cash in on the drug trade, their complicity, when discovered, going nearly unpunished. HSBC was found guilty in late 2012 of having laundered over $880 million for the Sinaloa Cartel and Colombian drug traffickers, among others. According to a report in *The Guardian,* "In order to handle the 'staggering amounts of cash', the bank even widened the windows at some branches to allow tellers to accept larger boxes of money."[103] HSBC was let off with a $1.9 billion fine—about five weeks of income for the bank—and none of its executives faced criminal charges for their role in facilitating the drug trade.[104] According to Antonio Maria Costa, head of the UN Office on Drugs and Crime, cash from organized crime essentially rescued banks during the market meltdown in 2008. "Inter-bank loans were funded by money that originated from the drugs trade and other illegal activities.... There were signs that some banks were rescued that way."[105]

In addition to organized crime, large corporations and public officials also participate in money laundering in Mexico and elsewhere.[106] A key aspect to any corruption scandal, where public officials steal money from government accounts, is money laundering or offshore bank accounts,[107] which corporations like Walmart have been accused of taking part in.[108] Narcotrafficking organizations are suspected of bankrolling candidates via campaign financing (in Mexico, the US, and elsewhere).[109] In addition, it has even been documented that large establishment media organizations like Mexico's Televisa have been involved in international organized criminal activity.[110]

Mexico is an important player in the world economy, and if the analysts' predictions are correct, it will have an even more important role as manufacturing continues to shift from China. A small transnational elite in Mexico, led by Carlos Slim, stands to make good off financial and other reforms, as do other important sectors, including the oil and mining industries, among others. The stakes are high, and the reforms brought in alongside the drug war are intended to reinforce and empower transnational capitalism in an increasingly stratified and unequal society.

CHAPTER 5:

PLAN MEXICO AND MILITARIZATION

ON February 23, 2012, forensic authorities delivered the remains of Jessica Leticia Peña García to her mother. Her bones were bleached and dried. She'd been murdered three years before and her body left under the desert sun in the Valle de Juárez, east of Ciudad Juárez in Chihuahua state. Coming up on what would have been the Jessica's eighteenth birthday, February 5, 2013, her mother, Maria García, asked Justice for Our Daughters (Justicia Para Nuestras Hijas), an organization led by mothers of missing and murdered women, to help her get permission to lay a wreath in the place where her daughter's body was found.

Norma Ledezma, founder of the group, submitted an official request in writing for access the site. "Our request was strongly questioned.... First they said yes, then no, and they made a bunch of excuses," she said, in an interview in her office in Chihuahua City. Ledezma kept the pressure on, something she had become an expert at since her daughter Paloma disappeared in March 2002. When Paloma's body was found, sixteen days after her disappearance, Ledezma swore on her daughter's remains that she would dedicate her life to finding her murderer. At the time, she admits, she thought it would be a matter of a few months. "Eleven years have passed this month, and I still don't know who killed Paloma," she told me. Eventually, Ledezma went all the way up the ladder to the state's top official, insisting that a grieving mother have the right to lay flowers and a cross where the killers dumped her daughter's body, and finally she got consent. On February 4, the day before Jessica's birthday, a convoy including García, Ledezma, and other families of disappeared and murdered women, together with police officers, psychologists, archaeologists, and officials, pulled out of Ciudad Juárez toward the Valle de Juárez to visit the exact site where Jessica's bones were found.

The cars pulled off to the side of the dusty desert road connecting Juárez with the valley. "They told us that to get to this creek, Arroyo el

Navajo, we would have to leave the vehicles behind, and walk between four and five kilometers," Ledezma told me. As the delegation walked, the mothers speculated about how the dead women found in Arroyo el Navajo were brought here by their killers: by donkey, helicopter, or four-wheeler. After laying flowers and crosses with Jessica's name on it, the team started back to the vehicles. At one point, not far from where women's bodies were found, Ledezma refused to continue. "They tried to confuse us, they walked us up and down, but when we arrived at the spot where the bodies were I realized that although they had us all turned around, there was a path."

Ledezma's instinct turned out to be correct: there was a direct pathway to the highway less than ten minutes walk from where Jessica's body was found. "I said to them all, I'm not moving from this spot. I'm not walking back to the cars, I'm not moving until they figure out where this path leads to," she recalls. Finally, the officials and experts accompanying the group agreed to take the women out to the highway on the shorter path. As they walked along, single file, Ledezma noticed a human bone on the trail, in an area authorities claimed to have combed time and again. The bone Ledezma found would lead to a male skeleton and a female skeleton, both fully exposed, and with their bones showing signs of having been there for an extended period of time. "It was so intense, so intense for us mothers, I couldn't move my head at all for days afterwards," said Maria García, Jessica's mother, who also saw the skeletons not far from where her own daughter's remains were recovered.

Finally, the delegation followed the path out to a collection of houses on the highway. "The most, how can I say it, the most incredible thing was that the soldiers had a military checkpoint right there," said Maria García. The checkpoint, which stopped every vehicle coming in and out of the area, was there from approximately 2008 to 2012, during the federal government's military surge in the Juárez area. Over the same time period, the Juárez Valley became one of the most dangerous places in the country, with mass displacements and locals forced to seek asylum in the United States. "The Valle de Juárez is very large, and it is held by organized crime, but it is supervised by the army, the army supervises the entrances," said Ledezma. The earlier walk had been an attempt to throw off the families; the authorities, archaeologists, investigators, and police were complicit in covering up the killers' tracks. I met with Ledezma in 2013, just as Felipe Calderón began his tenure at Harvard University: "I was with him three times, and I personally told him," she said, lowering her voice down to a near whisper, "The Federales took [our daughters], the soldiers took [our daughters]."

It was the arrival of federal police and soldiers in Ciudad Juárez and the surrounding region that caused murder rates to take off. Missing person posters, many featuring the faces of young girls, punctuate lampposts and public spaces throughout Juárez and Chihuahua City, the state capital. Juárez became synonymous with violence and tragedy during Felipe Calderón's term. As what officials called drug-related violence dominated the headlines, more and more young women began to disappear. "Beginning in 2008, when president Felipe Calderón, with the consent of the governor and the mayor, decided to implement operation Conjunto Chihuahua, which is a military confrontation against drug cartels, the assassination of women increased, but above all the disappearances of young women [increased]," said Dr. Julia E. Monárrez Fragoso, a professor and researcher at the Colegio de la Frontera Norte in Ciudad Juárez.

Indeed, the act of laying flowers on the tight dry earth where Jessica Leticia Peña García's body was found is just one of the harrowing stories her mother Maria García shared with me when I visited her residence on the extreme edge of Ciudad Juárez. García, who lives in a single, uninsulated room in the corner of a cold, empty warehouse with her partner and son, shivered and cried as she told me how her life has come apart since her daughter was disappeared and murdered in 2011. The warehouse faces the highway, and from the garage-style door hangs a plastic banner with her daughter's smiling face and a red rose in her memory. "I can't take it down, it is what keeps me going," she said. "I don't want to admit to myself that she's no longer here." Jessica Leticia was a beautiful young woman, which I point out in an attempt to put Maria García at ease. "That's what the police told me when I filed the report. They said, 'No wonder she was kidnapped, she was very beautiful.' Those were their words," she said, with anger in her voice. Like other mothers, including those who make up Justice for Our Daughters, García took the search into her own hands, going from cantina to cantina, from corner to corner, with a photo of her daughter. She was eventually directed toward a hotel, where she saw two young women, who were being held hostage, pulled out of their hotel room by armed men. When she called the police, they ignored her complaint. "They thought I had gone crazy," she tells me. The case of Jessica Leticia is far from an isolated incident involving a few bad apples, instead it is a manifestation of a form of structural violence that put Ciudad Juárez on the map, with a wave of women murdered in 1993. A word for the killings of women because of their gender was created: *feminicidio* in Spanish, or femicide, and eventually it was adopted by lawyers and activists around the world to describe the murders of young women for the simple reason that they were young women.

In the course of every work day, Itzel González scans local newspapers, looking for mention of violent attacks on women. More often than not, she turns to the whiteboard behind her desk and updates the previous day's total of women murdered in Juárez, the largest city in Chihuahua. Her makeshift tally is one of the few adornments in the understated, second-floor office of the Women's Coordinating Network (RMM), near the city's downtown. Gonzales is the coordinator of the RMM, a coalition of groups that work, among other things, on behalf of the rights of women in what has long been considered Mexico's most violent city.

"In the last few years the official discourse is that femicide has been eradicated, that it is a thing of the past and that it doesn't happen anymore," she said. In 2011, 196 women were killed in the city of approximately 1.3 million. "The situation continues to be very serious.... the problem has worsened.... Another one of the discourses or things that the state attorney's office here says is that the majority of, or a high percentage of, these women are being assassinated because they are part of organized crime. But the reality is that these crimes are not being investigated; 98 percent of these crimes don't even have an investigation file." Between 1993 and the end of 2011, 1,344 women were murdered in Juárez. A whopping 844—63 percent—of those murders took place after 2008, the year police and soldiers arrived to fight the war on drugs. The stories of the women whose daughters were taken from them are among the most heartbreaking I heard during my research, but to focus solely on the fate of these young women without talking about what has happened to men is to paint an incomplete portrait of violence along this small stretch of the Texas-Mexico border. Over the past decade, for every woman killed in Juárez, nine men were murdered. Molly Molloy, a librarian at New Mexico State University who keeps tabs on murders in Juárez, notes that "female murder victims have never comprised more than 18 percent of the overall number of murder victims in Ciudad Juárez, and in the last two decades that figure averages at less than 10 percent. That's less than in the United States, where about 20 to 25 percent of the people who are murdered in a given year are women."[1] Queer and transpeople in Chihuahua and throughout Mexico have also been murdered based on their gender and sexual preference.

It is difficult to make sense of the violence in Mexico, and it's hard to know if Jessica Leticia's killer(s) were after anything beyond cheap thrills. Their actions and the impunity granted them, however, goes beyond an isolated act and reinforces an overall climate of rampant sexism, racism, and classism. The actions of those responsible for Jessica's murder have impacts that permeate society as a whole, and were carried out in part because impunity is the rule, not the exception, in Mexico. When I asked Norma Ledezma how she defined impunity, she went much farther than to finger the state for complicity. "Impunity has been like an invitation from the authorities to the criminals," she said. They tell them: '*Es la tierra de no pasa nada*,' this is the land where nothing happens." After our interview she left with her bodyguard, who protects her throughout her busy workday.

The state's initial response to the femicides upheld what geographer Melissa Wright interprets as a gendered version of Achille Mbembe's necropolitics, by which the threat of violent death is used a governance tactic. She writes that the governor of Chihuahua "assured Mexican families that there was nothing to fear as long as they knew where their female family members were. The discourse of the public woman normalized the violence and used the victims' bodies as a way to substantiate the politics based on patriarchal notions of normality. Normal Mexican families, with normal, private women safely at home, had nothing to worry about."[2] This discourse criminalizes the victims of femicide, many of whom were working women without access to safe, accessible transportation to and from their workplaces. It is as though they are responsible for their own deaths. Similar discourses are at work in areas of Mexico that are impacted by the drug war, where one is made to understand from media and government reports that victims of violence linked to the war are blamed for their own demise.

"Juárez and a good part of Chihuahua are—and this should be made known nationally and internationally—truly in a situation of humanitarian emergency. The almost 4,000 assassinations that have occurred in the state in the last two years would be worthy of international attention in any other country, except this one, where the government continues to play dumb, thinking that they're winning a 'war' that increasingly has the characteristics of social cleansing," wrote Mexican activist and columnist Victor Quintana in late 2009.[3] Waves of killings of youth, small-time drug dealers, street-involved people, and the poor aren't just happening in Juárez. According to Gustavo de la Rosa, the former Chihuahua state human rights officer, "The majority of those killed ... are *malandros* ... people of no value in this war ... no use to any cartel ... people below poverty whose death has no explanation except as part of ... social cleansing ... the extermination of the lowest of the low. There are execution squads, another breed forensically killing *malandros*, planned assassinations of the unwanted. And if we look at exactly how they are done, they are experts in killing characteristic of training by the army or police."[4] One crucial difference in Juárez is that there are functioning activist groups and organizations that rally together to denounce and document what is taking place because of militarization, and a culture of journalism that has led writers take greater risks to report the news than they do elsewhere. Jessica Leticia's kidnapping in Ciudad Juárez in 2011 and the subsequent events that would test her mother's faith in Mexico's authorities are recounted here in order to provide a sliver of context for how—and why—Juárez residents have more reason to fear state security forces than to seek shelter from them. Writer Charles Bowden declared Juárez a "laboratory of the future." The city is without a doubt Mexico's most well documented test case for what takes place when federal police and soldiers are sent *en masse* to patrol the streets in the name of fighting organized crime.

US-Backed Police Programs in Mexico

Mainstream nongovernmental groups are categorical in their assessment of the impacts of the war on drugs: "The 'war on drugs' launched by [Enrique Peña Nieto's] predecessor, Felipe Calderón, had produced disastrous results. Not only had it failed to rein in the country's powerful criminal groups, but it had led to a dramatic increase in grave human rights violations committed by the security forces sent to confront them," according to a February 2013 report by Human Rights Watch.[5] "Rather than strengthening public security, these abuses had exacerbated a climate of violence, lawlessness, and fear." The Inter-American Commission on Human Rights found that the murder rate in Mexico increased by 50 percent each year from 2008 to 2010.[6] The United States plays an important role through its security programs in Mexico, which are focused on police professionalization and the provision of new equipment, as well as further encouraging militarization. The policing segment of the Mérida Initiative leads not only to better arming of long-time perpetrators of violence against the Mexican people (the police and army), but can also be seen as part of the state's long-term preparations to help enforce growing inequalities that will arise from the privatization and austerity regimes connected to US-backed initiatives, discussed in the previous chapter. This is connected to one goal of counterinsurgency, which is to deploy army and special forces temporarily so as to return to a framework where state violence is carried out by police forces, not soldiers, and where those who resist are criminalized and jailed or killed by police.

Similar to the way countries that take loans from international institutions like the IMF and the World Bank are required to carry out structural adjustment programs that further impoverish the population, drug war resources come tied to increased US involvement in internal affairs. Though the public doesn't generally have access to the process through which aid is disbursed, a confidential US State Department cable from Ecuador, which illustrates how political pressure and drug assistance go hand in hand, was leaked to Wikileaks. Rafael Correa's government wasn't prepared to accept conditions for anti-drug money, creating a problematic situation for the US government. In the cable, the former US Ambassador to Ecuador described the following situation: "Correa and [Government of Ecuador] officials were prompted into objecting to our polygraphing members of vetted units and were likely opposed to a set-up that ensured significant USG control over the actions of Ecuadorian law enforcement personnel and teams. During subsequent negotiations of agreements with [Department of Homeland Security] and [Drug Enforcement Administration], GoE officials regularly pushed [Narcotics Affairs Section] to give them counter-narcotics funds with few controls.[7]" In the end, the US government got its way, by "refusing to disburse funds until the agreements were signed."[8]

Police training, which is also called police professionalization, has long been an instrument in the US foreign policy arsenal. "Police assistance can accomplish many of the same U.S. foreign policy objectives as military intervention while appearing less political in the process," according to Martha Huggins, who has written extensively on US training of Latin American police.[9] "There is no evidence that almost a century of US assistance to foreign police has improved either the security of the people in recipient countries or the democratic practices of their police and security forces.... The outcome of such training may suggest that the training of Latin American police has deliberately been used to increase US control over recipient countries and those governments' undemocratic control over their populations." In 1974, after evidence of torture, kidnappings, and murders carried out by US-trained police overwhelmed proponents of foreign police training, Congress outlawed the training and equipping of foreign police. Interestingly, however, "The 1974 congressional ban exempted US police and military assistance for narcotics control."[10] In 1985, the training and equipping of police forces outside of the US was again made legal by Congress under Ronald Reagan, returning the practice of police training to a central strategy for US control over international security. The FBI began training Mexican border police in 1987, and in 1990, the Department of Defense spent $17 million on "training and equipment" in Mexico. "The equipment provided consisted of UH-1 helicopters and spare parts, ammunition, small arms, riot control equipment, radios and miscellaneous personal gear."[11] Ongoing programs to fund US police training took place over the following years, but it was with the Mérida Initiative that US police training in Mexico took off.

The *New York Times* reported in August 2011 that "the United States has trained nearly 4,500 new [Mexican] federal police agents and assisted in conducting wiretaps, running informants and interrogating suspects."[12] Since the beginning of the Mérida Initiative, the US has trained "8,500 federal justice sector personnel; augmented the professionalization of police units by providing training to more than 22,000 federal and state police officers, 4,000 of which are federal investigators; improved the capacity and security of its federal prisons, supporting the expansion of secure federal facilities from five with a capacity of 3,500 to fourteen with a capacity of 20,000; provided civic education and ethics training to more than 700,000 Mexican students; and improved the detection of narcotics, arms, and money at the border, reaching nearly $3.8 billion in illicit goods seized."[13] In addition to the United States and Canada, police from Israel, Colombia, France, Spain, El Salvador, Holland, and the Czech Republic are all actively training different branches of Mexican police.[14] Regardless of US training and vetting processes, generalized corruption among Mexican police forces has not diminished. "We do not want to overstate this finding: We see no evidence that police corruption is actually falling," reads a 2011 report prepared by right-wing think tank RAND Corporation.[15] In one high-profile incident in 2012, US-trained Mexican federal police ambushed an armored SUV with diplomatic plates, injuring two Central Intelligence Agency agents.[16] To this day it is not known why the ambush took place or what exactly the CIA agents were doing at Tres Marias, near the city of Cuernavaca.

Police training programs in Mexico are taking place at a time when an already large police force continues to expand and be rearranged.[17] In 2010, there were an estimated 409,536 police in Mexico, according to Insyde, a non-profit organization involved in US-funded police training.[18] All federal police, of which there are more than 30,000, also receive in-country military training, and many of them are, in fact, soldiers in police uniforms.[19] The United States is operating an intelligence Fusion Center in Mexico, but the National Security Agency has refused to disclose further information.[20] A training center dubbed Special Operations Command-North, based at US Northern Command in Colorado Springs, Colorado, plays host to at least 150 Mexican soldiers, police, and intelligence agents per year, who get training in counterterrorism and conducting raids. And if that were not enough, in early 2012, the US government extended its anti-gang training program to police departments in Mexico and Central America.[21]

In May of 2012, Mexico opened the Mérida Initiative-funded General Ignacio Zaragoza National Police Training and Development Academy in Puebla state, southeast of Mexico City. The Mexican government estimates that 6,000 Mexican police will receive training there annually.[22] The new police academy is built of modular housing, snapped together on freshly bulldozed land that was once part of the lightly forested rolling hills of rural Puebla. It includes dorms for men and women, firing ranges, mess halls and entertainment areas, a command and control center, among other facilities. There, Mexican police can receive shooting lessons, tactical fitness and combat technique training, lessons in high-risk prisoner transportation, courses in police investigation and the protection of high-ranking dignitaries, and a class in "Human Rights and the Rational Use of Force."[23] It must have slipped their minds that in life, the academy's namesake, Ignacio Zaragoza, fought the United States after the annexation of Texas—certainly not the kind of behavior they're promoting. A US-funded "tactical village" for police officer training was opened at the police academy in Puebla in late 2013.[24] American police are also training their Mexican counterparts at a similar center in the state of San Luis Potosí, and there are plans to open more US-funded and -staffed policing centers.

The drug war in Colombia provided a model for Mexico, and security officials and police from both nations have worked increasingly closely since 2006. "Colombia and Mexico are more united than ever in the fight against transnational organized crime and are also ready to collaborate with third countries in the region to combat this scourge, particularly with our brother nations in Central America," President Calderón said in 2011.[25] In 2012, Colombian police trained 12,000 Mexican police in specialized subjects ranging from anti-kidnapping to anti-drugs and civilian security.[26] French and Colombian police will train the 390 commanders of Mexico's new gendarmerie.[27] Mexico's new president, Enrique Peña Nieto, appointed Colombian police officer Oscar Naranjo as an advisor during his presidential campaign, and stated that Colombia provided him and the world with a successful model of how to achieve peace and security.[28] Naranjo returned to Colombia in early 2014 after the surge in self-defense groups in Michoacán.

The deployment of over 50,000 soldiers, as well as thousands of federal police and over 2,200 state and local police officers, in the name of combating drug trafficking, has resulted in an increase in violence throughout Mexico. In some states, like Tamaulipas and Veracruz, local police have been completely replaced by soldiers, marines, and military police. According to a 2011 report by Human Rights Watch, Calderón's militaristic security policy "resulted in a dramatic increase in grave human rights violations, virtually none of which appear to be adequately investigated."[29] The report documented "39 'disappearances' where evidence strongly suggests the participation of security forces," and "credible evidence in 24 cases that security forces committed extrajudicial killings, and in most of these cases took steps to conceal their crimes."[30] It also pointed out that Mexico's National Human Rights Commission "received 691 complains of human rights abuses committed by soldiers against civilians from 2003–2006; the number increased to 4,803 complaints in the 2007–2010 period [precisely the same period as the Mérida Initiative]. And while the commission issued five recommendations concluding federal authorities had committed torture from 2003–2006, it issued twenty-five from 2007–2010."[31] These numbers represent but a fraction of the total number of abuses; according to the same report, "National surveys have found that nearly 90 percent of crimes in Mexico go unreported."[32]

US support to the police and army has not prevented corruption or the collaboration of these organizations with organized crime.

Relations between state forces and organized crime groups in this hemisphere go back to earlier days of the narcotics trade. For example, following the Cuban revolution in 1959, anti-Castro drug runners moved their operations to Miami. "On occasion, the capos were protected by the CIA, since they represented an important bulwark in the anti-Castro struggle."[33] In Mexico, enough books have been written on the subject of government cooperation with cartels to fill a small library. One of the classics is Terrence Poppa's *Drug Lord*, which shows how the Institutional Revolutionary Party (PRI), which ruled Mexico for seventy years straight, worked with drug runners. Mexican journalist Anabel Hernández's book, *Narcoland*, takes on the task in another way, using detailed documentation to show how the National Action Party (PAN), which ruled Mexico for twelve years after the break with the PRI in 2000, came to agreements with the Sinaloa Cartel. Without getting embroiled in the details, it is easy to demonstrate how small the dichotomy between governments and traffickers really is. Professor William I. Robinson of the University of California–Santa Barbara puts it bluntly: "There's no Mexican Army and police war against *narcotrafico*." Rather, he says, what is taking place is a rearrangement of power among groups involved in the drug trade, which includes government officials and members of state forces.

In thinking about the artificiality of this binary, one has to wonder in what other battle situation are as many high-level state, army, and police forces exposed as collaborators working for groups that supposedly belong to the "other side"? In the war on drugs, there is no shortage of examples. "The army is part of the Mexican state, and the police are part of the Mexican state, and PRI and PAN and the political parties are at least in some way articulated to the Mexican state, and a good portion of them are so deeply involved in it themselves that it's really a war for who will control drug profits," said Robinson in an interview in Mexico City in 2011. "We know the army and the police actually give protection to the cartels in return for payments, that's so widespread." Moves to flush out politicians or police involved in criminal activity are often stopgap strategies to clean up the government's image. They can also be a way of taking privileges from one group, which are quickly redistributed to others.

In *Narcoland*, Anabel Hernández fingers Genaro García Luna, the head of the Public Security Secretariat during Felipe Calderón's term, as an active participant in drug trafficking, and it's not unusual to read of high-level officials being caught participating in the drug trade. In 2012, the Mexican and US governments opened investigations of three governors of Tamaulipas for their alleged money laundering and links with the Gulf Cartel and Los Zetas.[34] Or, take for example the Federal Security Directorate (DFS), a political police force responsible for repressing guerrilla movements throughout Mexico in the '60s and '70s: "Using their DFS credentials as shields, agents regularly escorted narcotics shipments, frequently even selling seized narcotics to favored organizations…. Later intelligence showed that the DFS embarked on an ambitious project to organize protection on a national scale, bringing as much of the nation as possible under a unified system."[35] Heads of policing organizations and anti-narcotics groups are routinely suspected of collaborating with organized crime,[36] and anti-kidnapping units of the Mexican police have been outed for running kidnapping rings. In 1990, President Carlos Salinas fired the head of the navy and fifty marines for their links with narcotrafficking.

It is widely known that rank-and-file police officers take state paychecks while working for criminal groups in cities and towns throughout Mexico's northeast.[37] Meanwhile, deserters of the Mexican special forces (GAFEs) formed the most feared paramilitary group in Mexico, Los Zetas.[38] Though they were among the last units to receive such instruction, units of GAFEs also received group training in the United States between 1996 and 1998.[39] Members of the Kaibiles, Guatemala's elite special forces, also US-trained, have turned up among Los Zetas, some while listed as active service members.[40] Many drug traffickers identified by the United States and Mexico are retired soldiers or police officers, some of whom have benefited from international training.

The binary between state and criminal forces is further undermined by the US connection to the drug business. The US Bureau of Alcohol, Tobacco, Firearms and Explosives (ATF) let 2,000 high-caliber weapons "walk" out of US gun shops in the hands of known cartel members and killers, supposedly to gain information in order to make arrests, but instead these same weapons turned up at crime scenes where over 150 civilians were injured or killed.[41] In Mexico and elsewhere, the DEA and the CIA facilitate the movement of narcotics among clandestine groups on the premise of eventually netting high-profile arrests. For example, in 2011, a son of one of the top-ranking members of the Sinaloa Cartel testified in US court that prior to 2004, the US government entered into an agreement with the leadership of the Sinaloa Cartel. "Under that agreement, the Sinaloa Cartel, through [Mexican attorney with Sinaloa Cartel links Humberto Loya Castro], was to provide information accumulated by Mayo, Chapo, and others against rival Mexican drug trafficking organizations to the United States government. In return, the United States government agreed to dismiss the prosecution of the pending case against Loya, to not interfere with his drug trafficking activities and those of the Sinaloa Cartel, to not actively prosecute him, Chapo, Mayo, and the leadership of the Sinaloa Cartel, and to not apprehend them.[42]" Government deal-making with segments of drug traffickers illustrates how the drug war is also used to attack a segment of traffickers and the political class, while others are given a free hand in ensuring their product makes it to market.

Ciudad Juárez is a devastating example of what can happen when thousands of police and soldiers are sent into an urban environment to fight the "drug war." The backdrop to the violence in Juárez, as in other violent border cities, is the manufacturing industry. According to one report, "The municipalities with the highest inequalities among the [northern] border states of the center and east of the Mexican Republic are those with the most developed maquila sector, that receive the highest flows of migrants and also contain important reserves of hydrocarbons or other natural resources."[43] In late March 2008, thousands of soldiers and federal police officers arrived in Juárez as part of a state surge against drug traffickers. Shortly after, the murder rate skyrocketed, violence increased, and kidnappings spiked. "What we've seen here in [Ciudad Juárez] is that the city was militarized on the last day of March of 2008, when federal forces arrived here, thousands of troops from the army and the federal police," Carlos Yeffim Fong, an activist and student, told me in an interview in late 2011.[44] At the peak of the militarization of Juárez, between 2009 and 2010, at least 5,000 federal police and 5,000 soldiers were in the city (one source in Juarez puts the combined number at 13,000).[45]

"Generally, before the soldiers came, there was an average of two murders a day, and when the soldiers arrived, that number began to rise, to five, and later to ten," recounted Fong, running a hand over his beard when he paused to reflect. "We've seen various cases where the army and federal police killed minors, as well as police and soldiers directly involved in robbery."

Over time I would run into Fong again and again, interviewing him a second time in a house being squatted by local anti-poverty activists near the city's downtown. Hyperaware of his surroundings, he moves carefully, watching the oncoming traffic and ensuring someone knows where he is at all times. These security measures are a minimum precaution when one is as publicly outspoken as he in a place like Ciudad Juárez. Locals also link Federales to kidnapping, which provides relatively low-risk access to cash through extortion. "When the wave of kidnappings grew, it was because of the arrival of the federal police," said Leobardo Alvarado, who runs the alternative news outlet *JuárezDialoga*. Just two months before our interview in Juárez, ten Federales deployed there were imprisoned for extorting and kidnapping civilians.[46] In early 2014, eighteen soldiers were charged and imprisoned for their role in a 2008 torture and murder during the Operacion Conjunto Chihuahua, in a rare case of investigation and persecution of soldiers for their crimes.[47]

In the ten years before the region was militarized, the state averaged 586 homicides a year, and never went above 648. Between 2008 and 2013, Chihuahua became one of the most violent states in Mexico. There were 2,601 homicides in the state in 2008; 3,671 in 2009; 6,407 in 2010; and 4,500 in 2011, according to the National Institute of Statistics and Geography (INEGI).[48] More than 10,000 people were murdered in Juárez following the troop surge between 2008 and early 2012. Officials often assert that the dead were involved in the drug trade, but murders are rarely investigated. "Yes, there have been standoffs of hitmen versus hitmen, as they say, or hitmen against soldiers who stopped them and detained them and they opened fire, but there's very few events like that. Most of the killings are between people.... Well, the people who died were unarmed," said Dr. Hector Padilla, a professor at the UACJ, with a dry chuckle. When I met Padilla, a father of two who splits his life between Juárez and El Paso, he was hard at work on a research project to qualitatively and quantitatively understand the violence in the city. "The majority [of the victims] are people who were in transit, or who were working, or in their homes and someone arrives and pluck," he said, making a gun with his fingers and pulling the trigger.

It's extremely difficult to understand the events in Juárez since the beginning of the drug war. One evening in 2011, while we drove through the deserted streets of the city, Alvarado offered his version. He described extreme violence in Juárez taking place in waves, which are discernible from media coverage of the killings. In 2007 and early 2008, a wave of assassinations targeted lawyers, owners of currency exchanges, and other middle-class residents. In January 2008, a wave of killings against police officers—particularly those in middle management with historical links to the drug trade—took place. "Then, in May 2008, what for me is the biggest episode of social cleansing started. They started killing many people from the lower classes. These folks were characterized as being inside the system of gangs, they lived in peripheral neighborhoods and in areas that have been conflictive historically in the city. It was incredible how they killed people then, in a massive and systematic manner. When we look at the statistics, we can see with clarity that at first the victims were over twenty-five years old, then, as time passed, the killings were against young men, in particular those who were under twenty-five, sometimes even young-er than fifteen years old." Alvarado, who has lived in Juárez since his teens, explained that gang membership grew in the city toward the end of the 1990s, and clarified that not all gangs are involved in the local drug market, though part of the gang system is dedicated to small-time trafficking. He says another wave of killings targeted kidnappers and extortionists who were working outside of organized crime groups—non-unionized criminals, he calls them—people who take advantage of the overall climate of insecurity and try their hand at kidnapping or extortion. "Because they were not inside the structures of organized crime as it's called, these people were easy targets for this social cleans-ing, which served to nourish the discourse that something was being done." Alvarado's explanation, based on careful study of newspapers and dozens of formal and informal sources in the city, is but one ap-proximation of what has taken place in Juárez over the past years. But it is an explanation that captures the crux of what took place in the beleaguered border city after it became ground zero for the drug war in 2008: the extrajudicial elimination of particular criminal, police, and popular sectors tragically expanded, transforming into massive social cleansing against poor young people in marginalized communities. The perpetrators were often police and soldiers, the killings serving as proof that, as Alvarado said, something was being done to combat crime.

Over the same time period, the level of police involvement in the drug trade in Juárez is believed to have deepened. "There's always been a really close line, or, well, they're the same," said journalist Ju-lián Cardona, who has lived in Juárez for over thirty years. "The police and the entire state apparatus, all of the institutions of the state, have always been the guarantors of the drug trade." As drug markets inside Mexico grew following an increasingly closed US border after 9/11, according to Cardona, police began to sell drugs themselves, to exe-cute people, and even to move bodies in patrol cars, all of which meant they earned more money. Instead of wiping out these occurrences, the militarization of the city seems to have exacerbated them. "What happens is that when the Federales arrive in Juárez, and the army, they basically displace local state or municipal police from their markets," Cardona told me in 2011. Tall and thin as a rail, Cardona has worked as a fixer for some of the most high-profile journalists visiting Juárez. When we met in the Starbucks on the Panamerican highway (which he, half jokingly, calls his office) it was just to talk, but he later insisted on taking me to see the city's highlights, including a nearly empty "narco bar" where he reminisced about what it was like in the city when there was ample money being spent. Another day, he took me to a historic downtown district once home to table dancing clubs, now half torn down. He was obviously nostalgic for old times, but deeply affected by the violence in the city. The last time I met with Cardona, in late 2013, he joked that now that police and soldiers had left the city, violence had dropped off and there was no longer much work for him there.

None of the reports of police and army involvement in criminal activity are particularly surprising, but what *is* astounding is that the majority of media reports and so-called expert commentary on the violence in Juárez and elsewhere didn't link the increased number of police and soldiers and the spike in violence. Take the work of Steven Dudley—who works for US-funded think tank InSight Crime, and moonlights for the Woodrow Wilson Center—for example: In early 2013, he wrote, "Last year was the least violent 12-month stretch since 2007, with the state government registering 740 murders. Homicide levels are a fifth of what they were at the beginning of 2011. Naturally, some analysts and authorities have focused on the criminal groups to explain why homicides have dropped so quickly."[49] This report ignores the link between the surge of police and army and the spike in killings in Juárez, and that when police and soldiers were withdrawn from Juárez and sent to other parts of the country, violence in Juárez dropped.

What Dudley missed is deadly obvious to Juárez residents. I'll always remember how, when I asked Cardona who I should interview about the role of police in the murders and the violence in the city, without giving it a moment's thought, he told me to ask anyone, anyone I met on the street. Over repeated visits to Juárez I took his advice, and he was bang on. His suggestion is confirmed by the statistics: a 2010 study carried out by UACJ found an average of one in four residents of Juárez were direct victims of police violence.[50] Your blinders must be security fastened in order to miss the connection between the mass deployment of police and soldiers in order to fight against internal enemies and systematic murders among poor and marginalized populations.

South of the Mexico-US border in Guerrero state, a similar pattern with regards to the arrival of federal troops and an increased use of violence emerged. In 2012 and 2013, the resort town (and port) of Acapulco played host to a federal police and army surge on the pretext of fighting organized crime. In 2012, Acapulco replaced Juárez as Mexico's most dangerous city, with 1,170 homicides, or a rate of 142.88 killings per 100,000 people.[51] An October 2013 case saw eighteen arrests of members of a kidnapping ring, thirteen of them federal police.[52] A government spokesperson told the media that the group of criminals and police had carried out seven murders and four kidnappings.

Prisons

The US rule of law program in Mexico falls in lockstep with counterinsurgency efforts, and it is clear that changes to the Mexican legal system are tied to the Mérida Initiative's funded expansion of the Mexican prison system. Remember, the United States has already "expanded secure incarceration at the federal level from five facilities with a capacity of 3,500 to fourteen facilities with a capacity of 20,000."[53] The statistics show that a move toward a US system is a transition to a model that incarcerates more and more people. According to the International Center for Prison Studies, incarceration rates in Mexico have been climbing—from 186 per 100,000 in 2004; to 197 in 2010; to 209 per 100,000 in January 2013.[54] Compare this to the United States, which incarcerated an estimated 716 people per 100,000 in 2011—by far the highest rate in the world.[55]

The war on drugs has been part of the impetus for the State Department's Bureau of International Narcotics and Law Enforcement Affairs program to provide prison training for foreign prison guards. Mexicans, Afghans, and others traveled to a women's prison, which was converted into the International Correctional Management Training Center, in Cañon City, Colorado.[56] "The threats are different; the cultures are different," training coordinator Bill Claspell told the *Denver Post*, which reported that "the strategies for neutralizing a cartel kingpin, a white-supremacist recruiter or a Taliban jihadist are the same: isolation."[57] According to a 2010 report on Colorado's training of Mexican prison guards, the exercises took place in a secret location, and the focus of the visit was on transporting high-risk prisoners from one jail to another: "Much of what they learn is about strategy. Ambushes most often happen because of breaches in intelligence. Drug lords pay underpaid federal agents to get information about when transports happen. In response, the Colorado authorities taught Mexican agents to limit how many prison officials know when transports happen, showed them how to use decoys and explained how to change when the transports happen. It makes sense sometimes to do them in the middle of the night."[58]

The *Wall Street Journal* reported that, by 2012, 5,000 Mexican prison officials had been trained in Colorado.[59] There are also training facilities for Mexican prison guards in New Mexico (canine trainings), California (emergency response), and Maryland (anti-gang trainings), as well as a Mérida Initiative–funded prison guard training program in Xalapa, Veracruz.[60] In addition to training for Mexican prison guards, the United States has provided "biometric equipment consisting of fingerprint card readers, voice recognition and DNA test kits.... This equipment will be placed in Federal and State facilities for positive inmate identification and registration in the National Database." The expansion of Mexico's prison system is a crucial if authorities are to maintain control south of the US border.

The Border

The US-Mexico border has become a linchpin in the drug war in Mexico. In the process of researching this book I visited and crossed the border dozens of times, between Juarez and El Paso, Nuevo Laredo and Laredo, and Reynosa and Pharr. On the way up to the United States, the experience is always rigorous and generally pretty high-tech, line-ups to cross can sometimes last for hours. On the way south, the situation is reversed. At most of these crossings, there is literally no control as you pass from the United States into Mexico; you could do it without a passport. The huge discrepancy between the levels of violence on each side lead me to believe the porosity of crossing into Mexico is a factor in why the level of violence in the United States is so much lower. It's not that there aren't enough resources for Mexican authorities to examine everyone that comes in, it just isn't a priority for the United States that they do so—since it is Washington that determines how these borders work. The militarization of the border on the US side, and the harsh and unjust restrictions on who (and what) can get in contribute to the concentration of criminal groups (including police, army, and authorities involved in trafficking) on the south side of the border.

Of course, there's a feeling that you are safer after crossing the border from Mexico into the States. Many Mexicans are fleeing violence, kidnapping, threats, and so on by going to Texas. In my case, I walked around Laredo alone in the evening and didn't feel afraid. When I visited Nuevo Laredo in early 2014, my contacts refused to take me for a walk through the city center in the evening, insisting that we drive. The same goes for when I was in McAllen and El Paso, compared to being in Reynosa and Juárez. On an individual level, stripped of context, it is much safer on the US side, but that doesn't change the fact that the worst of the violence taking place to the south is happening in places where the border area is militarized on both the US side and the Mexican side, as in Tamaulipas and Chihuahua.[61]

It is important to understand this militarization within the framework of counterinsurgency. Laleh Khalili notes that "Elbit Systems Ltd., the Israeli firm involved in the construction of the separation wall in Palestine, has also been contributing to the 'security' of the U.S.–Mexico border wall. In response to the moral panic about terror, many domestic police programs adopt military counterinsurgency tactics—and especially those of Israel—in their control of suspect urban populations."[62] In the case of the US-Mexico border, the suspect populations are obviously those south of the wall, and, in particular, groups of Mexican, Central American, and other migrants making their way north. In his book *Border Patrol Nation*, journalist Todd Miller reports that since September 11, 2001, the US government has spent $791 billion on Homeland Security, the agency responsible for border control. Miller reports that "in 2012, the $18 billion spent on border and immigration enforcement [outdid] all other federal law enforcement bodies combined including the FBI, Secret Service, Drug Enforcement Administration, U.S. Marshal Service, and the Bureau of Alcohol, Tobacco, Firearms and Explosives." *Border Patrol Nation* details that, prior to 1986, there were rarely more than 2,000 people deported each year. "By the late 1990s, the U.S. government was deporting more than 40,000 people annually, still only a fraction of what we see today. By the early 2010s, Homeland Security was expelling well over 400,000 people per year from the United States." This drastic increase in deportations has taken place just as a variety of US states—most famously Arizona but also Alabama, Georgia, Indiana, South Carolina, and Utah—have passed laws obliging local and state police to enforce immigration law. Communities of color, and especially those living close to the line experience the impacts of border militarization in the United States particularly harshly. However, the violence south of the border should not be considered an entirely separate phenomenon, as it can be considered, in some ways, a lurid reflection of the US policy of border militarization.

The Rio Grande area has been transformed into a testing ground for the rest of the US border with Mexico, from due west of El Paso and Ciudad Juarez to the Atlantic. "The intent is to use Texas as a model for a nationwide campaign that will stem the cross-border intrusion of these dangerous and insidious criminal groups," reads a 2011 report endorsed by the Texas Department of Agriculture. Senior Texas police officials told the retired military men who wrote the report that "much of their effort was derived from experience in recent campaigns in Iraq and Afghanistan."[63] In 2006, Texas, under the governorship of Rick Perry, launched the Unified Command (UC) structure in six urban centers along the Texas-Mexico border, bringing together federal, state, and tribal organizations, including the Joint Terrorism Task Force, Border Patrol, US Immigration and Customs Enforcement (ICE), local police departments, Parks and Wildlife, state military forces, the Bureau of Alcohol, Tobacco, Firearms and Explosives (ATF), and the FBI. At the UCs, these armed groups work hand in hand with other government agencies, including the US Postal Service and the Department of Transportation; corporations, including UPS and FedEx; as well as nongovernmental outfits like the reactionary Texas and Southwestern Cattle Raisers Association. To facilitate information sharing between the UCs, which are located in El Paso, Big Bend, Del Rio, Laredo, McAllen, and the Coastal Bend, six "unified tactical commands," known as Joint Operations and Intelligence Centers (JOIC) were created, one at the site of each UC. "UC/JOICs in effect replicate the military system of joint command and control that has proven so successful in Iraq and Afghanistan," reads the report.[64]

Borders play an incredibly important role in how societies are organized today. In *Undoing Border Imperialism*, writer and activist Harsha Walia describes the overarching nature of border controls as border imperialism. She summarizes border imperialism as emerging from a confluence of four central practices spearheaded by nation states and accompanied by ongoing processes of capitalist accumulation: The first is capitalism and empire, which underpin the entire system; followed by the criminalization of migrants; the production of racialized, sexist, and imperialist national identities; and the denial of legal permanent residency and citizenship to migrants.[65] "Border controls are used to deter those for whom migration is the only option to the plundering of their communities and economies due to the free license granted to capital and militaries," she writes.[66] But in addition to their role as locations for social control and the creation of a labor apartheid system, borders are increasingly used in the drug war context as launching pads for militarism and violence. For example, in order for the drug war to take root in southern Mexico, a program of border militarization along the Guatemala and Belize borders will be necessary in order to give the state a foothold and a venue from which to begin to interrupt flows of people and narcotics. The more open the borders are, and the less the state controls the movement of people through those borders, the less violence surrounding communities will experience.

Profits

It's long been clear that the boost in police in Mexico has been aimed at securing business interests. In August 2011, Mexico's former finance minister Bruno Ferrari told *Bloomberg* in an English interview that "Nowadays what we are seeing is that we are having a big fight against crime so that, as I said, [it] guarantees the future investments and the investments we are having right now because what we are seeing is that Mexico is fighting to prevail against crime."[67] Ferrari's statement is backed up by the experiences of the transnational business elite.

"Multinationals in Mexico practically haven't been affected, with exception of the mining sector," said Alejandro Hope, the Mexico City–based analyst. "Yes there have been some cases, but the extortion is more a phenomenon that is directed toward small and medium-sized businesses rather than large companies. There has been some kidnappings, but not much," he told me in the common room of the Mexican Institute for Competitiveness. According to Rafael McCadden, who works with Colliers International real estate group, "We don't see any companies leaving Mexico because of the security issues. We are experiencing expansions, which means they are here to stay."[68] Militarization that helps the corporate sector is often framed as benefiting society at large, like in this statement from a US military journal: "President Calderón promised to improve security, thereby enhancing prosperity for the Mexican people."[69] Though examined in the military and business press, the links between anti-narcotics programs and the economy are crucial, but are generally siloed off into separate categories or they are ignored.

According to a 2009 *Business Week* cover story, attacks on foreign staff and factories have been rare in Juárez and other border towns along drug trafficking routes, including Reynosa, Nuevo Laredo, and Tijuana.[70] Police are already deployed there with special instructions to care for transnational corporations. Following the kidnapping of a corporate executive, police suggested managers alter their work routines, leave Juárez by sundown, and stick to two key roads. Patrols were beefed up along these roads, "creating relatively safe corridors between the border and the industrial parks."[71] In other border areas, the level of repression and violence has been as intense as in Juárez, but there is less documentation of the situation. In Nuevo Laredo and elsewhere, local radio DJs would use codes like "it's hot outside" or "it's not a very nice day" to warn people to stay inside and avoid violence. Bazookas, grenades, and car bombs all made early appearances in the strategic border city, the busiest commercial crossing along the US-Mexico line. In 2010, the US consulate there was the target of a grenade attack. "Everything that the country is living through, all of the violence, started here in Nuevo Laredo," said a young lawyer from the city, just across the Rio Grande from Laredo. In 2003, during Vicente Fox's presidency, Nuevo Laredo was flooded with over 10,000 police (Federal Preventive Police [PFP], which preceded the creation of the Policia Federal) and soldiers. "On every corner there were four or five PFPs, from the edges of the city to the bridge," the lawyer told me. "As that happened, violence rose. The local police were infiltrated and they clashed with the federal police. Over time, we learned that another group had also infiltrated the federal police. In Nuevo Laredo there were clashes between municipal police and the army, and with federal police." On one visit, I walked across the bridge from Laredo and went over to a small Nuevo Laredo marketplace, which was once filled with restaurants and souvenir stands catering to day-tripping gringos. As I passed from stall to stall, I attempted small talk with various vendors. One man warmed to it, his voice dropping to a whisper when I told him I was a journalist. He was explicit that I couldn't record, but he wanted to tell me something important, he said. "The army is hunting young men on the edges of town. Hunting them like animals, and killing them, just like that."

I'll always remember an afternoon I spent in Nuevo Laredo in late 2011, a time when that city was considered one of the most dangerous in Mexico. The presence of organized criminal groups, working right under the army's nose, was apparent immediately, which is to say as soon as I hit the halfway point on the border bridge separating Laredo, Texas, from Nuevo Laredo, which is in the state of Tamaulipas. People I spoke to in Reynosa said going to their local, state-funded Human Rights Commission was like talking directly to narcos—there was no perceived separation between organized crime groups and the state government. Tamaulipas is famous, on one hand, for its horror stories, including the massacre of seventy-two migrants and the discovery of a series of mass graves in 2011, but it is also considered a state where "nothing happens"—where journalists are totally under state and cartel control, and local governments don't keep statistics.

I asked the young lawyer, who himself was kidnapped a few years before, what he thought would happen in Nuevo Laredo in coming years. "Our theory is that things won't change, this is the kind of government the PRI has always dreamed of running, with the army in the streets, with a form of control so that the people can't rise up against them. A totalitarian state, and the PAN did it for them, the PAN put the army in the streets and they won't, not even by accident, send the soldiers back to their bases," he said. His friends are organizers with Morena, the offshoot of the PRD that is organized under the leadership of Andres Manuel López Obrador. Since the violence took hold, they spend long evenings inside discussing the future of the city. "The country is militarized. In Nuevo Laredo there are no civilian police; it's been seven or eight years since we've seen a cop. There are no transit police. The soldiers do everything, and obviously that doesn't guarantee security. Rather, violence has exploded.... Today there is daily violence, violence that we didn't know before, social violence."

The drug war strengthens the power of the police and army, and fortifies the ability of the hegemonic political elite to rule. The Atlacomulco group, a neoliberalizing faction of the PRI, which was led by Carlos Salinas through the '90s, is also behind Enrique Peña Nieto, who was born in the municipality of Atlacomulco in Mexico state. At the same time as it creates internal enemies out of the population by linking them with drug trafficking, dealing, or using, the drug war is militarizing and modernizing the police and the army, and Mexico's network of jails. These elements together are useful in the exercise and preservation of repressive state power. In an interview with English journalist Ed Vulliamy, then-presidential spokesperson Alejandra Sota Mirafuentes said: "The president is clear: the fight is not against drugs, it is against the violence and the ability of criminal organizations to subvert the state. The president knows that drugs will not disappear."[72] Indeed they haven't and won't, and everyone knows this, but I can't help but wonder how things would be different if this was the tagline on the drug war that was repeated over and again on television and in newspapers.

Anti-Drugs Cops Help Canadian Mining Companies

Chihuahua, like other parts of Mexico and Central America, is experiencing an important expansion in transnational mining and state-led militarization under the pretext of the war on drugs. While disappearances and murders of environmental activists by state forces or paramilitary/cartel members are obvious examples through which we can understand environmental violence in Mexico, the overall rise in killings, kidnapping, and threats to civilians in Mexico is of utmost importance. I believe many of these events may eventually prove to be linked to environmental violence, which is to say violence related to the economic potential of the specific geographic location where it occurs. What now appear as indiscriminate murders may eventually begin to appear as patterns, which could be linked either, in rural areas, to the clearing of territory through terror for future resource extraction or, in urban settings, to capital flow facilitating infrastructure projects (like highways, airports, or border bridges). When government officials talk about reducing violence or improving security, what they are usually referring to is sending additional police and/or soldiers and/or marines.

Problems related to police deployments are not limited to urban areas. The mountain town of Madera, Chihuahua, lies a couple hours' bus ride west of the state capital. What happened after 10,000 federal police and soldiers arrived in Chihuahua state, in 2008, shows that an increase in police and soldiers in an area can prove beneficial to transnational corporate interests. Increased policing can precipitate the breakdown of community structures, in this case, of an ejido or community landholders group, who exercise legal title over their lands through assemblies and communal decision making. On an August afternoon in 2008, Dante Váldez Jimenez was giving a teacher training class in an elementary school in Madera, but before he finished his lecture, he was interrupted by a group of thirty men, some of them armed. In the minutes that followed, Váldez was savagely beaten in front of his students. While they beat him, his attackers yelled that he should keep his nose out of other people's business. Váldez was lucky to escape with his life. Five days later, Amnesty International put out an alert expressing concern for Váldez's safety, as well as that of members of a nearby community. The attack was political: Váldez is known for his work against Pan American Silver Corporation, a Vancouver-based company that operates an open-pit gold mine near Madera. Amnesty indicated that among the attackers were employees of the mining company. "There isn't a single authority in any of the three levels of government that is looking out for the people who are displaced, for people who have been mistreated or beaten," Váldez told me, his voice quiet and low. He pointed out that there was a classroom full of witnesses to the incident, but there was never an investigation. His attack wasn't an isolated incident, but a brazen reminder of the repression meted out to those who organized against the company, which began operating in Mexico in 1994 after NAFTA was signed. In 2007, Pan American Silver started construction on a low-grade, cyanide-leaching gold and silver mine near the town. Madera, which means "wood" in Spanish, is situated high in the Sierra Madre mountain range and has the air of a logging town, but the area is anything but tranquil: at that time, the dominant story was that in the Sierra Madre, the Sinaloa Cartel—Mexico's most powerful drug cartel—was battling it out with La Linea, the armed wing of the Juárez Cartel.

According to the official story, at stake were trafficking routes, as well as vast fields where peasant and Indigenous farmers cultivate marijuana and opium poppies. Certainly the region is home to illicit crop production and trafficking but there are other interests at play. Before construction of the Pan American Silver mine could begin, the historic town of Dolores had to be relocated to make way for the project, affecting more than sixty families. Locals were not ardently anti-mining, but many felt that Ejido Huizopa, the body that represents communal landholders in the area, was not getting a fair shake. By 2008, as construction gave way to gold production, tensions between the company and members of the ejido reached a breaking point. That May, after reaching a majority decision in an assembly, members of the ejido erected a blockade at the mine access route, demanding meaningful negotiations and a better agreement with the company. People working for the mining company were prevented from passing, but soldiers were allowed through the barricades.

The mining company soon found a way around the protesters, one that didn't involve sitting at a negotiating table. "At the blockade, there was always, permanently, soldiers traveling in the company trucks, dressed like civilians, [and] as many as eight company trucks watching the demonstrations, the blockade," said Váldez. Blockaders were intimidated by the soldiers' presence, and the company continued to access the mine, with workers passing through the blockade because they had soldiers in their trucks. After armed commandos linked to narcotraffickers attacked civilians in a neighboring village, police maintained a continuous presence at the blockade. The blockade lasted one year and five months, during which time residents say the company co-opted members of Ejido Huizopa through financial incentives and intimidation. "When the mining company saw that we had a majority of [communal land owners] supporting us, they began to manipulate in a certain way, using the same people from the ejido to manipulate other compañeros, to ensure that we didn't have a majority in decision making," said Luis Peña Amaya, a member of the ejido, who helped organize the blockade.

As on the blockades, the militarization of the region factored into the company's ability to win support for its open-pit mine. "The federal police had a presence and intimidated people on many occasions. In the decisive assembly, they took control and surrounded the inside of the hall where we held our assembly," said Peña Amaya. The intrusion of police into communal decision making is unconstitutional in Mexico. "When things turned against the other group, which was the group preferred by the mining company, [federal police] intervened to ensure that we didn't exercise our rights."

Then there's the case of Vasco Gil, a tiny ranching hamlet in the mountains of Durango. In the summer of 2009, approximately thirty soldiers showed up and began surveilling and harassing residents. A few days later, another ten or fifteen soldiers arrived, and twelve men from the area were kidnapped. "In a direct statement to *Riodoce,* [residents] commented that the soldiers showed up to the mountainous region approximately one month ago and began carrying out surveillance, then they began asking where the armed groups were, and especially if [locals] had any knowledge about suspected narcotraffickers Ismael El Mayo Zambada and Joaquín el Chapo Guzmán," reads an article printed in *Riodoce,* an independent weekly based in Culiacán, Sonora.[73] The criminalization and terrorizing of residents of Vasco Gil and nearby hamlets by soldiers was carried out in the name of the fight against drug cartels. Closer inspection reveals that there is a much larger interest in the region.

Vancouver-based mining company Chesapeake Gold Corporation has plans to build an open-pit mine in the area, removing 821 million tons of ore over nineteen years of mining operations. These plans would necessitate the displacement of all residents of Vasco Gil.[74] "The living conditions are primitive in this isolated, mountainous area, where the roads are sometimes impassable during the rainy season," according to the company's economic feasibility report on the mine, which proceeds to wrongfully characterize the local economy as based on ranching, rather than forestry, which is actually the predominant economic activity. The stakes in the area surrounding Vasco Gil are high: the company will need to invest about $487 million to operate the mine, and believes that the proposed Metates mine "project is one of the largest, undeveloped disseminated gold and silver deposits in the world."[75] For Chesapeake Gold Corporation, residents of Vasco Gil and the surrounding area are potential barriers to profit maximization. Chesapeake owns 5,776 hectares of concessions in the area, and actively drilled core samples for exploration in March and April of 2009.[76] Maybe it is a coincidence that almost four dozen soldiers arrived in the town months after a round of exploration drilling around Vasco Gil. Maybe not. But it seems useful to consider factors other than drugs (in this case, transnational mining interests) as potentially influencing violence aimed at local populations in resource-rich areas.

Territory, Community Police, and Self-defense Groups

In Mexico's Guerrero state, community members have prevented the army from entering their territories because they believe that where the army goes, transnational companies will follow. Guerrero's distinct history has meant that the drug war has differently impacted the state, which has long experienced violence and militarization at levels unknown in the rest of the country before the drug war began in 2006. "The war on drugs is no less than continuing to use military force to contain nonconformist, disruptive movements, groups in resistance, and collectives who raise their voices," said Abel Barrera, director of Tlachinollan, a human rights group based in Tlapa de Comonfort, Guerrero. Poppy growing in the region gives soldiers and state authorities a pretext to enter into community lands, but according to Barrera, it does even more than that. "What we've seen up until now is that the militarization is not only a way to enter into the territories, but that it serves to impose megaprojects. [The police and army] are the offensive front that goes and enters into territories in order to guarantee that transnational capital can be established there, and install itself via mines, megaprojects, dams, and ecotourism projects. Regardless of the fact that they are in their own lands, a village cannot go against a mine or a multinational company. Companies need a guarantee that capital is worth more than the lives of the peasants that are blocking it," said Barrera, emphasizing that the role of state forces in Guerrero is to provide that guarantee. Barrera, who is from Tlapa, dresses casually and his language is easy and informal, punctuated by local vernacular and street slang. A photo to his right shows him receiving the Robert F. Kennedy Prize for Human Rights, which he was awarded in 2010 for his work at Tlachinollan, and to his left is a heavy bust of RFK, sitting on a shelf beside dozens of reports produced by the human rights group.

According to Barrera, the re-militarization taking place as part of the drug war is a pretext to destroy community control over land and resources. "The other [role of militarization] is to not allow the community police and self-defense groups, which are controlling territory—this is another issue, the issue is that the people have understood that with the reforms and with all the privatizations, and with the mining companies, what do the people say? 'Well then we're going to protect ourselves, we are in our own territory, so how are we going to protect it?' And that's where the self-defense groups and the community police begin to take on a more proactive role, in saying, 'We're not going to allow the mining companies to come in.'" The places where community police and self-defense groups are active have been increasingly militarized since the war on drugs was declared and the Mérida Initiative launched. Barrera insists, though, that the suite of armed actors in the region be understood within a context where local armed groups are defending their territories while being faced down by state militarization at the service of transnational capital. "What we see is that there is a process of remilitarization, but it is with the intention of re-conquering territories and reinforcing a strategy of counterinsurgency, but also as an armed front of the state to re-conquer and impose projects, to help mega-projects set up in these regions."

Barrera is interrupted by a call on his old Nokia, and he takes it, signaling the end to the interview. He is a man known for having his finger on the pulse of social movements in Guerrero state, and for going out to a community gathering on a moment's notice if invited.

Unlike the self-defense groups in Michoacán, the community police in Guerrero didn't surge up from movements against drug cartels. According to Francisco López Barcenas, an Indigenous lawyer and human rights activist, community policing groups have a history that traces back to pre-colonial times in states throughout Mexico. "What we can see today is communities reorganizing," he said in an interview with *Vice*. "On the one hand, they are doing it to stop the violence, and on the other hand, to defend their natural resources."[77] Community policing experienced a revival in Guerrero in 1995 when the Regional Coordinator of Community Authorities (CRAC) was created to form a regional structure that incorporated numerous towns and included training and processes for trying and rehabilitating those deemed criminals through community service. "Officers of the CRAC community police are appointed by the Assembly. We don't cover our faces. The weapons used by the CRAC's officers are bought by the community," according to Pablo Guzmán Hernández, who previously coordinated the CRAC.[78]

Territorial control and the threat they pose to transnational capital is a crucial and oft-ignored role of these groups. "If we allow the army to enter communal territory, they will never leave. The government has its sights on exploiting the mines; they want us to fight amongst ourselves, so that they can come in and militarize the territory. That's the bottom line here," said Claudio Carrasco, former coordinator of the Regional Coordinator of Community Authorities-Community Police (CRAC-PC).[79] There are three producing mines in Guerrero state, a host of exploration projects, and vast expanses of mountainous land that has not yet been granted in mining concessions.

In his early days as president, Peña Nieto announced the creation of a gendarmerie, a heavily armed police force that would primarily patrol rural areas.[80] "Although falling under the Ministry of the Interior, the National Gendarmerie will mostly consist of soldiers who will remain under military/naval command. These troops will be heavily armed, uniquely trained in rapid assault tactics (rather than more standard evidentiary procedures) and specifically authorized to operate above force levels that typically apply to the police."[81] The national gendarmerie will increase police presence in resource-rich rural areas in Mexico, creating another layer of protection for mining companies and others active in these so-called under-policed areas. A 5,000 member gendarmerie was launched in August of 2014, and according to *The Economist*, "it will have special responsibility for protecting Mexico's economic assets—oil, mines, farms and so forth—from organised crime."[82]

The snapshots presented in this chapter are an initial attempt to look at how the deployment of police and soldiers has not brought security to the communities they patrol. Rather, these deployments act as a guarantee to investors seeking to insure their installations will be protected from community resistance, at great cost to men and women throughout the region. In addition, they've done little to stop the flow of drugs, but rather have contributed to shifting the flows to other regions. In the future, these other regions could also be militarized in the name of fighting the flow of drugs, extending into a kind of perpetual war.

CHAPTER 6:

MEXICO, PARAMILITARIZATION
& THE DRUG WAR

EARLY in 2014, I met with Javier Sicilia, a man who is today perhaps Mexico's most well-known peace activist, in a Starbucks in the south of Mexico City. He arrived with a friend, and though he left his trademark wide-brimmed hat and beige vest at home, he still garnered attention among the half dozen people sipping their coffees. As we chatted, one man patted Sicilia on the shoulder, telling him to keep up the struggle. The circumstances that plunged Sicilia into a life of activism are tragic. On March 28, 2011, his son Juan Francisco Sicilia Ortega was murdered along with six others in Temixco, Morelos, just south of Mexico City. The seven bodies were found inside a Honda Civic. Sicilia, a poet, vowed he would never write another verse, and began a national campaign known as the Movement for Peace with Justice and Dignity, that carried out marches, caravans, and events throughout Mexico and the United States. Sicilia places the blame for his son's murder squarely on the drug war strategy carried out by Felipe Calderón, and says that had drug trafficker Arturo Beltran Leyva not been murdered in 2009, his son would still be alive.[1] "I'm sure that if Beltran Leyva was still in Cuernavaca, if they hadn't killed him, my son wouldn't be dead," said Sicilia. His son was killed with six others when they were kidnapped after denouncing a robbery. The owner of the house where they were being held freaked out and called a local crime boss, paying him 300,000 pesos and giving him two trucks to get the kidnapped youth off his hands. All seven of them were murdered, and stuffed into a car. Sicilia believes that the war on drugs strategy is what ratcheted up the violence in Mexico. "This is my hypothesis: there's cartels out there, and when Calderón—with assistance from institutions that were involved in cartel activity—decides to mobilize the army, what he does is oblige the cartels to arm themselves like armies. Then he does another terrible thing as part of this strategy, he beheads the big *capos*, the ones who controlled those groups. So what was left were cells that cannot access drugs, which leads to the true diversification of crime."

The paramilitarization that has taken place in Mexico since Calderón declared war on drug cartels in December 2006 can be understood as stemming from two elements of US-promoted militarization in Mexico. Sicilia mentioned the first element in our interview above. The paramilitarization of drug cartels is an outcome of the police and army's piecemeal confrontations with well-financed drug trafficking groups that have a large supply of cash and almost unfettered access to weapons. As a consequence of state attempts to militarize their trafficking routes, drug trafficking organizations recruit and arm grunts to protect their trade. This is something that has been rigorously documented in Colombia, where "military and counter-narcotics aid to Colombia, rather than enhancing the state's monopoly on the legitimate use of violence, is diverted to empower non-state armed actors, increasing extra-legal violence with no apparent effect on its stated goal of curbing drug production," stated economists in a peer-reviewed paper released in December 2012.[2] "Our estimates display a distinct, asymmetric pattern: when U.S. military aid increases, attacks by paramilitaries, who are known to work with the military, increase more in municipalities with bases." Which is to say that the more the United States spends in Colombia, the more irregular forces have their way with local populations, generating terror and violence.

The second element is that historically in Latin America the so-called professionalization of the police, explored in the last chapter, leads to paramilitarization. "Professionalization's insistence on centralized and specialized police activities seems also to lead to the devolution (e.g. debureaucratization), as the activities of professionalized, specialized, and autonomous national police agencies increasingly diverge from the centers of authority that have produced them.... Devolution from bureaucratized militarization is often manifested in the emergence of social-control groups with less direct, more tenuous links to the state. These take the form of death squads related only in varying degree to police, or police-linked *justiciero* lone-wolf killers, or parts of the internal security system that have turned against other parts—as when one internal security organization spies on, or takes action against, another."[3] Seen in this light, we can understand that police training actually increases the possibility that paramilitary groups will form. Instead of calling the armed groups that work for narcotics traffickers paramilitaries, they are referred to in the mainstream press and by government officials (and by extension the majority of the population) as drug cartels, or in some cases the "armed wing" of a given drug cartel. Many of these groups are initially formed by deserters from state security forces in the pay of crime groups. The notion that they are loyal to a particular organization (or more absurdly, to the trade of a particular commodity) is vastly overstated in hegemonic discourses about drug cartels. (The same is true of members of state security forces, who as noted above have defected with incredible frequency to work with organized crime groups.)

The notion of drug cartels presented in the media is very simplistic, and could be said to hide more than it obscures. Julián Cardona, the journalist who explained to me how in Juárez the police carried out the functions of a drug cartel, had the following to say to journalist Ed Vulliamy. "It simply doesn't make sense, as the media and government think, to draw lines between cartels in Juárez. Along the smuggling corridors into the U.S., maybe, but not on the streets. The cartels cannot even see those lines themselves anymore. Of course the drug cartels exist, they are players, but they are no longer the main reason for the violence here. You have a product and a production line. There are bosses, managers, middle management, line workers, accountants, bankers, shippers—they are all part of the process but they never meet each other and most of them are not directly employed by the corporation. We'll have counted seventeen hundred dead in this city by the end of the year [he predicted, rightly, in September 2008] and in most cases, the executioners don't even know which cartel, if any, they're working for. If they change sides, from someone far from here who is in the Juárez cartel to someone far from here in the Sinaloa cartel, they won't know it. All they have is their assigned task, their piece of turf, and maybe an order to do this, do that, or kill someone. Not why or who for. They have no idea about the big money, or who their bosses are."[4]

There are, of course, differing views on this matter and there are people who don't believe drug cartels are functioning as paramilitary groups, carrying out the bidding of corporate or other sectors. In an interview, National Autonomous University researcher Gian Carlo Delgado hesitated at the idea of classifying cartels as paramilitary groups. "Paramilitaries have always existed, they've always been here, since there have been armed resistance movements or armed movements, there have been paramilitaries…. For my part, it is difficult to link or to say that organized crime is paramilitarism; if we included the armed elements of organized crime under the category of paramilitaries generally, I still have a hard time making a clear link to the state."

Violence and Small Business

The violence in Mexico has decimated local economies, especially in the north. According to a priest I interviewed in Tamaulipas—who preferred to remain nameless for fear of being targeted—extortions and insecurity have undermined the entrepreneurial spirit of the people in northern Mexico. "The economic situation has destroyed the border [area], especially taking into account the situation of insecurity that people are living through in the city, which has meant there are less jobs, and the people are fearful and are not able to be entrepreneurs, which is characteristic of people from the north."

"The businesses that are most affected by the violence are the smallest and those that are located in the states of northern Mexico.... The lack of security hurts small and medium producers, businesses and vendors to a larger degree, due to the fact that organized crime has 'a higher ease of penetration with them than with the directors of large companies, which, in many cases, operate from outside the country.'"[5] According to COPARMEX, a Mexican business association, 160,000 businesses closed because of security concerns in 2011. "There is a reconversion of the economy taking place at the national level that is favoring [large companies], and it is making more [Mexicans] into employees instead of entrepreneurs," said Dr. Correa-Cabrera during a presentation in Baja California Sur in February of 2012.

Correa-Cabrera's observations were made plain on my first visits to Reynosa and Ciudad Juárez, both in 2011. Unlike other cities I'd visited in Mexico, here I was surprised to find large, popular areas in these cities without the food stands or little corner shops that are usually ubiquitous. Between 2009 and 2011 in Ciudad Juárez, "almost 6,000 small grocery stores were closed down, out of 7,000 such stores that were formally registered. The reason: an increase in robberies, extortions, and kidnappings."[6]

The disappearance of local businesses meant that when I visited Juárez the only place with an open patio was Starbucks. The patio looked on to the parking lot of a Walmart, built over top of one of the city's historic bullfighting rings. Activists held their press conferences at Sanborns, a cookie-cutter restaurant chain owned by the country's richest man, because it was one of the few safe places open later into the evening. Those who can afford it use their cars more, shop in big department stores, and eat at restaurants, which are generally considered safer areas further outside the reach of organized crime. It is more difficult for criminal groups to operate with total impunity and threaten and extort owners and workers at transnational food and beverage chains than it is for them to do the same to a local business whose owner has lived his or her entire life in the area.

The experience of Carlos Gutierrez is one of the most public examples of how extortion can ruin someone's life. And it's public for two reasons: first, because he survived a bloody attack against him, and second, because he was able to leave Mexico and gain temporary legal status in the United States. These factors are what enabled him to speak out about what happened. Gutierrez ran a successful concession stand in Chihuahua City until extortionists began to demand monthly payments of up to US$10,000 a month. After about a year, Gutierrez could no longer make the payments, and one night, while he was hanging out in a park with friends, four armed men attacked him and cut off both his feet, with either a machete or an axe.[7] Those responsible for the extortions and attack were never publicly identified or captured, and Gutierrez has tried to start a new life with his family in Texas.

Correa-Cabrera notes that attributing the violence in Mexico only to narcotics trafficking is no longer a useful way to understand the conflict. "The new organized crime corporation in Mexico has a transnational character and includes various divisions or key areas, which include: drug trafficking (buying and selling); money laundering (which would be part of the financial division); human trafficking; paid assassins (which operate as a kind of marketing area, with the task of generating terror and sending messages to various actors so as to negotiate with or to threaten them); a more recently created division, which is dedicated to extortion, kidnapping, and charging rents (which represents a diversification of the traditional activities of so called drug cartels); among others."[8]

When drug trafficking patterns eventually shift away from Mexico, which history indicates that they are bound to do, those who can afford to pay members of paramilitary groups will be people connected to the state and the so-called legal economy. But the extortions carried out by these groups with impunity will likely continue, meaning that ironically it will be the poor, working, and middle-class Mexicans who are forced to pay for the ongoing survival of these paramilitary groups, chief among them Los Zetas.

Tamaulipas state is a crucial node in understanding the drug war in Mexico. There the lines between the PRI and criminal organizations are blurred to the point that there is no longer any way to differentiate between them. "[Cartels] have all the control, they monopolize the legitimate use of violence, and they are performing activities that are of the state," said U of T professor Correa Cabrera when we spoke in 2011. According to a 2010 report by the Committee to Protect Journalists, "It's hard to be sure when the Gulf cartel gained the power over the city [Reynosa] that it has now; it didn't happen in a single blow, reporters said. Most traced the change to three or four years ago. Before then, the cartel ran a kind of parallel government from which it strongly influenced institutions such as the police and the city government.... Journalists say the cartel is fully embedded in the government and gets nearly whatever it wants."[9] The Gulf Cartel got its start running liquor across the border during alcohol prohibition in the United States in the 1920s. In the 80s, its main business was marijuana trafficking, by the 1990s, official estimates held that the Gulf Cartel was responsible for 30 percent of the cocaine moving through Mexico.[10] Through that time, some of the highest-ranked members of the Gulf Cartel were former police officers, and traffickers had links to the highest echelons of PRI officialdom.

In 2010, Reynosa was home to the clashes that gave birth to a new armed group, Los Zetas. The emergence of Los Zetas has proven to be a transformative element in the reconfiguration of Mexico's military and paramilitary forces under the rubric of the war on drugs. The official story has it that the very first Zetas were men recruited from the GAFEs, an elite airborne unit of the Mexican Army originally created to provide security at the 1986 FIFA World Cup in Mexico. French Special Forces from the National Gendarmerie Intervention Group trained the first GAFEs, and after the Zapatista uprising in 1994, they went on to carry out counterinsurgent activities against the EZLN, the Zapatista army. According to a US State Department cable released by Wikileaks, GAFE-turned-Zeta Rogelio López Villafana was trained in the United States, possibly at Fort Bragg.[11]

Osiel Cardenas Guillen, who took over the Gulf Cartel in 1999, was able to broker the participation of Mexican Special Forces in the narcotics-funded protection market. In 2003, the Mexican Army arrested Cardenas Guillen, accusing him of threatening to kill an undercover US sheriff, and threatening FBI and DEA agents in broad daylight.[12] He was jailed at La Palma, near Toluca in Mexico state, and in 2007 he was extradited to the United States.[13] That same year the relationship between the Gulf Cartel and the Zetas began to sour, as Cardenas Guillen was jailed and could no longer negotiate between them, creating the initial split between the Gulf Cartel and the Zetas that would eventually tear wide open.

By the time Cardenas Guillen was put in jail, the Zetas had appropriated protection rackets long held by municipal police in Nuevo Laredo.[14] It is said that, around that time, the Zetas and the Gulf Cartel agreed that the Gulf Cartel would continue to control trafficking routes through Tabasco, Veracruz, and Tamaulipas (along Gulf Coast), and the Zetas would control Nuevo Laredo (the busiest commercial land crossing on the US-Mexico border), as well as exercising influence in other parts of Tamaulipas, including Ciudad Victoria and San Fernando. Their pact was totally broken in January of 2010, with the assassination of El Concord, a representative of Los Zetas in Reynosa.[15] After the break, other Mexican crime groups, including La Familia Michoacana and the Sinaloa Cartel, under the name "La Nueva Federacion" declared that they would unite in a war against the Zetas.

Part of the reason the Zetas are perceived and presented as being so powerful is because their members often have military training superior to those in other cartels, which are portrayed as recruiting inexperienced eighteen-year-olds—although ex-police and ex-soldiers play an important role in the paramilitarized element of every drug cartel. The Zetas did not emerge as a traditional drug trafficking organization, and thus do not exercise the same kind of territorial control as the other groups. This is because, since their inception, the Zetas have been involved in extortion and other ways of making money—including trafficking in migrants.

Following Correa Cabrera's conception of cartels as corporations, the Zetas are sometimes described as a kind of franchise operation, where local criminals can access weapons and branding in exchange for a cut of the proceeds. Affiliating with the Zetas brand gives criminals the potential to extort greater sums of money from kidnapping and other forms of extortion, including charging *derecho de piso*, and trafficking in migrants. Greater amounts of money can be extorted based on the reputation of the group one associates with, and, in the case of the Zetas, that reputation has been established through mass graves and terrible murders.

People who associate themselves with the Zetas have taken over the edges of the economy, including the so called "illegal economy" of human trafficking (of women and migrants), as well as forms of informal commerce like pirated DVDs. Colonizing these informal segments of the economy has created a new pattern of territorial expansion for the Zetas, one that is different from what other organized criminal groups have traditionally done (control a series of plazas and physical transshipment routes). With these methods, the Zetas have extended their zone of influence along, within, inside, and around territories previously of little interest to drug traffickers, areas that have little to no strategic value in terms of moving product. The Zetas also exercise their own form of control in regions monopolized by other criminal organizations (for whom movement of product has traditionally been the key focus of activities, requiring contiguous territorial access). In San Fernando, Tamaulipas, for example, it is known that local police actually assisted in training Zetas.[16] In Monterrey, state police looked on as Zetas hung banners from the State Congress.[17] Police cooperation locally, and active impunity granted by higher levels of government and reinforced by world powers willing to turn a blind eye, give the Zetas, and other paramilitary groups, a free hand to enforce and fulfill the desires of their higher-ups.

The Zetas are not simply some kind of warped end-product of transnational capitalism, nor are they an organization beyond comprehension or logic. Instead, there has been an active transnational-state-media role in their formation. As mentioned earlier, Los Zetas were allowed to flourish and consolidate when the United States supported Mexico's decision to make Juárez a focus of the fight against cartels, instead of interrupting Los Zetas in Nuevo Laredo. The killing off of many of the Zetas' original members has resulted in an increasingly fractured and dispersed group of trained killers, each of whom could easily recruit and train others to carry out the orders of those who can pay them, in order to do what was required to make a profit once the group is out on its own. One of the innovations of Los Zetas, which could come from the model of Central American gangs, is that they create and maintain zones of total silence: journalists do not publish stories about them, and on every street corner someone on the Zeta's payroll keeps an eye on the neighborhood. The intense surveillance of urban areas by Los Zetas and their workers, combined with the terror generated through their actions, is enough to smother not only dissent but also mobility and communication about life under occupation.

The structure and style of Zeta control has been copied and applied outside of their original area of influence. Groups who rebelled against Zeta leadership in the state of Michoacán would later take on many characteristics of Los Zetas as they formed La Familia Michoacana, which later splintered to form Los Caballeros Templarios (Knights Templar). Events in Michoacán have proven that the model of Los Zetas is one that can be copied and applied elsewhere, so long as authorities guarantee impunity.

"The Zetas are a paramilitary force," said William Robinson, the professor and author whom I interviewed in Mexico City in 2011. "Basically it's the creation of paramilitarism alongside formal militarization, which is a Colombian model."[18] One barometer of paramilitary activity is the level of displacement experienced in areas where these kinds of groups are active. Those most strongly impacted by paramilitarization in Colombia are primarily poor people in urban and rural areas, and the same generally holds true for Mexico. According to the Mexican Human Rights Commission (CNDH), 120,000 people were displaced in Mexico between 2006 and 2014, especially from the states of Chiapas, Guerrero, Michoacán, Tamaulipas, Sinaloa, Chihuahua, Coahuila, Sinaloa, and Baja California. "In Sinaloa alone 30,000 people have fled their homes, and in Guerrero, according to the CNDH, over 7,000 people have changed their places of residence due to the fear created by criminals in diverse areas of the region."[19]

Paramilitarized Migration

Where paramilitary groups and cartels go, a strikingly similar brand of terror follows. In Colombia an important variable in counterinsurgency and counternarcotics efforts is the presence of guerrilla groups, but in Mexico it is the presence of migrants that is probably the largest variable. The men and women moving through the country are not necessarily organized or ideologically driven; the presence of migrants from Central America, and also from South America and elsewhere, is a significant occurrence in certain parts of the country. Controlling the flow of migration through Mexico is a key concern for Washington, and paramilitarized cartels are playing an increasingly important role in doing it. The mass kidnapping of migrants took off over the same time period as Calderón's war on drugs spread around the country. During a six-month period between late 2008 and early 2009, Mexico's National Human Rights Commission documented 198 cases of mass kidnappings, in which 9,758 migrants were kidnapped. A later study by the organization found that between April and September of 2010 there were 214 documented mass kidnappings, resulting in 11,333 victims.[20] The ransoms associated with these kidnappings provide a new revenue stream for organized crime groups, and the kidnappings lessen the flow of migrants, effectively extending border control to the Mexico-Guatemala border, something the US government has thus far not objected to.

The situation facing migrants traveling through Mexico has long been complicated by extortion and abuse, but over the past years, the experience of migrating through Mexico has been transformed as drug war militarization has led to better equipped and more disperse armed groups. The long-functioning coyote system, in which migrants pay (often through loans) to be guided over part or all of their route by experienced border crossers, was slowly dismantled as coyotes were threatened or killed by criminal groups. The illicit activities of migration authorities and police were either assumed by cartels, or they began to function in a complimentary fashion with them. "In reality migrants always complained of abuses by authorities, especially police, not just here in Nuevo Laredo but also in Chiapas, in Veracruz, and in Tabasco; the stories they tell reflected the total fear they feel toward the authorities," said a man I interviewed who was involved in the migrant shelter in Nuevo Laredo, Tamaulipas. "The situation they are facing became more complicated because of organized crime. Initially the kidnappings started in 2004 or 2005, when the group the migrants feared were the Maras (Central American gangs).... Those groups have since been substituted by cartels like the Zetas or the Gulf, who are responsible for this whole disaster, especially of kidnappings and the extortion of family members—that's been the new element." Migrants don't generally travel with cash, they are detained and forced to give a phone number of a relative in the United States; it is that person who is then extorted for sums nearing $5,000. In dozens of interviews with migrants, I heard over and over again about groups of people traveling above one of the trains to the United States being corralled or detained by migration officials, only to be abandoned by authorities and turned over to criminal groups. They described how, from the moment they crossed into Mexico, they were subject to open recruiting by members of criminal organizations, and how once they were at the north border they would be forced to pay quotas to the Zetas or other crime groups in order to cross.

Dramatic events in Chiapas and Veracruz provide some examples of how this informal border enforcement takes place. At the crime scene, one of the women lay face up, her torso cutting a diagonal line across the railway track. The other lay face down, her right leg splayed over the same track at the thigh. Both wore reddish tank tops and pants that went down just below the knees. A police officer with an automatic weapon watched over the bodies. It was far too late to do anything to help. Little yellow numbers, from one to six, were placed on each piece of ballistic evidence, dotting across the tracks. According to local media, the women were shot and stabbed in the late afternoon of May 30, 2013.[21] A preliminary report suggests they refused to pay the quota charged by a criminal group after climbing up on the train.[22] Their bodies were found later that same day just north of the Mexican tourist town of Palenque, in Chiapas. Both women were from Honduras—Mexicans don't risk traveling on cargo trains when they migrate through their country toward the United States. Most Central Americans traveling through Mexico do so as undocumented migrants, which means they are not afforded the right to free movement.

If undocumented migrants board a bus in Mexico, they can be pulled off by soldiers or immigration agents at numerous checkpoints along the roads, and deported. Without paperwork, they can't make it past the airport service counter. Thus, the train is the most accessible means of transport for Hondurans, Guatemalans, Salvadorans, Nicaraguans, and others who hope against hope they'll make it to the US and find employment. But the train represents another set of risks, as it is completely under the control of criminal groups. Groups of migrants I met with in Palenque explained in hushed tones that they are expected to pay three $100 quotas in order to advance through to Tamaulipas state sandwiched on top of a cargo train, which for the purpose of comparison, is more expensive than it would be to buy a cheap plane ticket from Chiapas to northern Mexico.

The double murder on the train tracks in Chiapas took place on the heels of an attempted mass extortion of migrants in the same region on May 1, when hundreds of Central American migrants making their way through Veracruz state on top of a cargo train experienced first hand what it is like to live through absolute horror. After nightfall, the train passed Las Barrancas, a community of about 3,000, in the southern part of the state. As it neared the village, a group of people linked to the Zetas began demanding that those riding the train pay them a quota. According to the testimonies of people on the train, members of the Zetas demanded each migrant pay US$100. As the train chugged along, people who resisted or couldn't pay were beaten, shot at, stabbed, and thrown from the train over the course of nine kilometers. Approximately twenty-five people were hospitalized with injuries, one of which was serious. One boy survived because bullets lodged into his backpack. Hundreds of people jumped off the train to safety, landing on the gravel road that follows the tracks and leads to Las Barrancas. Amid the confusion, someone got word to Julio Pérez Zabalza, a spry seventy-year-old with the energy of someone half his age. He got on a loudspeaker mounted on a twelve-foot pole in front of his house and called for the migrants to come up to the plaza. "I started to make announcements on the loudspeaker; five or ten minutes later the migrants started to come out to the soccer field; within an hour or an hour and a half the field was full, with 500 or 600 migrants," he said. Residents of Las Barrancas fed and sheltered the migrants, most of whom have since continued on toward the United States. The few who remain in the community, because their injuries prevented them from carrying on, preferred not to speak to journalists.

Ruben Figueroa helps run a migrant shelter on the Guatemalan border, which for many is a point of entry into Mexico, and the first place they'll climb up on the train heading north. He says that abuses of migrants in Veracruz have reached epic proportions because of the government's close relationship with criminal groups. "By its nature, migration is a humanitarian tragedy, but when there are governments that are complicit with organized crime, it becomes a holocaust."

Some have accused the governor of Veracruz, Javier Duarte, of covering up for the criminals who attacked migrants in Barrancas on May 1st. Duarte stated in a press release that the incident was actually caused by infighting between the migrants themselves.[23] But Guillermo Cortes Moreno, the adjunct mayor of Las Barrancas, rejected that version, reiterating that the conflict was related to the extortion of migrants. According to newspaper reports, no one was killed when the criminal group attacked the passengers on the train. Local journalists, however, say they think it is possible that people were killed that night, but because police were in control of the area for ten hours following the attack, no bodies were seen. Without bodies, there are no dead, they said. According to members of Grupo Beta, a government-funded group that provides food and water to migrants and minimally interacts with them, what happened in Las Barrancas isn't necessarily unusual. The difference is that this time it was denounced by local authorities, and picked up by the media. "Events like this aren't rare; they are common here," said Figueroa, the migrant rights activist. "It's normal that the government tried to deny what happened, but this got out thanks to the media." Figueroa works at La 72 in Tenosique, Tabasco, a slow-moving town in the humid lowlands on the Guatemala-Mexico border. La 72 was opened after the August 2011 discovery of the corpses of seventy-two migrants, who were killed after refusing to work for Los Zetas. There were at least two survivors, from Ecuador and Honduras. The bodies of fifty-eight men and fourteen women were bound and stacked in the back of a ranch in San Fernando, Tamaulipas. The shelter was named in honor of the victims, who were said to have been killed by the Zetas after failing to either pay extortion or join the ranks of the organization.

"Effectively, this is the beginning point for the sinister Gulf route— the route through hell is what we call it," Figueroa told me in 2012. "[The migrants] take about 25 days to arrive to the north border. They use trains, they use buses, they use many means to arrive to the north border, and from there they try and pass over to the United States." Figueroa went on to explain why he calls the Gulf route, which sees migrants travel north through Veracruz and Tamaulipas, the route through hell. "There's a lot of economic interests at play on the part of organized crime; for them migrants are like merchandise. What [members of organized crime groups] don't seem to realize is that this is a poor migration, a forced migration, and that the migrants don't carry money. But they want money anyway. They torture [the migrants] until they give them the phone number of a family member in the United States, and if they don't have it, they'll be murdered."

It's a short walk to the church from the shelter, or you can hop on a three-wheeled moto-taxi, locally called a *pochimovil*, and be there in minutes. There I met with Fray Tomás Gonzáles Castillo, a Franciscan who also works in Tenosique supporting migrants passing through. "I've heard various testimonies of mass kidnappings, and when they tell me what happens to them, honestly it is incredible and it's only after many testimonies that one starts to believe it. It sounds like something out of a horror movie, when people tell you about the mutilations," he told me, in the small, unevenly lit backroom of his parish. The horrors faced by migrants transiting Mexico have generally been kept out of the headlines in Mexico and the United States.

Paramilitarized Extraction

In the last chapter, we looked at how formal militarization can benefit transnational corporations, as police and soldiers form security corridors and quell dissent. Concretely, there are also a number of cases where paramilitarization linked to the drug war is taking place in areas where resource extraction is a key economic activity. These cases differ from the formal militarization documented in the previous chapter, because the government formally distances itself from paramilitary violence, or is made to look as if it is struggling to control it. Take northern Tamaulipas, the Zetas stronghold: it is also home to the Burgos Basin, which is rich in oil and gas. The US Geological Survey said in 2003 that Burgos could contain more than six billion barrels of undiscovered oil, and over seven trillion cubic feet of gas.[24] The Burgos Basin is centered on Reynosa, Tamaulipas, covering an area about the size of Ireland, in a border region that has become one of the most dangerous parts of Mexico. Much of the violence in Tamaulipas stems from the 2010 split between the Gulf Cartel and Los Zetas, as well as the deployment of 8,000 troops throughout the state.[25] Ciudad Mier, which sits atop the Burgos Basin, experienced intense, midday gun battles through 2009 and early 2010. "The scale of the upheaval increased at the beginning of November 2010, when the Zetas issued an open threat to all of Ciudad Mier's inhabitants, saying that those who remained in the town would be killed. As a result, as many as 400 people who had not been able to leave throughout the year fled to the nearby town of Ciudad Miguel Alemán, where they took shelter in a community hall."[26] Gun battles and kidnappings of oil workers have also forced Pemex to shut down oil production at drilling rigs in the Burgos Basin. "Pemex hides cases [of kidnappings]. There's more than twenty people disappeared in our union," said a man I talked to in Reynosa, who has been with the company his entire working life. "They just are marked down as missing work," he said. Theft of petroleum products by organized crime is also a common occurrence. As much as 40 percent of natural gas condensate production from Burgos is rerouted and stolen, something generally blamed on Zetas.

In 2011, Pemex filed a lawsuit in Houston against ten US oil and pipeline companies for collaborating with organized crime to purchase condensate stolen from the Burgos Basin in Mexico. "The cartels built tunnels and even their own pipelines to facilitate the thefts.... All of the Defendants have participated and profited—knowingly or unwittingly—in the trafficking of stolen condensate in the United States and have thereby encouraged and facilitated the Mexican organized crime groups that stole the condensate," says the complaint.[27] The significance of this lawsuit cannot be ignored, as it alleges a direct relationship between paramilitary groups and various Texas oil companies. The Burgos Basin is just one of the oil- and gas-rich areas along Mexico's northern border. The new discoveries of shale oil are recoverable through hydraulic fracturing, or fracking, and Mexico has passed reforms allowing US oil companies to do so in these areas. The recently announced deposits are in northeastern Mexico, including in the states of Coahuila, Chihuahua, Nuevo Leon, Tamaulipas, San Luis Potosí, and Veracruz.[28] These regions have all been militarized as part of the war on drugs, and some of them also have high levels of displacement because of violence linked to the drug war. Following a pattern set in Colombia, there is little doubt that the abilities of residents to organize or even protest against the thousands of wells to be drilled in these desert areas will be massively compromised by the intense violence that precedes the projects.

The overlap between paramilitary activity and transnational mining is particularly evident in Chihuahua, Mexico's largest state by territory. Chihuahua is, at once, experiencing an important expansion in transnational mining, militarization, and paramilitarization, under the pretext of the war on drugs. Because of this, it presents us with a microcosm of what is taking place in areas throughout Mexico, parts of Central America, Colombia, and Peru. The fact that there is a resource rush taking place in tandem with the militarization (and paramilitarization) linked to the drug war is an open secret, one which provides a more adequate explanation of why governments (host and foreign) are promoting drug control strategies that do little to control drug trafficking or lessen consumption.

The Reyes Salazar family is the most high-profile family to have been displaced and targeted by organized crime activity in Chihuahua State. I met Saul Reyes Salazar in El Paso, Texas, across the border from where two of his sisters, his sister-in-law, and two of his brothers were murdered between January 2010 and February 2011. The Reyes Salazar family was known for their environmental activism, having successfully fought a proposed nuclear waste facility in Texas and carried out campaigns against contamination and toxins being illegally disposed of in Juárez. They were also among the loudest critics of the army incursion into the Juárez Valley.

Today, Saul Reyes Salazar lives in El Paso, Texas, with his family. He and his immediate family were granted asylum in January 2012, and his activism is now focused on denouncing the killings and the war that destroyed his family and forced him to flee Mexico. "Today there's pretty much no one who talks about this, but the Juárez Valley is still contaminated by a 100 km canal that carries Juárez waste water, the farming lands are contaminated by chemicals from various maquilas who dump their chemicals in the water, there's oil from the mechanics shops, and of course all of the human waste from all of the houses in Ciudad Juárez end up in the valley, which is basically the septic tank of Juárez," he told me in March 2013. Environmental and protest actions in the border region have fallen off in the face of the violence, which has been extreme in many locations of the Juárez Valley. "We're not the only ones who have suffered this tragedy. In Chihuahua, there have been more than forty social, environmental, and human rights activists who have been murdered. I consider it like a cleansing ... an ideological cleansing."

In order to explore this phenomenon in more detail, let's look closer at what's at stake in Chihuahua. According to the Mexican Geological Service, in 2010 Chihuahua was the second most important state in the country in the production of all of gold, silver, lead, and zinc.[29] More than half of the land in Chihuahua state, which is almost the size of Texas, has been granted in mining concessions.[30] The volume of precious metals mined in Chihuahua has increased since 2006, with silver extraction almost doubling between 2006 and 2010.[31] As mining has increased, so has the violence in there. As we shall see with the story of Ismael Solorio Urrutia and Manuelita Solís Contreras, drug cartel–linked violence can work to the benefit of mining companies or their boosters seeking to silence dissent.

Ismael Solorio Urrutia and Manuela Solís Contreras were two more victims of the cleansing described by Saul Reyes Salazar. They both breathed their last breaths seated inside their truck, which was parked beside the highway leading out of the city of Cuauhtémoc. According to video footage acquired as part of the investigation into the murder, Ismael pulled his pickup off the road, and turned the car around as if to talk to the driver of a car that had pulled in behind him. As the killer approached, Ismael pulled 160 pesos (about $13) out of his wallet as if planning to pay him. He was still clasping the bills when his body was found. When I asked Martin Solís Bustamante, an activist and lifelong friend of the family, how exactly they died, he got up from his chair and walked around behind me, pressing two fingers to my lower skull. Two shots passed through Ismael's skull and lodged themselves in Manuela's breast and shoulder, killing her. Their killings are the first of opponents to Canadian mining in Mexico's northern

Chihuahua state. The double murder shocked the people of Benito Juárez, a desert town with a population about 12,000. Benito Juárez spreads out from a small central park, where vendors sell ice cream and burritos and elderly men rest on benches in the shade. After a few blocks, the paved roads leaving the park turn into dusty gravel roads, which lead for kilometers into a harsh desert. Water flows from a reservoir at the foot of the Carmen River through a small canal, providing farmers with the raw material for cattle ranching, chili growing, and cotton harvesting—the economic mainstays of the area. Benito Juárez is also an ejido, with 53,000 hectares of land collectively owned and farmed by about 400 families. The mining concessions supposedly grant the right to explore and exploit minerals below ejidal land, but in order to access the minerals, the company that holds the concessions must secure surface rights. The road out to where MAG Silver—a Vancouver-based mining exploration firm—was drilling core samples cuts through sunbaked desert plains, flanked by mountains in all directions, the stark landscape interrupted only by chaparral bush and spindly spikes of ocotillo. Without irrigation, little survives here, and securing water in the desert is no small feat. In Benito Juárez, the effort to ensure the survival of the local economy and a way of life based around family and farm is multi-generational and involves hundreds of residents. Ismael Solorio and Martin Solís, for instance, studied together at an agricultural school in Juárez. Returning to the ejido in the early 1980s, they got their start in activism, organizing in defense against predatory banking practices after the peso was devalued in 1987, and using direct action to help improve the lives of the ejido's members.

Later, Solorio and Solís helped form the Barzón movement (a *barzón* is the yoke-ring on a plough), whose members captured the attention of the nation when they entered the country's national Congress on horseback after riding fifty-four days from the US-Mexico border crossing in Ciudad Juárez to Mexico City. The bold tactics of the Barzonistas brought back memories of Mexican revolutionaries at the turn of the twentieth century. They successfully forced the first change in the rural budget anyone can remember, and later secured electricity subsidies for rural farmers whose livelihoods were under threat following the unequal terms of the North America Free Trade Agreement. In the last years of his life, Ismael Solorio, who was known to his friends as "Chops," continued to grow chili peppers and raise cattle, while devoting his spare time to water and mining issues in the region. A far cry from a full-time activist, Solorio devoted most of his time to working on the land, speaking out when he felt outside forces threatened the future of his community. First was a host of off-the-books deep wells drilled by Mennonite farmers, which sapped the Carmen River of the flow that had long provided water for farming in Benito Juárez and other desert communities. Then there was MAG Silver, which was carrying out a controversial drilling program at its "Cinco de Mayo" project to explore for silver, gold, copper, molybdenum, and tungsten in lands locals claim are communal.

Ismael and his wife Manuela, a primary school teacher and ardent supporter of her husband's activism, had faced off against many powerful forces: banks, governments, and wealthy well drillers, but something was different this time. Tensions rose quickly; the conflict heated up, and in a matter of months Manuela and Ismael were dead. In the months before he was killed, Solorio denounced death threats he received and aggression by people he said were paid by the mining company, and demanded the government provide protection. His requests were ignored.

"Since 1985 we have been involved in different actions and mobilizations as part of social resistance," said Solís, who spoke to me at El Barzón's Chihuahua City headquarters. "We always confronted the government, and we had never confronted organized crime." The decision to kill Manuela and Ismael didn't come from the head of a drug cartel, Solís emphasized. Far from drug lords, the killer and his accomplices were local men who had been involved in carrying out the dirty work for a crime group known as the Juárez Cartel: "Hit men, armed men, people who previously had threatened Ismael related to the actions he was taking against the mining company," Solís told me, confidently and steadily.

Dozens of statements collected by police in the months following the murders make it plain that MAG Silver's exploration program was a source of conflict in Benito Juárez. Testimonies included in the state investigation of the murders, which I reviewed, include references to men claiming to be plainclothes federal police without badges or a legitimate arrest warrant threatening Ismael, and fights between mine exploration workers and those who didn't support the mining project. A geologist working for the company was also questioned. The man believed to be Solorio's assassin was murdered by police on January 19, 2013, but Solorio's friends and family refuse to stop their quest for accountability. "We have maintained that justice must be done and the other material authors must be detained, but so must the intellectual authors of this crime," said Solís.

Today, instead of working in the fields or sitting around a table talking with friends and family, Manuela and Ismael are gone. Their bodies are buried under the desert earth they once farmed. Their names, along with dozens of others, grace a rebel monument erected to remember victims of violence in Chihuahua state, among them other activists, Indigenous community members and young women.

Instead of calling for a proper investigation and denouncing the murder of the highest-profile community opponent of its "Cinco de Mayo" exploration project in Chihuahua, Dan MacInnis, president and CEO of MAG Silver, chalked the killings up to the government's fight against organized crime. "It was kind of an odd situation considering that 60,000 to 100,000 people have been killed in Mexico in the last six years by organized crime in the so-called drug war," MacInnis told Canadian online magazine *ipolitics.ca*. "And rather than the obvious being reported, it was everything but that was being reported."[32] When I asked him to clarify, MacInnis responded: "It is currently a very sad reality in Mexico that between 60,000 and 100,000 deaths have occurred over the past six years due to the country's ongoing struggles with organized criminal activity. We remain puzzled why certain groups made assumptions about the involvement of mining companies, utility companies, or farmers."[33] Essentially, the company's position is that it is normal for civilians to be killed in the country where they are operating. When 100,000 people may or may not have been killed over six years, one or two more deaths by firearm are a drop in the bucket. This position would have been far more difficult to maintain before the drug war was launched in December 2006.

The police investigation into the murders also said that it was a community dispute that triggered acts of violence ending in Ismael and Manuela's murders, but it also makes clear that the prospect of well-paying jobs MAG Silver would bring to Benito Juárez was at the heart of the dispute. "That's what is so painful for us, you know, the fact that members of the community handed over Ismael and Manuelita. That's something we know, that here in Benito Juárez the deal was made and everything so that they would be killed," said Siria Leticia Solís, a long-time resident of the community and a member of the Barzón, in an interview. "We blocked the company, and because of that people are being killed."

Since the killings, mining exploration work in the community has stopped, but tensions haven't fallen off. "[MAG Silver] never showed up to a general meeting of ejido members. The paperwork that they did with the corresponding authorities were fictitious because they never went before the assembly, which is the maximum authority here," said Fausto Albión Jiménez Holguín, president of the ejido of Benito Juárez. Following the murders, an assembly was held with more than half the members present, and the ejido of Benito Juárez voted in November of 2012 to ban mining activity on its lands for the next hundred years. The company acknowledges its exploration program in Benito Juárez is currently inactive, claiming it is "working through delays in the exploration permits for its Cinco de Mayo project." The murders of Ismael Solorio and Manuela Solís took place at the crossroads of environmental activism and organized crime, in a region where all armed groups act with almost total impunity. Ismael and Manuela's three orphaned sons and their extended family will live with the loss for the rest of their lives. Their community, Benito Juárez, is deeply divided over the prospect of future mining activity in the territory. Despite the hundred-year ban, MAG Silver plans to pick up again as soon as possible. More violence seems like a likely outcome should the company attempt to have workers restart exploration.

As word of October's double murder made its way through anti-mining networks around Mexico, Manuela and Ismael's names were added to a growing list of activists killed. The list already included Mariano Abarca, who was killed in Chiapas by hitmen connected to Blackfire, a Calgary-owned mining company, in November 2010, and Bernardo Vásquez, murdered March 15, 2012, because of his activism against Vancouver-based Fortuna Silver in Oaxaca state.

Today the existence of the local mining project is something that residents of San José del Progreso, Oaxaca, couldn't ignore if they tried. The main access road into the town passes directly in front of Fortuna's operations, complete with its own power station, offices, and a huge stockpile of ore, all surrounded by high chain link fence. Vásquez was murdered gangland style, in a spray of bullets aimed at his vehicle. His cousin Rosalinda and his brother Leovigildo were both wounded in the gunfire. When the company first came around, locals saw the mayor meeting with people who were not from the community. "There were various meetings between the ejidal commission and the mayor, and the people asked, 'Who were those people?' until the ejidal commission finally realized it was a mining company that wanted to exploit the minerals." This is what Bernardo Vásquez told me approximately one month before he was murdered. "[The company] went after the folks in the ejidal commission individually," ignoring the assembly process, he explained. Before he was killed, threats against him were spray painted on the wall of a dam, and signed "Los Zetas."

Paramilitary violence is taking place in resource-rich areas across the country. Violence has also been wrought against members of the ejidal commission in Carrizalillo, Guerrero, whose president was murdered in May 2013.[34] His murder came after years of protests by the ejido, including blockades against a local subsidiary of Vancouver's Goldcorp Inc. A couple of months later, two workers at the same mine in Guerrero were murdered when their vehicle was sprayed with more than a hundred rounds from AK-47s.[35] Other incidents in Guerrero include the July 2013 displacement of 300 people—most of them children—from seven villages of San Miguel Totolapan and Coyuca de Catalán after they'd received threats from organized crime groups.[36] Approximately 2,000 people have been displaced from the region.[37] "It is said that there are mining concessions, but most of the territory consists of ejidos. The state leaves the dirty work of depopulating the area to organized crime, and when the mining companies arrive, there will be no one to oppose them," Manuel Olivares from the Guerrero Network of Civil Organizations for Human Rights (RGOCDH) told *Desinformémonos*.[38]

In February 2014, I traveled to Tlapa de Comonfort with Juan Pérez, an activist with Holistic Processes for Community Management (PIAP) in Guerrero state. Pérez draws a clear line between the arrival of large mining companies and the exercise of territorial control by organized crime groups. "There is a new logic that organized crime groups are imposing, they are establishing themselves but in such a distorted way that they are not controlling territory for the purposes of arms or narcotics trafficking, rather for the purposes of extortion," he said. He explained how two crime groups, one protected by the army and the other by the marines, control the territory between Iguala and Chilpancingo, which is traversed by the Balsas River. "These areas are extremely well cared for; there are marines from the river to Iguala, and soldiers from the river to Chilpancingo," he told me. A crime group linked to the Beltran Leyva Cartel or a splinter group known locally as Los Rojos extorts community members in these areas. "If you are in the middle and you are part of a process of extortion by, for example, Los Rojos, but you have to take your child to the hospital on the other side [of the river], you are unprotected.... [Forms of territorial control] including kidnapping, disappearances, and killings are carried out simply because you are considered to be supporting the other group, even though your support for them is more of an exercise of fear because it is based on 'either you pay me, or I kill you or I fuck you over.'"

For Pérez, it is no coincidence that Goldcorp operates its Los Filos-Bermejal mine near the Balsas River, in the middle of this contested region. Pérez is active in the Mexican Network Against Mining (REMA), and part of his work is helping community and ejido members trying to prevent the entry of mining companies. But the paramilitarization of the region, with the presence of organized crime groups, has prevented activists from being able to reach out to local communities. He gave me an example of this: "In an area called El Limón [not far from Goldcorp's Los Filos-Bermejal project], we were trying to do an informative process in order to prevent the entry of the mine. Well by the time we went for our first visit there were already four people murdered [by crime groups]. There simply were not conditions for us to carry out an assembly. That was in 2010, and the company has since entered," he said.

"What company?" I asked. "Goldcorp, through a local subsidiary."

Controlling local protest against mining is but one form of cartel/ paramilitary involvement in mining. There are also examples of criminal groups extracting minerals and commercializing them themselves, specifically in Michoacán and Coahuila. According to Humberto Moreira, the former governor of Coahuila and head of the national PRI party, Zetas steal coal from mines in the northern state and sell it to third parties, who then resell it to the Federal Electricity Commission (CFE).[39]

The Knights Templar in Michoacan have been involved in events that appear quite similar to those linking the Zetas to US companies accused of buying stolen condensate. In Michoacán, the Knights Templar steal iron ore and export it via third parties to China. Britain's Channel 4 interviewed a man who they said worked in one of the iron ore mines operated by the cartel. "The companies that actually export the mineral are Chinese, they know that the mineral is illegal but, well, they have found their little gold mine here, as the saying goes, and the companies that you call illegal are the ones that export ... they sell [the mineral] to companies that are legal in order to be able to export the mineral. It's worth US$13 million per boatload.... We're talking about more or less thirty boats a year, so you can imagine the quantity of money that brings in,"[40] said the miner, who was not identified. He estimated that between 50 and 75 percent of the iron ore shipped out of the port of Lázaro Cardenas, Michoacán, was taken from mines operated by Knights Templar affiliates. The journalist then asked the mine worker if mineral sales would bring in more money than drugs, and he responded "of course."

In 2013, leaders of a self-defense group in San Miguel de Aquila, Michoacán, told Mexico City–based alternative news website *SubVersiones*: "They are exploiting our natural resources, primarily iron. The day that the state government arrived, we told them the community's mine was being exploited by organized crime. The government, instead of going after them, actually protected them and even more people came to work at the mine. We no longer believe in the state government, that's why we want the federal government to intervene and give guarantees for our families, for the natural resources in our community.... We have so many natural resources in San Miguel de Aquila; we are very rich in resources but at the same time we are among the poorest, because transnationals are those who take advantage of the resources of the community."[41]

In 2014, the group wrote another communiqué, which stated: "The period of July 24 to August 13, 2013—when the indigenous community guard from the community of San Miguel Aquila was active in the area—was one of immense calm. The rapes, kidnappings and payments of protection fees disappeared as the criminals fled. Seeing the results of the community movement, we were inspired to support the community's cause. However, on August 14, a joint state and municipal government operation, together with the Marines, entered Aquila and dismantled the community movement. They took forty-five prisoners. The Special Operations Group (GOES) and State Judicial Police killed two and also beat women, children, and the elderly who called for them to return the men who were defending them from organized crime. When the community guard was dismantled, the Knights Templar, under the auspices of the state and municipal governments, decided to 'exterminate' all the residents of San Miguel Aquila."[42] Following the state incursion, three men from the community were kidnapped, tortured, and murdered; another three were disappeared; and the Knights Templar again began to exert control over iron ore extraction, extorting the community for the royalty payments they received from the company Ternium, a Luxembourg-based transnational steel company.

Displacement and Real Estate

According to the Norwegian Refugee Council, "Evidence of forced displacement in the localities of El Porvenir and Práxedis G. Guerrero in Valle de Juárez is unquestionable: virtually all houses are empty, burned out, and vandalized."[43] But exact figures are difficult to come by: "In the small towns of Guadalupe, Praxedis G. Guerrero, Porvenir, Esperanza and the even smaller hamlets that dot the valley, there's been no official census in recent years, so no one knows exactly how many people have left, or how many residents have been killed or forcibly disappeared," wrote journalist Melissa del Bosque.[44] She was sure to point out that the violence and displacement did not fall neatly at the feet of drug cartels. "The official story is that the army was sent in to protect residents and drive out the cartels, but townspeople tell a different story. They say the soldiers, working in league with the Sinaloa cartel, perpetrated much of the violence."

Just as paramilitary displacements in Colombia depopulated lands which were later used for palm oil and extractive projects, the displacement of thousands of residents in the Juárez Valley has not transformed the region into a land of ghost towns, cemeteries, and cartel free-for-alls. On the contrary, the Juárez Valley area is currently slated for redevelopment, and plans include the construction of a $400 million housing and industrial park project in San Agustín, which is about thirty kilometers from downtown Ciudad Juárez. The housing project, which will cover 2,470 acres of ejidal land in San Agustín, is being developed by Fortune 500 corporation Prudential Financial, together with one of its local partners in Mexico.[45] "It is a complete, ambitious project, almost like a new city," Leopoldo Canizales, a city official in San Agustín, told El Diario.[46] The housing project will be built just over ten kilometers from a new border bridge between Tornillo, Texas, and Guadalupe, also in the Juárez Valley.[47] The San Agustín development is being erected in anticipation of a boom in the maquila industries, as massive expansions in Mexico's manufacturing sector will be necessary should analysts' predictions about the sector come true. "[Mexico] has the enormous advantage of bordering the U.S., which means that goods can reach much of the country in a day or two, as opposed to at least 21 days by ship from China.... In addition, by 2015, wages in Mexico will be significantly lower than in China."[48] More maquilas are certainly not something all of those who reside in the area are keen on: "It is exactly because of the maquila industry that things are how they are; what the maquilas have left is nothing but criminality; they obliged parents to leave their children home alone," said San Agustín resident Ignacio Ibarra.[49] "Right now things are calm here but if they bring maquilas and all the new housing, well, then we'll see what the good life was."

Acapulco is another city that has suffered through the worst of what the drug war has to offer. "The resort town has also become a major theater of the drug war: On a single weekend this year, more than 30 bodies were found, including night-club workers abducted after hours and later found hanging from a bridge."[50] Fourteen tourists were tied up and threatened in a single incident in 2012, and later, six of the women (who were Spanish citizens, hence the fact that it became a national scandal) were raped. Following the rapes, the mayor of Acapulco said that what took place was bad for Acapulco's image but that "this could have happened anywhere, in Mexico or in Acapulco."[51] Tourism to Acapulco, a resort city nestled between cliffs, white sand beaches, and the crashing waves of the Pacific, dropped off 50 percent between 2006 and 2011.[52] The spike in violence has, just like Juárez, taken place in tandem with the deployment of state forces as part of Operacion Guerrero Seguro. In Acapulco, "Components [of Guerrero Seguro] include new lighting along Costera Miguel Alemán, the placement of more than 600 surveillance cameras in the tourist areas and the deployment of federal security forces to oversee nighttime law enforcement."[53]

Far from scaring away investors, the height of the violence in Acapulco inspired magnate Carlos Slim, who has repeatedly been named the world's richest man, to bring together some of Mexico's richest and most powerful in a consortium for the economic revival of the city. While thousands of families suffered through devastating losses of friends and loved ones and were forced to live in an increasingly cruel context of kidnappings, tortures, and massacres, Slim stayed focused on investing. "Those who do not invest and go slow because they have doubts will be left behind. I am not afraid of investing here in Acapulco," he said in 2012.[54] Slim has invested heavily in Acapulco real estate, and now owns a hotel and other properties in the resort city. Violence against the poor in Acapulco, one of the most unequal cities in Mexico, has provided investors like Slim a clean slate for kick-starting a new development plan.

Farmers and ranchers have also been displaced from rural areas in northern Mexico because of threats and violence. By the end of 2010, 5,000 farmers had been displaced in Tamaulipas state, according to a report prepared by Mexico's intelligence agency (CISEN).[55] "Ranchers and farmers have been victims of kidnapping and extortion and all of that, and now many of them are asking me to sell their lands, and their ranches, but who can I sell them to?" said a real estate agent I interviewed in Tamaulipas state in 2011. "They're kidnapping ranchers and farmers, so they don't go to their ranges anymore; their ranches are abandoned."

"They forced me out of my truck near Loma Prieta, a ranch I have near Jiménez [a city close to the capital of Tamaulipas]," a farmer told Mexican newspaper *Milenio*.[56] "There were a handful of kids, no more than twenty years old, armed with machine guns and with Central American accents."[57] After the threat against him, the farmer stopped going to his land. "I don't know if I still have cattle, but the way things are, I'd rather lose them." According to press reports, narco groups, especially Los Zetas, used the abandoned lands for training camps and bases.

Avocados and Limes at Gunpoint

In 2011, Mexico's agri-food exports were valued at $22 billion, just slightly more than the country's mining exports of $21.6 billion. The overlapping presence of armed actors in some of the country's most productive agricultural regions has had severe consequences for the lives of farmers and has impacted the price of fruits and vegetables in Mexico, the United States, and elsewhere.

Attacks against and extortions of small and medium-sized farmers are taking place in areas that had previously undergone rapid changes to their agricultural sector as a result of neoliberal policies and changing market structures. Dr. Donna Chollett documented the transformation of the local economy in the Los Reyes region of Michoacán from one where sugar cane workers could earn a subsistence living because of state subsidies, to one where contract workers picked blackberries for luxury consumption in the United States. "The retraction of government assistance for *campesinos*, withdrawal of price supports, and reduction of import tariffs create markets in which small farmers are unable to compete, thus opening the door for transnational agribusiness.... Transnational blackberry agroindustries form a commodity chain that establishes hierarchies of power linked to broader initiatives of the WTO and NAFTA. As men are displaced from cane production, a segmented labor force that relies on unequal compensation divides workers by gender and separates capitalized growers from small-scale campesinos who lack the resources to compete in the new transnational order."[58]

Avocados and limes are grown in the area Chollett describes, part of which is known as the Tierra Caliente region of Michoacán. The state is Mexico's number one producer of avocados and one of the most important producers of limes in the country. In fact, the very first drug trafficking group in Michoacán, Los Hermanos Valencia, had its roots in avocado farming.[59] Michoacán is also an area that, over the last decade, has been occupied by various armed groups, from the Mexican Army[60] to La Familia Michoacana, which has morphed into what is known as the Caballeros Templarios (Knights Templar).

Michoacán has been a hotbed of political activity, including disputes between parties, Indigenous movements, student uprisings, and otherwise. Like Tamaulipas and other embattled Mexican states, it has also been an area where deep links between state governments and organized crime have contributed to the consolidation and dominance of criminal economies. Some of the most gruesome public acts of terror in Mexico since 2006 have taken place in the state: five human heads were tossed onto a dance floor at a bar in Uruapan in fall 2006; and grenades exploded at Independence Day celebrations in the capital of Morelia in September 2008, killing eight. Mexico City–based analyst Alejandro Hope notes that the family of Governor Leonel Godoy had "all kinds of links with people from La Familia, which later became Los Templarios. There is a taped phone call between [the governor's] half-brother and La Tuta, the leader of the Templarios…. Where Julio Cesar Godoy, half-brother of the governor, calls La Tuta 'Godfather' and La Tuta tells him, 'Don't you worry, my son, you have already won, we already spoke with the boys, we told them.'" Godoy's term ended in 2011, and new elections brought Fausto Vallejo to power in Michoacán. "He won, but he was very sick and he left his post temporarily right at the beginning of his mandate. He left the position to his secretary of government, equivalent of a secretary of the interior, and that individual has all kinds of links with the Templarios." Hope says that historically, "What drug trafficking [in Michoacán] there was, and what organized crime there was, was strongly connected with the traditional PRI structure of control." As an example, take the case of Tepalcatepec, where locals accused Mayor Guillermo Valencia of being the "big Templario." Valencia, who denies the accusations, was elected to Congress as a member of the PRI in the embattled state ten years ago at the tender age of twenty-three, and then served as youth leader of the PRI, before being elected mayor.[61] Where they exist, these high-level links ensure impunity for criminal groups, whose actions do not threaten the state government so much as contribute to the rearrangement of land ownership and the economy, at a high price for small farmers and common folk.

A report on the alternative Mexican news website *Sin Embargo* reveals that, as of November 2013, the Caballeros were charging small avocado growers 3,000 pesos per hectare if they were exporting the fruit and 1,500 pesos if it was for the internal market. Humberto Padgett and Dalia Martínez, the journalists who reported the story, asked a group of small farmers how the crime group could know how much land each of them had planted. In an answer the journalists attribute to the whole group, the farmers respond: "Ahh, that's easy! They know how much we have because they have direct access to the guides (permits) that the Local Council for Vegetable Sanitation gives, which depend on the Secretary of Agriculture, Ranching, Rural Development, Fishing and Alimentation (SAGARPA) and the State Committees of Vegetable Sanitation. The Council controls and physically inspects every meter of every hectare, every bush, every tree, and the quality of each fruit."[62] Agricultural authorities are in the pocket of organized crime groups, who charge additional extortion fees from the growers. According to the reporters, "The incursion of organized crime in the avocado production chain has hit the small farmers who have less than 10 hectares especially hard, as well as those new to the business and who, faced with the excessive payments, have opted to abandon their lands and sell or rent them." Indigenous and farming communities throughout Michoacán are up against organized crime groups that are increasingly taking control of the land. "First we found marijuana plantations, but the real use of the land was for planting avocados. They wanted to take over the territory. In a handful of nearby villages, in Zacapu, the same thing happened, the same thing happened there and where they're cultivating used to be forest, and now it's only avocados," said Trinidad Ramírez, a member of the Council of Chéran.

Chéran, an Indigenous Purépecha village, made headlines in April 2011 when a group of women chased out illegal loggers that were associated with La Familia Michoacána. Margarita Ambrosio Magaña, whose husband was killed by illegal loggers when he tried to protect some forested lands in 2009, participated in the blockades from the early days. "Before, the forest cutters would come in and we were all afraid. Now with the barricades bad people don't come in anymore and the kids can go out and play," she told Desinformemonos.[63] Chéran was the first example in Michoacán of a self-defense group formed (in this case by assembly) to prevent organized crime groups from operating in the area. Since the uprising, Chéran has been an autonomously run community, without state police or political parties, and the violence and illegal logging have dropped off considerably. Rural communities have responded to the presence of paramilitary and state forces in their territories by creating their own armed groups, sometimes in the form of self-defense groups and other times community police. Lime growers in Michoacán have met much the same fate as avocado growers, forced to choose between their lands and livelihoods and extortion under threat of death or kidnapping by the Caballeros Templarios. In April of 2013, eight lime farmers were killed and at least sixteen wounded when they joined a protest against extortion. After the massacre, marchers were evacuated by the Mexican military.[64] Buenavista Tomatlán, a tiny town in western Michoacan that depends economically on lime crops, made international news when a federal prosecutor claimed the self-defense group there was in fact working in tandem with one drug cartel against another. Lime growers from the town of Apatzingán claim to have been threatened against receiving limes from farms in Buenavista for packing at their local plant.[65] In a story that reinforces why banners hung by supposed narcos should not be trusted, the lime growers from Apatzingán later allegedly hung a banner with the same accusations against their neighbors.[66] Instead of defending the lime growers against the Caballeros Templarios, the state accused them of being with the other cartel. The violence continued after the army raided the town and police and soldiers took over self-defense patrols in the community of just over 42,000. Six people were murdered there in July 2013, another four bodies were hung from a welcome sign crossing a rural road the same month, and nine more were killed in August 2013.

Self-defense groups operating without a clear mandate from their communities must be evaluated on a case-by-case basis. Though their name harkens back to the United Self-Defense of Colombia (AUC), a right-wing paramilitary group allied with the Colombian state, and their white T-shirts may appear in the same vein as Miami's reactionary Cubans, many of the self-defense groups that have formed in Mexico appear to be protecting the will of the people against the collusion of state and cartel/right-wing paramilitary groups. Often sparked by the kidnappings, murders, or extortions of community members, these self-defense groups organize to guard the roads in and out of their community, checking each vehicle, armed with basic weapons and machetes. But the formation of these armed groups can also be understood as a strategy to defend community and small holder territories from ongoing theft and pillage.

"In reality we're prisoners in our own village, but at least we're safe there," said a community member from a town in Michoacán, which has been protected by a self-defense group for eight months.[67] Within the boundaries of each village, these groups can ensure locals are not being kidnapped or otherwise impacted by paramilitary/criminal groups, but once they travel on highways connecting their villages, locals risk their lives. After a march of self-defense groups from their communities to Apatzingán was met with grenades and gunfire, soldiers told a reporter with *El Pais* that the army is merely a referee in the conflict, and that things would get worse when night fell.[68] As a solution, it was agreed that members of the self-defense groups would patrol with the army to ensure that they didn't let criminal groups through the main roads back to their villages.

In reading information from the US government and the status quo media, one finds a careful reiteration that the war in Mexico is non-political. "The Mexican gangs are motivated by profit, and have no visible ideological agenda. Their only political goal is weaker law enforcement," reads a 2011 report by the Soros-funded research group InSight Crime.[69] The effort to present criminal groups in Mexico as apolitical has echoes in the effort to rebrand Colombian paramilitaries as criminal bands (Bacrim). But it is deceiving to ascribe "political" status to a war only when there is a national liberation movement or a guerrilla struggle. The war in Mexico is political: it is a counter-revolution, a hundred years late. It is decimating communities and destroying some of the few gains from the Mexican Revolution that remained after NAFTA was signed in 1994. Conceiving of drug cartels as paramilitaries politicizes their actions and creates space through which to have a more informed discussion of the ramifications of drug war violence in Mexico and elsewhere.

CHAPTER 7:

DRUG WAR CAPITALISM
IN GUATEMALA

THOUGH Guatemala and Mexico were both subject to Spanish colonization (the first genocide), the countries' histories have diverged
dramatically since. Access to land, and land reform (or lack thereof),
has put the two countries on markedly different paths in the twentieth
century. Unlike Mexico, Guatemala didn't undergo a revolution or a
period of nationalizations early in the last century, instead it was in the
1940s and the early 1950s that the country experienced what some call
the "Guatemalan Spring." Democratically elected presidents Juan José
Árevalo and Colonel Jacobo Árbenz Guzmán began making reforms,
but both remained committed to the capitalist economic model and to
a Western liberal conception of democracy.

US leaders characterized Árbenz's main misstep as daring to ex-
propriate land owned by American banana companies. According to a
report by the Food and Agriculture Organization, "The election of Árbenz in 1951 resulted in a period of intense but brief reform beginning
with the enactment of the Agrarian Reform Law (Decree 900) on 17
June 1952. The declared objectives of Decree 900 were to 1) eliminate
feudal estates 2) obliterate all forms of indentured servitude 3) provide
land to the landless and land poor 4) distribute credit and technical assistance to smallholders. The developmental goals of the reforms was
to develop a capitalist economy among the peasants and in agriculture
generally and to facilitate the investment of new capital in agriculture
by means of the capitalist rental of nationalized land. The reform involved the expropriation of *idle* land and its redistribution to the landless and land-poor."[1]

Regardless of the capitalist nature of his land-reform program, Árbenz was labeled a communist, and, shortly after, his government was
overthrown in a coup d'état planned in Washington and backed up

by the CIA in a mission called PBSuccess.[2] The CIA-backed Guatemalan coup in 1954 and the US government's refusal to allow elections in 1963 in order to prevent the participation of Árevalo marked the beginning of a series of events that would push the country toward a thirty-six-year war that culminated in genocide. More than 200,000 people were murdered over this time in Guatemala, primarily Indigenous Mayans, as well as leftist activists, union organizers, and otherwise. An additional 50,000 people remain disappeared.

Though the conflict in Guatemala was often dressed up as being a war against communists or insurgents, in many regions it is clear that what was really motivating the assassinations of Indigenous people was access to their lands. One example of this is the municipality of Rabinal, where approximately one-fifth of the population was assassinated between 1981 and 1983. Efraín Osorio Chen is from Rio Negro, a community in Rabinal, where Maya Achi people make up the majority of the population. Osorio was ten years old when he survived the massacres that killed his family. I met him as I traveled with Jesús Tecú Osorio through the village of Pacux, where many of the survivors who were displaced from Rio Negro were resettled in the 1980s. I mentioned to Tecú Osorio that I wanted to talk to someone who had directly survived the violence, and the first person we saw was Osorio Chen, riding his bicycle down the road. Tecú Osorio called out to him, and he rode up and met us at a monument to the dead—a plain rock reminder pointing toward the sky.

"I am a survivor, I lost my whole family. They killed my father, my mother, an older brother, two sisters, and a younger brother. When they killed my mother, she was pregnant," Osorio Chen told us. "The army destroyed our community. They wanted to eliminate the whole community, but still, thank God, we survived. I don't know how, how we could survive all of that, but thanks be to God that here we are, alive." Survivors like Osorio were eventually required to settle in the model village of Pacux, which he likened to a cage, a place where community members no longer have access to firewood or land to plant and harvest their crops. Entire communities were fragmented and decimated through mass murder, survivors forced into military-controlled model villages like this one. After the massacre, Osorio Chen spent two years hidden in the mountains, sleeping under trees and eating plants to stay alive.

In a pattern repeated throughout the country, members of the community were labeled guerrilla supporters and communists to justify the massacres in the Rio Negro area, of which there were five. Beside the memorial where I first met Osorio Chen sits Pacux's one-room community hall, the walls of which are painted with even more names of people killed. "We're talking about approximately 700 people, because what you see on the list are about 450, but there are people who were disappeared, children; we still don't know if maybe there are some people who live nearby but who won't come back to Rabinal out of fear," said Tecú Osorio, who was a boy when he witnessed the killings of his relatives by the army and the Civilian Patrol in 1982. He says the genocide against his people, the Maya Achi, was carried out to make way for the construction of the Chixoy Dam, a project funded by the World Bank. "What was called communism, in Rio Negro, was the community's opposition to the project and defense of their territories. The fight was because the peasants were defending their territories, and the government was responding to the demands of transnational corporations with interests in building the dams." Tecú Osorio's words would continue to echo for me as I navigated a present deeply marked by the wounds of the past.

Massacres weren't the only terror technique deployed in Guatemala. In 2012, I spoke with José Samuel Suasnávar, the executive sub-director of the Forensic Anthropology Foundation of Guatemala. When we met, forensic anthropologists had just turned up over 400 skeletons at a military base known since 2006 as the Regional Training Command for Peacekeeping Operations, or CREOMPAZ, in Cobán, Guatemala, in what fast became one of the largest discoveries of a clandestine mass grave in the country. During the country's thirty-six-year internal armed conflict, which led to acts of genocide, the base at Cobán was a center of military coordination and intelligence. "We have a few more than 400 trenches, where we've found I think sixty graves, and we've found 426 skeletons, mostly men, like everywhere else, but there's also women, and what's particular to CREOMPAZ is that there are also many children," Suasnávar told me. "What is radically different about this military base … is that here there are up to sixty-two people buried in one single grave, representing a single event." Suasnávar explained how incidents of massacres and those of forced disappearances during the internal conflict responded to economic logic. Most of the massacres during the war took place in the Guatemalan highlands, in areas inhabited by a Mayan majority, but many of the disappearances took place in the fertile lowlands, where Guatemala's land-owning elite ran cotton, coffee, and sugar plantations. Laborers would come from all over the country to work during harvest season. Suasnávar said the economic costs of carrying out open and massive counterinsurgency in the lowlands in the Pacific Coast region were far higher than the political costs. "If they carried out massacres there, as they did in other places, who would work in export agriculture?" he asked. "The disappearance of people, the disappearances of leaders, this was what took place there in a more selective way than how it transpired in other areas."

Many of the disappeared may have eventually been taken to places like CREOMPAZ, in the interior of the country, and murdered there. There are few bullet wounds among the dead; most of the skeletons still show evidence of being bound, and many reveal bones that had been broken, healed, and re-broken, indicating that the dead had been tortured and interrogated, some for lengthy periods of time, before they were killed and thrown in the pits. The dig in Cobán is revealing the gruesome reality of the country's internal armed conflict, where people labeled subversives—political and student activists, Indigenous leaders and community members, and others—were kidnapped and tortured *en masse*. Children were also murdered before being dumped in graves at the base.

The work of identifying the country's disappeared is monumental. Of the 50,000 disappeared, the names of 42,000 are known. Eighteen thousand bodies have been found in clandestine graves, but so far only 500 have been identified.

But what set the dig at CREOMPAZ apart is that it took place at an active military base: foreign military and police arrive regularly at the base to train troops from Guatemala, El Salvador, Nicaragua, Honduras, and the Dominican Republic. The killings took place within the protective confines of a military-controlled area where today blue-helmeted peacekeepers from the United Nations are trained.

In 2013, General Efraín Rios Montt and Mauricio Rodríguez Sánchez, his head of intelligence, were tried for the genocide of the Maya Ixil people during the former's dictatorship in 1982–1983. The dig at CREOMPAZ and the recent genocide trial are two ongoing efforts by activists and nongovernmental organizations in Guatemala to force official acknowledgment, reparations, justice, and closure for the millions of survivors of the internal conflict. While some officials like Attorney General Claudia Paz y Paz have pushed hard for justice, others in the Guatemalan legislative and executive branches actively deny genocide. This was blatantly displayed when the Constitutional Court overturned the Guatemala City court's guilty ruling against Rios

Montt on procedural grounds. Terror in Guatemala is far from being a thing of the past; instead it exists in the memories and daily lives of millions of survivors, and it continues to manifest in systemic racism, discrimination, and violence against the Indigenous majority.

Guatemalan president Otto Pérez Molina is a perfect example of how power and impunity reign in Guatemala. Pérez Molina was a major and head of intelligence in the Guatemalan Army and served in the Ixil triangle during the genocide, for which Rios Montt stood trial. He eventually became a general and received training at the School of the Americas. Nearly thirty years later, in September 2011, Pérez Molina was elected president. "He held very important positions inside the military high command in these settings, therefore even if he did not participate directly in a massacre, he obviously made decisions and directed and coordinated military actions, operations which led to massacres," asserts Luis Solano, a Guatemalan journalist and researcher. "Otto Pérez Molina arrives to the Presidency of the Republic with a curriculum stained by his past in counterinsurgency, his dark passage through military intelligence, and his tight links with the conservative business elite."[3] Pérez Molina campaigned on hands, head, and heart: an iron fist against crime, a head for development, and a heart in support of the poorest Guatemalans. Pérez Molina described his own style of governance as one inspired by Colombia's controversial ex-president Álvaro Uribe. He also promised to use Kaibiles, Guatemala's elite special forces (whose members have been linked to Los Zetas) in the war on drugs. After his election, Pérez Molina tapped numerous retired military men from his party, called the Patriot Party (PP), to become ministers in his government. One of them, General Ulises Noé Anzueto Girón, the minister of defense, was accused of participating with eight others in the torture and murder of Efraín Bámaca, a member of the since-disappeared guerrilla group, Organization of the People in Arms (ORPA).

Pérez Molina has made public calls for drug legalization. Some analysts believe that he and his Patriot Party, which has an important support base among soldiers and veterans, is between a rock and a hard place. To effectively interrupt the flow of drugs, he'd have to fight against his own: the army has long been known to be enmeshed in the drug trade. "My perspective is that [Pérez Molina's] proposal is a smokescreen, something designed to distract from the confluence of problems of Guatemalan society, and particularly those of the rural peasant farmers," said Kajkok Maximo Ba Tiul, a Maya Poqomchi' analyst and university professor based in Cobán, Alta Verapaz. "What is in dispute is territory, and especially the territory of Indigenous peoples, and so, while he's consolidating his process of control, he comes up with this, knowing full well that he can't fight his friends and colleagues, and that he has no capacity to pressure the United States." Regardless of Pérez Molina's rhetoric, Guatemala continues to arm more soldiers and police, supposedly to fight drug trafficking, following the US State Department's strategy in the region. Instead of fighting communism, today's military buildup is justified by the war on drugs. This is a crucial backdrop to understanding the introduction of the drug war in Guatemala, the imposition of a new war on a society still reeling from genocide, where perpetrators and supporters of terror continue to live in impunity, while their victims face a new round of militarization.

Enter the Drug War

Peace accords, signed in 1996, promised to cut the military budget and reduce the army's power and control, but demilitarization remains a distant promise. Since 2000, the army has been back patrolling in the streets on the premise of fighting organized crime. "The state needs something to make the population believe that there needs to be militarization, in order to control everything. That something had to be invented, and it's called drug trafficking," said Ba Tiul, when I interviewed him at his home in 2012. We sat around the kitchen table as his partner prepared tamales for lunch, their conversation drifting from threats against community members resisting power lines to a comrade who had been knifed for organizing in his community. Just as, in many instances, the internal conflict in Guatemala unraveled in areas deemed important for energy projects or resource extraction, militarization today is taking place in areas where there are fierce social and land conflicts related to the imposition of mega-projects.

"In less than ten months, this government has inaugurated three new military bases, and there's talk about a fourth that could be up and running by the end of this year or the beginning of next, all with the argument—and this is what worries us—of the supposed fight against drug trafficking. This has been the pretext for the participation of the army in civilian law enforcement," said Iduvina Hernández Batres, of the Guatemala City-based NGO Security and Democracy (SEDEM) in an interview in late 2012. Hernández points out that the construction of new military bases is taking place in areas already steeped in social conflict. The positioning of new military bases in areas of heightened social conflict has raised alarm bells for local activists. One of the new bases is in San Juan Sacatepequez, which is the site of a major struggle against a highway project and a cement company; another in Panzós, near a proposed nickel mine in El Estor and where surrounding areas are steeped in land conflicts related to the industrial production of African palm; and the third in Petén, the huge northern region of the country, which is currently undergoing a wave of oil investment and development.[4] "While it is true that there is narco activity on the Atlantic coast, the military base there isn't in that area of the territory, but below, right near a community in the area of Panzós.... Where there are intense conflicts in the community because of the presence of a nickel mining company, this company has already had a serious record of human rights violations, including suspicions that there have been extrajudicial executions. And it's in this area that the base is being installed. We think that it's a pretext to return back to the level of militarization that existed during the harshest stage of the armed conflict, which resulted in acts of genocide," Hernández told me in her Guatemala City office in 2012.

Maria Magdalena Cuc Choc lives in a palm-roofed house near Lake Izabal in El Estor, not far from Panzós. For her, this new wave of militarization hits close to home. Her brother-in-law was killed by private security for his activism against the nickel mine mentioned by Hernández Batres. Her brother is in jail for the same reason. The mining project was first proposed by Canada's Inco, and later taken up by Vancouver-based Skye Resource, which sold it to a third Canadian company called HudBay Minerals (it's now owned by Russia's Solway Investment Group). "Here in Guatemala the big struggle that we have as Indigenous peoples is against the state of Guatemala and large landholders. Here there are many multinational and transnational companies, foreign companies, that are buying lands that belong to our grandparents," said Cuc Choc. "Here there are mining companies, oil companies, companies that plant monocultures like African palm, there are also rubber companies.... We enter into a conflict dynamic, because we want to recuperate the land.... They displace us from our properties."

She talked about how police and the army defend corporate interests against Indigenous resistance, and how paramilitary groups are formed by elites looking to protect their interests. "When we were removed from our lands, or when communities are displaced, the first thing they do is bring in the armed forces of the state, which are members of the army, Kaibiles, as they're called, and the national civil police. But in addition to that, the companies, or their owners, or large landholders, contract our Q'eqchi' brothers who have already served in the military, and they contract them as security guards, and then they also contract others, people that we could call private forces. They give them guns, they give them machetes, they give them ski masks so that they can go and displace people, kill people, abuse people—all of this equipment that they give them is like a way of saying, 'Go do whatever you want, no one will recognize you.'" The strategies Cuc Choc identifies are generally ignored in the media and in analyses of the violence in Guatemala, which instead focus on drug cartels and the like.

Amilcar de Jesús Pop Ac is a lawmaker and head of the congressional transparency commission. He was first elected when Pérez Molina was brought to power, as the lone representative of Winaq, a left Indigenous party. Pop also thinks national security policy in Guatemala is driven by the extractive industries, not opposition to drug trafficking. "This government especially, which is of military persuasion, bases Guatemala's national security policy on the needs and desires of social control dictated by the extractive industries, all the industries linked to extractives: hydroelectric projects, mining, oil, now generate the directives of national security policy." I had arranged a meeting with him after we were introduced in a bar in the city's historic old downtown, where he was drinking whiskey with a group of progressive lawyers. "We're seeing that the army has detachments in all of the physical spaces where these industries and companies are setting up," he said.

Communities that resist displacement and the extractive industries have been tarred with accusations that they're involved in the organized crime, and in some cases entire peasant villages have even been labeled narco-communities. "The strongest impacts in terms of human rights, which also occurred during the national security doctrine, which here led to genocide, is the idea that an entire community can be criminal," said Claudia Samayoa. She's the coordinator of UDEFE-GUA, a group dedicated to monitoring attacks and threats against activists. "You can't denominate as narco an entire community, including everyone from the baby that was just born to an elder who is dying," she told me in her bustling Guatemala City office. In the cases investigated by UDEFEGUA, Samayoa says there may be one or two members of a given community involved in drug trafficking, and the rest of the community stays silent because of fear and intimidation. "As community-based opposition to natural resource extraction projects and hydroelectric dam construction has grown, governmental and business sectors increasingly have made public statements to the press to suggest that current grassroots activism is inherently 'terrorist' in nature, alternatively suggesting that drug trafficker influence is involved or that the sentiments are manipulated and/or funded by outsiders and specifically international entities," reads a 2013 report by the United Nations High Commissioner for Refugees.[5] This pattern was brought into evidence during unrest in Santa Cruz Barrillas in 2012. As locals engaged in blockades to prevent the installation of a new hydroelectric company in their lands, Pérez Molina claimed that protesters were backed by drug traffickers and funded by international interests.

In early 2012, I visited Nueva Esperanza, in Petén, which was denominated a narco-community by the government of Álvaro Colom (who preceded Otto Pérez Molina). To get to Nueva Esperanza, we boarded an old school bus, which left from a busy backstreet in the city of Tenosique, in the southern Mexican state of Tabasco. The bus does a twice daily milk run through half a dozen small agricultural communities, ending at the Guatemalan border. The temperature was over 100 degrees, and the bus so full at the beginning that a couple of young men hung out the door as we drove. We continued on for about two hours until there were just three of us left. On a dusty strip of road surrounded by small houses and facing a soccer field, we stepped off the bus at the end of the line. The tiny Mexican ranching town of Nuevo Progreso ends a couple of hundred meters away, where a gathering of shelters built from scrap wood, old galvanized roofing, and USAID tarps marks the border into Guatemala.

In 2000, forty landless farmers formed the agroecological Community of Nueva Esperanza. "We needed more people to live in the community, and so when we met someone who needed land, we would tell them [to come], and support them, and we all supported each other to build our community, and that's how it grew to a total of 150 families," said Marcelo Martínez Morales, who moved to Nueva Esperanza after being displaced by Hurricane Mitch. "We started to work the land, planting corn, beans, chiwa, sweet potato, yucca, macal, peanuts, sesame—that's what we planted." From the beginning, the community tried to get legal title to the land. "We tried for a long time, and instead of recognizing our community we were evicted for the first time" in 2007, he tells me. A second eviction took place in 2008. Both times, soldiers and police who said they had orders to protect the forest forced them from their homes. Some families fled in fear, but with nowhere else to go and no other options, most returned.

The last eviction, which took place on August 23, 2011, was different. This time families fled the area to the sound of gunfire. They watched as their homes were destroyed with chainsaws, doused in gasoline, and set on fire. Many of them ran to the hills, hiding out for days in the forest, eating what they could scavenge. One family hid with their then four-month-old baby, scared and hungry. The majority of the families in the community have young children.

The soldiers didn't leave the remote village after the eviction, neither did the police or the armed park rangers. Instead, they occupied the few buildings they hadn't burned to the ground. During my visit to the community, armed men were constantly present, standing in the forested areas on the edge of the settlement, limiting residents' free movement.

After the August eviction, the community decided there was only one safe place to go, one place where the Guatemalan army and police couldn't come after them: Mexico. They set up lean-tos and tents in a five-meter-wide strip that marks the border between the two countries, an area sometimes referred to as no man's land. This marked one of the first times since Guatemala's thirty-six-year internal conflict officially ended in 1996 that an entire village has crossed into Mexico in search of safety. After being forcibly removed by Mexican authorities in January, the community returned and set up their makeshift shacks a few meters from the line. They drink and bathe using water from shallow wells dug alongside a stream that trickles across the border from the Mexican side. On April 10th, just a week after I left the community, a one-year-old named Yorleni Yolet Zacarías Escobar died from fever, dehydration, and diarrhea. Her death was entirely preventable.

"The people are very tired. There is a kind of collective depression. They've been in the camp for seven to eight months, living under tarps, eating whatever they can, with no drinking water," said Brother Tomás González Castillo, the Franciscan priest based in Tenosique, Mexico, the closest urban area to Nueva Esperanza. "It's tragic." Castillo and others have organized church support for members of the community, who were prohibited from planting crops until their situation is resolved. Some of the men work for local Mexicans as farmhands when they can, pocketing about $9 on a good day.

A short walk along a narrow dirt trail from the cramped, muddy camp is the former village of Nueva Esperanza. Mynor Morales, who accompanied us to the old village, with his young son and another youth, pointed out the remains of the destroyed houses still visible under the weeds. Over the deep cries of howler monkeys that live in the lush forest, he explained how the community tried to live in harmony with nature, showing us a sign indicating where animals could and could not graze. "Now pretty much all you can see is bush, because everything grows fast here," said Morales, who pointed out that the police and army also cut down the community's fruit trees. As we came toward a clearing we saw one of the only structures still standing—the former community center. Music blasted out from the building and we could hear the voices of men who seemed to be in full party mode when we arrived at around eleven. Noticing us, a handful of officers hushed the party and came toward us, taking our picture with a digital camera and recording our names. It became clear that the party was in fact a gathering of the security forces tasked with protecting the area.

We told the police we were missionaries assisting the community, and carried on to a pristine stream that widened out under dense forest cover. As Mynor Morales's son swam, police armed with semi-automatic weapons approached, and it was made clear that we were not welcome in Lacandón National Park. Other community members told us the army still bothers them, sometimes even patrolling at night, and that soldiers have threatened that women who try to access the stream for washing, bathing, and drinking water will be raped. Even with small children and no other safe source of water, people like Yorleni's parents now stay away from their stream. "It hurts us a lot, in our souls, to see where we lived before. This is where our children were born, where we lived for years, where we had dreams of a better life," said Morales.

The official reason for the eviction was that the people of Nueva Esperanza were illegally occupying private property. Others say it was a move by the Colom government to clear the area as part of Cuatro Balam, a mega-project in Petén that includes the promotion of tourism in the region. After the August eviction, Carlos Menocal, the former interior minister of Guatemala, claimed the families of Nueva Esperanza were involved in drug trafficking. For their part, residents said they've been told cocaine traffickers use a corridor that runs through the park, but they say their community has never been involved in the drug business. "A drug trafficker wouldn't live under a tarp for eight months; they wouldn't live here and sleep right on the ground," said Morales, pointing to a piece of cardboard that served as a bed for an entire family.

If there are drugs moving through the park today, which seems a likely scenario, trafficking is carried out under the direct supervision of the army, and in territory under the care of "Defensores de la Naturaleza," a private nongovernmental organization, and the National Commission of Protected Areas. "We're not criminals, but the government chased us out of our country as if we were," said Mynor Morales. "The government kicked us out.... They care more for animals than they do for humans, they want to go back to the time of war, back to the '80s, when there were evictions throughout the country."

The community accepted resettlement to another part of Petén in 2012. Whoever is moving drugs through the park today is doing so with little risk of being spotted by a civilian.

The Oil Factor

In May 2011, the municipality of La Libertad, Petén, was the site of the deadliest massacre in Guatemala since the conflict ended. Twenty-seven day laborers were killed on a ranch called Los Cocos. When authorities entered the ranch the day after the massacre, they found twenty-six bodies and twenty-three severed heads. On the wall beside the bodies, a message written in blood, in Spanish: "What's up, Otto Salguero, you bastard? We are going to find you and behead you, too. Sincerely, Z200"—supposedly from a local cell of the Zetas.

Images of the carnage at La Libertad were posted online. They showed heads scattered in the grass, and soldiers guarding decapitated bodies whose hands were bound. They shocked the world and evoked memories of the darkest years of Guatemala's history when these kinds of events were almost commonplace in some rural areas. But unlike the old days, it wasn't men in government-issued uniforms overseeing the killing. This time, it was blamed on the Zetas. The rise in violence in Guatemala "has a lot to do with the beginning of the war in Mexico and interests of territorial control on the part of actors who didn't involve themselves in territorial control because that was the job of local narcotraffickers," said human rights monitor Samayoa. Following the massacre in Los Cocos, the government declared a state of emergency in Petén that lasted until January 2012.

"More than controlling the distribution chains and infrastructure needed to run the day-to-day operations, the Zetas are focused on controlling territory," reads the introduction to a September 2011 series prepared for InSight Crime.[6] The report, based mostly on information from government sources and newspaper articles, points to the massacre in La Libertad as the first incursion of the Zetas into Petén. It does seem that drug traffickers who identify as Zetas are active in Petén, and Fox News even reported on a banner, hung in the state's capital, threatening death to civilians in Petén and signed by Z200.

To claim that Petén is Zetas territory, however, is to ignore other important interests in the resource-rich region, which is bigger than Belgium. For one, there are established drug trafficking families in Petén who haven't ceded control of the lucrative transshipment market to the Zetas. But the armed groups with the most visible presence in the region are the Guatemalan police and army, and they were an ever-present part of the daytime street life in the half-dozen cities and villages I visited there, driving around in the backs of pickup trucks or walking around in groups. The Lacandón National Park, where Nueva Esperanza was located, is in the municipality of La Libertad, as is the Laguna del Tigre Park, where we were warned against entering because our presence at the various army checkpoints on the way into the park could create problems for the people we wished to visit.

Both of these protected areas are heavily militarized, and both are reported to be places where drugs are moved into Mexico, but they're also home to dozens of peasant communities and are among the areas of Guatemala with the most abundant natural resources. The events unfolding in Petén are less familiar to many than those in Mexico, and merit closer attention. To get into the Laguna del Tigre National Park, you have to travel through El Naranjo, a busy frontier town bordering a river that flows to Mexico. While we visited, soldiers kept watch over the riverfront; rickety, wooden motorboats came and went; other armed men without uniforms stayed back under the shade of nearby shop fronts; and a small sign at the loading area displayed the logo of another powerful group operating in the area: Perenco. A Paris-based oil company, Perenco produced and exported over 3.6 million barrels of crude oil in 2011, when oil displaced cardamom as Guatemala's fourth largest export, after coffee, sugar, and bananas. The firm operates forty-seven wells in what is known as the Xan Field inside the Laguna del Tigre National Park, forming a footprint anyone with access to Google Maps can see. The oil travels down a 475-kilometre pipeline, also owned by Perenco, which leads to the company's refinery near La Libertad town center, and then continues on to the company's terminal near Puerto Barrios on the Atlantic coast. Perenco acquired the operation from Canada's Basic Resources in 2001.

According to one local resident, who asked that his identity be concealed for fear of reprisals, the militarization of the area has more to do with protecting oil interests than it does with fighting organized crime. "In the case of Perenco, it's a company that's providing financing for the army of Guatemala to install itself in the area," he said, pointing out that six small military bases and at least 250 soldiers—part of a so-called green battalion that is framed as protecting wilderness—exist inside Laguna del Tigre. Some of these soldiers have taken part in forced evictions of communities living inside the park and are currently responsible for what amounts to a state of siege for those still living there. Not only are the twenty-five to thirty communities within the park forbidden from cutting a tree without a permit, they are under constant pressure from soldiers and armed park rangers.

"First, the mere presence of soldiers is something that makes the communities feel uncomfortable because of the memory of the people—when they see a soldier, they see someone who is there to kill," said the resident, who travels regularly into the area. "Second, they built a military outpost on the road, fifteen or seventeen kilometers from here, from El Naranjo, where they are controlling everything that the communities bring into the park." He said soldiers prevent community members from bringing in provisions, work tools, and materials they need for their homes, like corrugated zinc, cement bricks, sand, and rebar. "They're pressuring them by denying them access to things they need, which is another way of pressuring them so that they'll leave the area on their own," he said.

Perenco has deflected attention from its impacts on the park by stating on its website they "recognize[s] the serious nature of the problems facing the Park, such as those caused by migrant communities [sic] illegal slash and burn farming techniques." The government of Guatemala also blames people living inside the park for environmental damage to Central America's largest wetlands. "I will not tire of saying that the biggest threats to the Laguna del Tigre Park are cows and not the pipes of Perenco company," said former president Álvaro Colom in 2010.

Ex-Petén governor Rudel Mauricio Álvarez claims that during his administration, which ended in 2012, the choice was between oil or drugs. I met Álvarez in an open, modern café in Flores, the picturesque capital of Petén, following a Twitter exchange spurred by the word *narcoganadería*—or narcoranching, meaning large-scale ranches used as cover for drug trafficking activity. "That's the question: What's worse, what's more damaging: oil that only impacts the 450 hectares where the fields are, or narcoranchers who have 140,000 hectares?" he asked. "Everyone, the environmentalists and everyone else went against oil.... They make the real problem of the protected areas invisible," he said, pausing briefly before coming back to his own question. "The problem isn't oil extraction. The problem is narcoranchers."

No one I spoke to denied that Laguna del Tigre was part of a trafficking route where Colombian cocaine arrives on private airstrips and is then moved out to Mexico. Opinions differ on how involved the dozens of communities inside the park are with trafficking. Álvarez claimed that most of the communities are invaders, funded by narcodollars, but unlike parts of Mexico where the drug trade dominates, I didn't see a single showy SUV while I was in Petén. My source in El Naranjo said the narcos keep to themselves, flying in and out of the area, while the communities—many of which were settled by families displaced during the internal conflict—survive off of their basic crops of corn, beans, and squash. One thing is clear: the presence of drug traffickers in Laguna del Tigre hasn't affected oil production, and in fact, oil companies are showing a renewed interest in Guatemala's crude. A handful of Canadian oil companies have made their own moves into Guatemala, including Calgary-based Quattro Exploration and Production, which actively extracts oil in Saskatchewan. Between November 2011 and mid-2012, Quattro acquired almost 350,000 hectares' worth of oil concessions in Guatemala, including a concession block adjacent to Laguna del Tigre, itself within the Maya Biosphere Reserve. Other companies, like Pacific Rubiales and Latin American Resources Ltd., are also active in Petén.

Oil is only one of the super-profitable industries in Guatemala. The Cuatro Balam project proposes biofuels and large-scale agriculture in the south of Petén as well as increased spending on infrastructure for mass tourism, partially funded by groups such as the Inter-American Development Bank. Corporate-linked conservation groups, like the New York–based Wildlife Conservation Society, continue to claim vast tracts of land as park. There is also the threat of new hydroelectric projects, four of which are proposed along the Usumacinta River, which activists say would flood 35,000 people off their land. Few, if any, of the profits from these illicit or licit economic activities will ever make it to Petén's poor majority. They remain the most likely to be displaced from the land they depend on for survival, and they are the most likely to lose friends and loved ones as the drug war escalates in Guatemala.

US Marines, Beyond Mérida

In August, 2012, 200 US Marines were stationed in Guatemala as part of the war on drugs.[7] The deployment of US combat troops to Guatemala was part of Operation Martillo, a military plan meant to disrupt cocaine trafficking routes that pass through Central America from Colombia to the United States. "We have the sense that [fighting narcotrafficking] is a pretext to return to the level of military deployment that was maintained during the height of the armed conflict, which resulted in acts of genocide," said Hernández Batres. The Guatemalan army was called upon to fight drug trafficking in early 2012. "Today, publicly, I want to lay out for the army an important goal of collaborating, coordinating, and cooperating with other security institutions, and that is to put an end to the external threats and contribute to neutralizing illegal armed groups by means of military power," said Otto Pérez Molina, following his inauguration as president of Guatemala in January 2012.[8] Pérez Molina, a former general and head of army intelligence, promised to increase military spending, and so far, he's kept his promise. According to *Plaza Pública*, a Guatemalan investigative journalism outlet, spending on military and security equipment in 2013 surpassed all such spending between 2004 and 2012.[9]

The arrival of US Marines to Guatemala in 2012 represents more than a military maneuver to disrupt drug trafficking. It demonstrates that in allied countries like Guatemala, the United States can champion a military invasion under the discourse of the war on drugs with little fanfare or criticism. The deployment of troops to Guatemala is arguably the most blatant example of an evolving military strategy that the US military establishment is betting on in order to continue to exercise control within a framework of democracy and law and order. "The predominant hemispheric security challenges no longer stem principally from state-on-state conflict, right-wing paramilitaries, or left-wing insurgents," reads the US Western Hemisphere Defense Policy Statement, released in October 2012. "Today's threats to regional peace and stability stem from the spread of narcotics and other forms of illicit trafficking, gangs, and terrorism, the effects of which can be exacerbated by natural disasters and uneven economic opportunity."[10]

Guatemala, and Central America as a whole, is a testing ground for one iteration of the US military's evolving strategy of control, which is being applied unevenly throughout the hemisphere. In Guatemala, it includes US combat troops—something the United States can't get away with in Mexico, whose constitution explicitly forbids foreigners from carrying weapons. Like Mexico, anti-drugs efforts in Guatemala also include the involvement of military officials from Canada, Chile, and Colombia as trainers in regional security matters.[11]

While Mexico has been a central focus for US anti-narcotics funds and media attention, its neighbors to the south have already seen their share of action. The deployment of US Marines to Guatemala came just three months after a massacre of civilians in Ahuas, Honduras, when a US-backed anti-drug effort there went awry. In an incident we'll examine in the next chapter, human rights groups say DEA agents were present when Honduran police shot from State Department helicopters, killing four Indigenous people in the country's northwest in May 2012. [12] "The aircraft that were used in that operation were at that time piloted by officials of the Guatemalan Army," said Hernández. "Later, [Operation Martillo] appeared publicly in Guatemala, getting its official start midway through this year, but the operations had already begun." According to official sources, between July and October 2012, members of the US Marine Corps Forces, South—the naval component of the US Southern Command—flew helicopters destined for trafficking interdiction efforts in Guatemala out of Santa Elena, Petén. They also flew aircraft out of La Aurora in Guatemala City, Retalhuleu, and Puerto San José, as well as coordinating with the Guatemalan Navy in Puerto Quetzal, on the Pacific coast.[13]

Beyond a handful of wire stories, news of the deployment of active-duty US combat troops in Guatemala made barely a blip in the media.[14] It also seemed to go largely unnoticed in the Central American nation itself. Few outside military and security research circles were aware of the details of the agreement between the US Embassy and Guatemala's Foreign Relations Ministry. Nineth Montenegro, second vice president of Guatemala's Congress, said she found out about the operations through reports in the newspaper. "I found out through the print media, here in Congress there was no request to permit the transit of troops, maybe because they were not troops, maybe because they're unarmed, maybe because they're coming, in effect, to help support [the fight] against organized crime, a scourge that is killing our country.... There was no discussion in Congress. It was an agreement [made by the executive] that the president approved.... Some here think there was a violation, because legislative power is independent and it is the only one which can authorize the arrival of troops or military or support, but it never went to Congress," she said in an interview in Guatemala City.

Instead of moving through constitutional channels, on July 16, 2012, the US Embassy in Guatemala delivered a verbal note to the Minister of Foreign Relations, proposing the conditions for the regularization of US defense personnel in Guatemala. The note from the embassy, which was later transcribed and published in Guatemala's congressional gazette, makes reference to military and aviation cooperation agreements signed between the two countries in 1949, 1954, and 1955.[15] Castillo Armas, the military dictator who took power after the coup against President Árbenz in 1954, signed one of the documents referenced in the agreement. Such references make it clear that the legal elements permitting present-day US military engagement in Guatemala were created in the wake of the coup in 1954, and have been maintained ever since.

The day after it received the request from the US embassy, the Guatemalan government responded in the affirmative. While researching in Guatemala City, I obtained the exchange of notes between the US and Guatemala that legalized the presence of US troops and private security contractors hired by the US Department of Defense in Guatemala for 120 days, beginning July 17, 2012.[16] The agreement allows US personnel to carry arms, to import and export goods without inspection or taxation by the Guatemalan government, to freely transit into, out of, and throughout the country without interference by the Guatemalan government, and to make free and unlimited use of radio frequencies.[17] US soldiers and contractors are granted immunity from prosecution in Guatemala should injury or death of civilians or military personnel result from the operation.

According to members of the US Navy, their mission in Guatemala, led by the Joint Interagency Task Force South out of Key West, Florida, represents a move back to what the organization has traditionally done in the region. "For decades, the Marine Corps has supported engagement in Central and South America with the intent of building partnership capacity and improving interoperability," wrote Captain Greg Wolf on the Marine Corps official website. "In recent years, though, the wars in Iraq and Afghanistan have curtailed some of that engagement. The Marines of Detachment Martillo relished the opportunity to partner with Guatemalan authorities and strengthen ties in the region."[18] According to New York University professor Greg Grandin, whose book *Empire's Workshop: Latin America, the United States, and the Rise of the New Empire* documents the US military's shift from Vietnam and South Asia to Central America in the late 1970s, the discourse of the US military today masks a continued attempt to control local armies and police.

"We've come a long way from the robust language of the cold war—which hailed Latin American death squads and dictators as 'freedom fighters' on the frontline of a global anticommunist crusade—to the anodyne babble of 'building partnership capacity and improving inter-operability,'" wrote Grandin in an email interview. "But basically the goal has remained the same, to coordinate the work of national security forces on an international level subordinated, either directly or indirectly, to Washington's directive." That said, Grandin thinks the reach of the US in the hemisphere has shrunk, making the importance of what takes place in countries like Honduras and Guatemala even greater. "What is different is the degree that the US's reach has been reduced, from all of Latin America to basically a corridor running from Colombia through Central America to Mexico. But even there, US's hegemony is threatened by a degree of independence that would have been unthinkable just a few years earlier, whether it be in Juan Manuel Santos' Colombia or Daniel Ortega's Nicaragua."

The steadfast allegiance displayed by the government of Guatemala toward Washington, as well as the presence of US troops in Guatemala—both overt and clandestine—has a strong historical precedent. In 1960, the CIA coordinated directly with Guatemala's right-wing president José Miguel Ramón Ydígoras Fuentes, who offered support for the Bay of Pigs invasion against Fidel Castro in Cuba. According to declassified CIA documents, "Not only did Guatemala sever official relations with Cuba, but before the end of February 1960, President Ydígoras offered the use of his territory to support propaganda activities directed against Castro; and he also made a special offer through the CIA 'to groups favorably regarded by us [of] training facilities in the Petén area of Guatemala.'"[19] The US continued to be openly involved in all manner of military operations in Guatemala through to 1978, when official military aid to Guatemala was cut off by US Congress after evidence of massacres, rapes, and disappearances by the army became insurmountable. US assistance to the Guatemalan army has come in the form of supports for anti-narcotics initiatives, including the Central America Regional Security Initiative (CARSI), a nearly $642 million program, which started in 2008 under the Mérida Initiative and continued to 2014, with assistance, equipment, and training going to Central American police and armies.

Mexico falls under the jurisdiction of the US Northern Command, but south of its borders, it is the US Southern Command, which operates from a $400 million headquarters just west of Miami, that is responsible for all US military activities in Central and Latin America.[20] The presence of US troops in Guatemala is ongoing. For example, the "US Southern Command-sponsored, joint foreign military interaction/humanitarian exercises" named Beyond the Horizon took place in Honduras and Guatemala, ending two days before US Marines were deployed to Guatemala for Operation Martillo in July 2012.[21] Two days after Operation Martillo troops left the country, members of the United States Navy construction battalions deployed to Cobán as part of a "theater security cooperation mission" with the Guatemalan army.[22] But there is a new twist to the engagement of US Marines in Guatemala for Operation Martillo. "This is the first Marine deployment that directly supports countering transnational crime in this area, and it's certainly the largest footprint we've had in that area in quite some time," Marine Staff Sgt. Earnest Barnes told AP shortly after news of the deployment broke in the US.[23]

In an October 2012 speech in Virginia, US Secretary of Defense Leon Panetta outlined his army's plan in the face of budget constraints, explaining that rotational deployments and joint exercises with local militaries are to become an increasingly important element of US defense strategy. "We build new alliances, we build partnerships, we build their capacity and capability to be able to defend and provide their own security. So we're gonna do that. We're gonna do that in Latin America. We're gonna do that in Africa. We're gonna do that in Europe. We're doing it in the Pacific. Just have a rotational deployment of Marines going into Darwin. We're gonna develop the same capability in the Philippines. Gonna do the same thing in Vietnam. Gonna do the same thing elsewhere."[24]

The US-Guatemala military partnership includes a law enforcement role. "The military's role is not to act as a law enforcement force, but the unfortunate reality is that it has been called upon to deal with this problem on an interim basis in several countries," said US Deputy Assistant Secretary of Defense for Western Hemisphere Affairs Frank Mora in June of 2012. "When asked to do a job that many of them do not want to do—which is to do law enforcement, like in El Salvador and Guatemala—they have tried to do it the best that they can."[25] In 2012, using CARSI funds, the US trained 900 Central Americans at the International Law Enforcement Academy in San Salvador—El

Salvador's capital.[26] The connections with Colombia are strong, and have been reinforced by CARSI. In 2013, Brownfield, the US drug war czar in the Western Hemisphere, stated that "right now the Colombian national police is training more police and law enforcement in Central America than all of US law enforcement put together. Now, we support some of it. So in essence it is CARSI funding, Plan Colombia funding, or in some cases, even Mérida funding that does this. And it does it because it is cheaper for us to have the Colombian national police provide this training than us doing it ourselves. Sometimes it is the Colombians themselves providing that training. They are at this point training in four of the seven countries in Central America. They are providing training and support in the Dominican Republic in the Caribbean. They are open to further engagement. I actually believe we get excellent value either by Colombians training in third countries or by us bringing law enforcement personnel from those third countries to train in many of the Colombian training institutions that we helped support and set up during Plan Colombia from the year 2000 to 2010."[27]

One of the least acknowledged difficulties of increasing US support for the Guatemalan armed forces is the role the army has played and continues to play in drug trafficking. The Guatemalan army is widely documented to have been involved in drug trafficking, but that hasn't stopped the United States from partnering with it and providing it with technology and training aimed at controlling the flow of narcotics. "Evidence from various sources, including information from DEA reports, indicates that beginning in the 1980s, Colombian traffickers gained access to trafficking networks along key routes throughout the south and west of Guatemala," according to a publicly available research paper prepared by Navy-linked CNA Analysis and Solutions. "These networks were composed of military intelligence officials, their subordinates and former colleagues, and informants and partners—including military commissioners."[28]

By the mid-1990s, Guatemala's top drug lord was Byron Berganza, a former soldier whose "profile had risen and his security detail was comprised exclusively of military officials."[29] At that time, Berganza was also a DEA informant and the local Guatemalan go-between with Colombian and Guatemalan drug trafficking groups. Berganza was extradited to the United States in 2003, opening up new space in the country's drug transshipment market, which would eventually be filled by members of a handful of powerful Guatemalan families. In 2011, activist and writer Jennifer Harbury said the rising drug violence in Guatemala "is being carried out by military leaders who took their uniforms off after the war, created large mafias to run drugs, and hired and trained gangs such as the Zetas—that's very well documented—to help them run the drugs."[30] Little has changed in the three years since. In addition, weapons including rockets and grenade launchers belonging to the Guatemalan military have been found in the hands of Los Zetas members.[31]

It was a former Kaibil (member of Guatemala's elite special forces) who was accused of directing the single most violent act in Guatemala yet linked to drug trafficking. Hugo Gómez Vásquez was accused of supervising the massacre in Los Cocos, Petén in May 2011.[32] Some Kaibiles trained in the United States, as did some of the original members of the Zetas, who defected from the GAFEs, an airborne unit of Mexico's elite special forces, in the late 1990s. The Kaibiles also trained the GAFEs, and have been involved in training with US Marines.[33] "It has become normal that when they find an official on active duty among Zetas, or a Kaibil who is still in active service, two or three days go by and the army claims 'it's that they deserted,' but the internal process regarding what discipline was applied, and what disciplinary procedures there are aren't documented," said Hernández of SEDEM. Regardless of evidence of collaboration with the Zetas and other drug trafficking groups and a history of participation in massacres, Guatemala's Kaibiles maintain a privileged relationship with the US military.

Then there is the role of US troops in Guatemala. "These guys, the marines, they aren't just here to control narcotrafficking, but to train the Guatemalan military for what I call the continuation of the Cold War," said Ba Tiul. "A cold war that's more refined, more academic, more intellectualized, if you'd like. But one that will be just as brutal and damaging for all of us here in Guatemala, and which I don't think … I don't think is destined only for Guatemala." Beyond his connections with an influential elite connected to the extractive industries and the energy sector, there are also important links between Pérez Molina's government and a powerful sector of organized crime.

"Fernández Ligorría, a military man from Cobán, was one of the most important figures in the Patriot Party, and was very close to the current president, Otto Pérez Molina," according to a Guatemalan analyst who requested anonymity out of fear for his safety. Ligorría was an instructor to the Kaibles, a former chief of national defense, and later the head of the national police (PNC).[34] Sylvia Gereda Valenzuela, who is closely linked to one of Guatemala's most powerful families (the Novella family, owner of Cementos Progreso, which has a monopoly on cement in Guatemala), links Ligorría to various organized crime activities, as well as drugs and arms trafficking beginning in the mid-1990s. By the time of his death in January 2011, various media outlets described Ligorría as the head of Los Zetas in Guatemala. "One of his sons, José Fernández Chanel, is currently a sitting congressperson with the [Patriot Party]. It's complicated, because a direct fight [against drug trafficking] on the part of the government would implicate their own colleagues, ex-colleagues, and high ranking military officials," said the Guatemalan analyst. "This could unleash wars of another kind, power disputes that could put at risk not only the stability of the government of Pérez Molina, but also the stability of the state itself."

Military personnel from Cobán make up an important part of Pérez Molina's support base. Cobán is in the department of Alta Verapaz, where former president Colom also declared a state of emergency in 2010, allegedly because of the presence of Zetas there. For all the talk of a new strategy in the drug war, on March 30, 2012, the Guatemalan defense minister announced the creation of a new, anti-narcotics military task force called "Tecun Uman," which will benefit from technical and financial assistance from the United States.[35] Four days later, on April 3rd, US officials and Guatemalan authorities captured Horst Walter Overdick Mejía, a drug trafficker affiliated with the Zetas who was active in Alta Verapaz and Petén, in Guatemala.[36] "After Overdick's arrest, the narcos began to reposition, and the Zetas as well, under the careful and close watch of the military," said Ba Tiul. "It's not about controlling the narcos, but ensuring the business stays in their hands ... as well as controlling social mobilization, which is very powerful."

As explored previously, after more than a decade as a testing ground for a US drug policy that has victimized millions, Colombia has the fastest growing economy in Latin America. The hard lesson from Colombia is that, unfortunately, drugs and oil do mix. "We need to keep in mind that Colombian president Santos, like Pérez Molina, wants to expand Plan Colombia, which doesn't just mean strengthening the fight against narcotrafficking but actually means converting it into a form of paramilitarism in order to generate a new kind of counterinsurgency—not against social movements but against Indigenous communities," said Ba Tiul. "It's the remilitarization of Guatemala as a patriotic project."

CHAPTER 8:

DRUG WAR CAPITALISM IN HONDURAS

HONDURAS is a place where the gap between the tiny elite and the poor majority is so great that it is almost invisible on the street level. The rich simply do not walk around or go out in the same neighborhoods as the poor. I traveled to Honduras from Guatemala to cover the 2013 elections, and kept a diary of what I saw on my first day in the country. After a long process of passport stamping, the bus I was on crossed the border, and immediately there was a banana truck that had burst a tire; green bananas were spilled all over the road. As soon as I arrived at San Pedro Sula, I spied four military police, toting modern automatic weapons and looking at cell phone cases in the bus station. From there, I caught a shared cab downtown for about $4, made my way to a hotel with a window out onto the street and a whirring fan to fight the intense humidity. Down the street, the Despensa Familiar (Walmart) featured a little corner with slim pickings of fruit and vegetables. Most of the store was junk food and processed food wrapped in plastic. It struck me that the baby formula is kept under lock and key at the front of the store, so that parents who worry about feeding their babies enough protein won't steal. There were at least eight people in the four-block walk back to the hotel looking through garbage, sorting, carrying garbage bags. By nightfall, most places downtown were closed and few people were out on the streets. At dawn, from my hotel window, I noticed a man cooking over a garbage fire. All of this was taking place downtown in San Pedro Sula, Honduras's second largest city, at the heart of the region considered the industrial belt of the country.

Violence in Honduras is sometimes presented as random and wanton, or as somehow involving drugs, but it can't be separated from the acute poverty imposed on the country's majority. The war on drugs is the government's latest justification of extreme violence in Honduras. It cannot be a surprise that the drug war is providing useful cover for

Honduras' skyrocketing murder rate following the 2009 coup d'état, and according to one of the country's most respected activists, its designs go beyond Honduras's borders. "In reality this is a dangerous pretext because it means that territories are occupied and human rights are violated, and of course it guarantees the pillage and appropriation of the common goods of nature by the United States, which is exactly why they're here, and of course for the geopolitical interests, because Honduras has a particular, privileged location between two oceans and with countries like Venezuela, Cuba, Nicaragua, and in reality the occupation of Honduras is to help impede the advance of emancipatory processes throughout the continent," said Berta Cáceres, General Coordinator of the Council of Indigenous and Popular Organizations of Honduras (COPINH).

The US-backed war on drugs picked up in Honduras when the United States began renewed anti-drugs funding in Central America in 2008 via the Mérida Initiative. The Mérida Initiative was later split, and the Central American Regional Security Initiative (CARSI) became an independent program in 2010. The program has five overarching goals, which are comparable to those of the Mérida Initiative: to "help make streets safer, disrupt criminal networks, support the development of strong government institutions, bring services to at-risk communities, and promote greater collaboration among the region's governments, not only within Central America but with Mexico, with Colombia, and beyond."[1] US aid to Honduras climbed from $62 million in 2010 to $90 million in 2012, thanks in large part to increases in Department of Defense spending and CARSI. As elsewhere, the more US aid to the drug war flowed, the higher the murder rate climbed, peaking in 2012 when US aid for the drug war topped out. Under CARSI, "Honduras received $12.1 million in FY2010, nearly $14 million in FY2011, and an estimated $24.8 million in FY2012."[2] By 2014, CARSI funding had dropped off to zero, and the US directed the majority of $49.3 million in aid to Honduras to development projects.[3]

In the fall of 2012, when Hillary Clinton was still the US secretary of state, she addressed the Central America Citizen Security Meeting and boasted of improvements in the region following an increase in US spending through CARSI. She claimed the homicide rate in Honduras was down 25 percent in the first six months of 2012 compared to the first six months of 2011. "In some communities, we are told that the fear of violence is beginning to fade for the first time in many years," Clinton said.[4] Whoever was telling the State Department that things were improving was a creative statistician, to put it mildly. The Honduran Observatory on Violence, an organization comprising police, the Attorney General's Office and the National University of Honduras, recorded 3,594 reports of homicides in the first six months of 2011, compared to 3,614 over the period of 2012.[5] By December, they said that the number of homicides in 2012 was in fact one percent higher than the previous year, at 7,172.[6] Those numbers don't include many others who are killed in Honduras each year but whose deaths are not classified as homicides, like the 360 people killed in the Comayagua prison fire in 2012. Regardless, the number steadily climbed each year, increasing from 2,155 homicides in 2004 before peaking in 2012.[7] In 2013, the number of homicides fell to 6,747, or about nineteen each day and an average of 563 per month.[8] In 2013, the government changed the system it uses to count murder victims, which has not yet affected the number of dead counted by the observatory, but has already made the Honduran murder rate appear to decrease.

The devastating present-day ramifications of US aid in Honduras, and the link between military assistance and increased insecurity, can best be understood in the context of Honduran history. Washington's influence in Honduras throughout the twentieth century was primarily devoted to protecting American investors, to building up a transnational faction of the Honduran elite, and to using the country as a staging ground for military attacks on neighboring countries.

US Military History in Honduras

Early US political involvement in Honduras rose with the banana industry, which reached its apex in the 1920s. By way of example, in 1914, John Ewing, a US minister in Tegucigalpa, sent a letter to the US State Department, in which he explained the reach of the United Fruit Company thus: "In order to obtain these concessions and privileges and to secure their undisturbed enjoyment, it [the United Fruit Company] has seen fit to enter actively into the internal policies of these countries, and it has pursued this course so systematically and regularly until it now has its ramifications in every department of the government and is a most important factor in all political movements and actions."[9] In 1924, a platoon of 200 marines entered Honduras and traveled to Tegucigalpa after civil war broke out between Liberals and Nationalists. The peace treaty between Honduran parties took place under US supervision aboard an American warship.[10]

After 1932, the United States oversaw the seventeen-year dictatorship of General Tiburcio Carías Andino of the Liberal Party. Carías's strategy against the opposition parties was known as "*encierro, destierro y entierro,*" or "round them up, throw them out, and bury them."[11] Carías "gagged the press and jammed the prisons. He created an institutionalized dictatorship that combined political, military, and economic force."[12] Turmoil followed, and the military seized power from the National Party in 1956 and governed for one year, until it was replaced by the Liberal presidency of Ramón Villeda Morales.[13] In an agreement "probably underwritten by the United Fruit Company and the US Embassy," Villeda Morales signed off on giving the military autonomy from civilian control.[14] After paying off a debt to the US in 1953, the Honduran state, through the US Alliance for Progress program, again began to incur foreign debt in 1958. From the 1950s to the 1980s, the US trained at least 1,000 members of the Honduran army and provided $6.4 million in military assistance to the country.[15] By 1965, the military had become Honduras's "most developed political institution," controlling the government between 1963 and 1971, and again from 1972 until 1982.[16] The evolution of the Honduran Army is directly linked to US-financed military training and equipment provisions.[17]

In the early 1960s, the Bank for Central American Economic Integration and the US Agency for International Development (US-AID) began to make large loans, of which the primary beneficiaries were the elite merchants and factory owners of San Pedro Sula, who joined together to create the Honduran Financing Bank (FICENSA). The creation of FICENSA was crucial in facilitating the extension of US resources to the Honduran private sector, as previously the military had been the main organization to take advantage of US "aid" to Honduras. Historian Edelberto Torres Rivas argues that the integration of Central American economies through the Central American Common Market (CACM) in the post-WWII period caused new social groups to emerge, including "the state, the local industrial and financial bourgeoisie, and children of the landowning oligarchy," together creating the social base necessary for foreign investment.[18] Though the functioning of the CACM was seriously disrupted by the 1969 soccer war between Honduras and El Salvador, the social and economic base created during this long period of military rule would serve as a jumping off point for the project of democratization in Honduras. It also served as the soil from which the transnational economic project would germinate and grow to dominate the country's bipartisan political system by the end of the 1980s.

Pressure from the United States pushed the military to aid in a transition toward a civilian democracy, and "although the Carter administration never severed military assistance to Honduras, it pressured General Paz to relinquish power."[19] The transition to democracy was finalized in 1982, with the election of Liberal Roberto Suazo Córdova. After the 1981 elections, the US immediately came out with a series of recommendations known as Reaganomics for Honduras, released by then ambassador to the United States, John Dmitri Negroponte, days after Suazo's election.[20] Regardless of the democratic opening, according to the US Congressional Research Service, "the military continued to operate as an autonomous institution."[21]

Dr. Robinson defines a polyarchic system as having an exclusive focus on elections, which limits "the focus to political contestation among elites through procedurally free elections; the question of who controls the material and cultural resources of society, as well as asymmetries and inequalities, among groups within a single nation and among nations within the international order, becomes extraneous to the discussion of democracy." For Hondurans, the transition toward democracy looked a lot like a transition to polyarchy.[22] It resulted in the closure of traditional political spaces, an increase in repression, and the imposition of economic and military programs at odds with popular opinion.[23] The Suazo/Reagan years saw the implementation of a "national security" doctrine in Honduras. That doctrine transformed Honduras into a staging area for US-led counterinsurgency efforts on the isthmus, and included the construction of twelve military bases where hundreds of thousands of US and third-party soldiers were trained. "Honduran society was altered by becoming the location of three non-national armies and was converted into the aggressive military axis of US foreign policy" in Central America.[24] US troops in Honduras had a three-part mission: crush incipient revolutionary (armed and popular) movements inside Honduras, provide a military backbone of stabilization during the transition to democracy, and wage war on revolutionary movements in neighboring countries.[25]

In 1981, US military aid to the country spiked, and over the next four years, the US would provide $41.48 million in military assistance to Honduras, second only to El Salvador in the region.[26] Between 1985 and 1992, the US would give another $83.33 million to the government of Honduras, earmarked for military spending.[27] During the

1980s, Honduras received $1.6 billion in economic and military aid from the United States.[28] By 1983, there were death squads in Honduras targeting political activists for murder or disappearance.[29] During the 1980s, there were at least 180 people disappeared, and hundreds of political dissidents were murdered—a significant number in such a small country, but still only a fraction of the level of violence wrought in Guatemala and El Salvador.[30] According to former US ambassador to Honduras Jack R. Binns, "one of the bitterest ironies was that Honduras's human rights record deteriorated sharply under a democratic government, in part because US policy makers deliberately closed their eyes to growing abuses."[31] Not only was there a build-up in the presence of the US military, but the United States also funneled money into Honduran civil society and the private sector often via USAID. According to the US State Department, at this time, "Honduras became host to the largest Peace Corps mission in the world, and nongovernmental and international voluntary agencies proliferated."

"That era was one of disappearances, of torture, of the organization of death squads," said Dr. Juan Almendarez about the 1980s, when I interviewed him in his clinic, off a small street near downtown Tegucigalpa, in 2009. Almendarez is a well-known activist and medical doctor who served as rector of the Autonomous University of Honduras. In person, he is soft-spoken, cycling back between history and the present in order to make his views understood. "I am a survivor of torture. I was condemned by the death squads during the decade of the '80s, and it's important to remember that there are still some [death squad members and members of the military and government] from that era who are today part of the coup d'état in Honduras." Having participated in movements for decades, Almendarez was clear about the difference between the struggles in Honduras in the 1980s and those today. "It's important to understand that in the '80s the direct confrontation was more [against] the political sector working together with Army. Today, the struggle is precisely about the neoliberal economic model, imperial globalization, and this whole campaign by financial capital to gain power over our lands, to take our resources."

Transnational '90s

The Honduran elite is understood historically to be lacking power and coherency, and it is sometimes said to constitute the weakest oligarchy in Central America. With the onset of formal democracy in the 1980s, a transnationally oriented segment of the national elite began to gain coherence in Honduras, and toward the end of the decade they gained the upper hand over national capitalist groups.[32] "During the 1980s, as the country was being militarized, AID bankrolled the formation of almost two dozen business associations and private sector organizations that responded to the demands of transnationalism."[33] According to the University of California's Dr. Robinson, these included the Foundation for Investment and Export Development (FIDE), the National Council to Promote Exports and Investments, the Federation of Agro Export Producers, the National Association of Honduran Exporters, and the Honduran American Chamber of Commerce, among others. Half of the $711 million in economic aid that funneled in between 1980 and 1990 went directly from the US government to private sector groups, "entirely bypassing the government."[34]

In one of the early political moves toward institutionalizing transnationalism, the US government signed the Caribbean Basin Economic Recovery Act (CBERA) in 1984. CBERA was part of a series of policies known collectively as the Caribbean Basin Initiative (CBI). The CBI would provide favorable conditions for export-led development in the maquila sector. According to the World Bank, while "this act did not grant textiles tariff-free access to US markets, it did exempt them from the Multifibre Arrangement (MFA) as long as they were assembled using US inputs."[35] By encouraging Caribbean countries to assemble garments using imported US cloth, the CBI explicitly made clothing production into a transnational activity. In addition, the CBERA carried with it a number of mandatory criteria for all countries that participated in it, which among other things stipulated that they not be communist, that they not nationalize property of US citizens, and that they be party to an extradition treaty with the United States.

It wasn't until 1990 that the government of Honduras would introduce economic measures and policies that fully institutionalized the open markets and government policies synonymous with neoliberalism. President Rafael Callejas "agreed in March 1990 to the first of three major structural adjustment programs negotiated with the IMF, USAID, and other international lenders," including the World Bank and the Inter-American Development Bank.[36] This agreement, known in Honduras as *"el paquetazo"* (which translates as "the big package") encouraged foreign direct investment in nontraditional exports, tourism, free trade areas, *maquiladoras* (sweatshops), and ushered in currency devaluation and fiscal austerity measures. In 1990, Honduran exports to the United States, by far the country's largest trading partner, were worth $429 million; by 2007, exports from Honduras to the US were worth $3.728 billion.[37]

The Structural Adjustment Program (SAP) signed by Callejas eliminated protectionism for small and medium-sized businesses in Honduras, which would find they could no longer compete with larger corporations.[38] According to Honduran economist Alcides Hernández, the SAP and the economic stabilization program embarked upon by the Callejas regime "legitimized the rising rate of unemployment, the fall of net salaries, the deterioration of social services in the public sector, and the conversion of the state into a subsidiary of private export capital, which would likely become the most important emerging source for capital accumulation in the current economic crisis."[39]

The maquila sector, operating from free trade zones and paying little tax, became Honduras's contribution to global capitalism. Neoliberalism continued to deepen, and the international finance institution (like the IMF or the World Bank) oriented macroeconomic policies, which were promoted throughout the 1980s and adopted formally in 1990, became the norm in Honduras. Even while local economic conditions declined, the transnational elite continued to benefit from so-called austerity measures within Honduras. "Creating a good investment climate means creating a climate against working people," said Yadira Minero, of the Center for Women's Rights in Honduras (CDM), in an interview in San Pedro Sula. "Foreign investment isn't our salvation."

Demilitarization began to take place at this time, with support from the private sector and as a result of the fact that militarization had become "unnecessary and unproductive for the transnational agenda," whose backers felt constrained by the military.[40] "During the 1990s, successive Honduran administrations took steps to reduce the power of the military. Mandatory military service was abolished, the police and several state-owned enterprises were removed from military control, and—after the ratification of constitutional reforms in 1999—the military was subordinated to a civilian-appointed defense minister."[41] Military cutbacks were in part a response to the changing geopolitical context of Central America at that time. US funding for the Honduran military began to drop, to $500,000 in 1995 and $325,000 in 1995.[42] Revolutionary movements in Guatemala and El Salvador had been violently repressed, and peace accords were drafted and signed.

When Hurricane Mitch hit Honduras in October 1998, 11,000 people were killed and two million were made homeless.[43] Mitch was used as an excuse to change national law, including the Mining Law, in order to improve conditions for foreign direct investment. Though following Mitch the country was allowed to suspend payments on US$4.4 billion in debt (amounting to 46 percent of its annual budget), "this restructuring of Honduras's debt and the extension of additional loans required the [Carlos Flores Facussé] administration to pursue structural adjustment policies while pledging to reduce poverty."[44]

The Honduran Elite and the 2009 Coup

Deepening economic inequality and social unrest was the backdrop when Manuel "Mel" Zelaya Rosales, a member of the Liberal Party, was elected president in November 2005. He was removed from the presidency on June 28, 2009, via a coup d'état. Throughout most of his presidency, he could have been considered a political moderate, though he did make concessions, including putting a moratorium on controversial new mining deals, proposing a plebiscite on constitutional reform, raising the minimum wage and teachers' pay, and cutting elementary school tuition. Zelaya is from an elite family, and worked in the logging and agricultural industries and later in government before being elected president. In fact, coup backer Adolfo Facussé told AP after the coup that "Mel Zelaya is one of us and—well—it just got out of his control. But the people think that he is an instrument of [Venezuela's Hugo] Chávez and that the fight is with Chávez."[45]

Zelaya's presidency came at a time of increased protest and resistance among Honduran social movements, who were unhappy with the policies that impoverished so many people. According to *The Economist*'s assessment of Zelaya's first year in office, "Simmering social tensions have resulted in around 200 protests since the government took office, and there is a risk of more of these in the future."[46] Eventually, Zelaya began ceding more and more ground to popular movements. Dario Euraque, a Honduran historian and author, explained to me that "for the first time in Honduran twentieth-century history and actually nineteenth-century history, you have a president, with all his failures and problems and issues that most of the opposition points to, but the fact is that this president, who himself comes from the elites of Honduras, put out not only a discourse but even many policies that fundamentally questioned the political system of Honduras."

Zelaya's steps toward a constitutional assembly garnered massive opposition from elite factions in Honduras. The significance of the possibility of a *Constituyente* (constituent assembly, as it is known in Honduras) was not lost on members of the country's poor majority, many of whom saw changing the constitution as beginning the kind of systemic change necessary to make Honduras more equitable. Zelaya was removed from his home and flown to Costa Rica by the army early in the morning of June 28, the day that a preliminary vote on constitutional reform was planned. Euraque relates that Zelaya drove the already precarious situation of the bipartisan political system toward a crisis by opening up the possibility of a constitutional assembly.

The Honduran National Business Council (COHEP) sent out a press release the day after the coup, stating, "What occurred today [*sic*] was not the changing of one president for another; today, framed in national unity, respect for the Constitution, national laws and institutionalism was achieved."[47] Honduras's National Industrial Association (ANDI) also sent out a press release in support of the coup, claiming the event marked a return to constitutionality. "President Zelaya provoked with this attitude a rupture in the rule of law, as a consequence, it is the same ex president Zelaya who has provoked a coup d'état by disregarding and disobeying the ruling of the judiciary while invested with presidential powers."[48] The Honduran Association of Manufacturers (AHM) provided a huge Honduran flag and white T-shirts for people who took to the streets in unprecedented pro-coup marches in San Pedro Sula and Tegucigalpa. In an interview not long after the coup, Euraque explained, "Never in the history of Honduras has there ever been a mobilization along the lines of this white T-shirt [march].... Part of the way to try to see how new that was, was that they didn't have a culture of resistance, of mobilization, so a lot of their music and placards and the paraphernalia ... was not even local. A lot of it was borrowed from Venezuela, Cuban Americans, lots of it was in English, peppered with English phrases, and so forth, and very manufactured, placards and so forth."

The 2009 coup is different from previous coups in Honduran history, which were generally either carried out under pressure from the United States, or carried out by the army for its own sake. This time an important section of the Honduran elite, specifically the transnational elite as represented by people like Camilo Atala and Jorge Canahuati and the Facussé family, as well as organizations like ANDI, AHM, and COHEP, encouraged the army (some might say manipulated the army) in removing Zelaya from his private residence. Even though it was clear to observers from all points on the political spectrum that the Honduran armed forces violated the constitution when they removed Zelaya to Costa Rica, Honduran business elites and the Honduran army, along with some members of the judiciary, Congress, and the Catholic Church insisted that the coup did not represent an interruption in the country's democracy. This again contrasts with previous coups in Honduras, which were blatant military operations whose leaders did not attempt to mobilize the civilian population so as to appear to be fulfilling a democratic mandate.

I traveled around Tegucigalpa six months after the coup, and graffiti against "turcos"—a Honduran slang term for the Arab businessmen that are among the most influential in the country—was impossible to ignore. There was also anti-Semitic graffiti, aimed at the handful of Jewish families among Honduras's elite. COHEP itself has claimed that graffiti and public statements against "turcos" could be taken as direct assaults on the Honduran business community. "Traditionally, the term 'turco' has been erroneously associated with people of Palestinian descent and to the service activities and more specifically to the large capital generated by them."[49] Euraque explained that negative sentiment against this group had never been publicly demonstrated in the past, and that it stemmed from the role of these elites, consisting of some of the families mentioned earlier, including the Facussés, the Ferraris, the Canahuatis, and the Atalas. According to Euraque, "What the elites basically decided to do, and especially that sector of the Arab [elite] which is, you know, the most important sector as I mentioned.... They basically said there is no way out here other than to cajole the military into thinking that what's at stake is not just the defense of us, it's the defense of the nation against Hugo Chávez."

Since the 2009 military coup removed President Manuel Zelaya from power, the number of people in poverty has increased significantly in the small Central American nation. On another trip to Honduras in 2013, I waited for the country's former finance minister, Hugo Noé Pino, in the air-conditioned lobby of one of the country's fancier hotels. He arrived looking fresh, though I knew he'd been pulling long days and long nights, since we met a couple days after the elections, and he was deeply involved with the process. In the course of a long and detailed interview about the state of Honduras' economy, I asked Noé how he characterized the country's elite. "It is an elite that has diversified its investments, and whose principal characteristic is the use of the state as a mechanism either of direct accumulation or of the facilitation of accumulation. It is an elite that does not pay taxes, or that pays them at the lowest rates, and that represents such a large profit for them that it isn't surprising to look at the Gini coefficient and learn that 10 percent of highest earners in Honduras control 42 percent of national income, and the lowest 10 percent of earners only receives 0.17 percent of income nationally." The Center for Economic and Policy Research released a report in late 2013 showing that Honduras is now the most unequal country in Latin America. Honduras's tiny elite runs the country's maquilas, owns the media, and controls the telecommunications, banking, and energy sectors.

For months after the coup, activists would gather every day in Tegucigalpa to march against the change of government, and against the faction of the elite perceived as being responsible for it. State repression against anti-coup activists was intense, including ongoing detentions, disappearances, the use of torture, and the beatings and murder of social activists and everyday Hondurans mobilizing against the coup. Between June and December 2009, the Committee for Relatives of the Disappeared in Honduras (COFADEH) documented 708 human rights violations, including the murder of fifty-four activists. On November 29, 2009, the de facto government presided over the country's regularly scheduled presidential elections, which led to the election of National Party head Porfirio Lobo Sosa. Almendarez, the doctor who was also once a presidential candidate, called the 2009 elections a second coup. "We are faced with a situation that's very delicate, where there was a military coup, where a president is named, and then there is a second coup, which was the election, the fraudulent election," he said. The resistance movement against the coup actively promoted an elections boycott. "There is no doubt that there was fraud, because they were illegitimate elections," he told me. The Organization of American States didn't send monitors, and many countries in the region took years to recognize the government of President Lobo. Canada and the United States, however, quickly heralded the elections as a return to democracy.

The deepening of the neoliberal program and the intensified re-militarization of the country were the hallmarks of Porfirio Lobo's administration. For example, in 2011, the government passed the Law for the Promotion and Protection of Investment, which provides legal certainties and guarantees for large investors that they will not face tax increases or lawsuits. The law was passed with an English name, under the slogan "Honduras is Open for Business," and is expected to benefit over 350 foreign investors. Under the law, foreign companies can open a subsidiary in four days, and mega-projects valued at $50 million or more will be able to access a sped-up permitting process, allowing them to gain all of their state and local permits within thirty days.[50] Lobo's government also passed laws decimating labor rights and allowing foreign companies to purchase nationally owned land and resources.

Throughout the Lobo administration, legislative and executive initiatives increasingly blurred the lines between the Secretariat of Security, which oversees police, and the Ministry of Defense. First, the use of soldiers in policing, a practice begun during Zelaya's term, became the norm. Later, the use of soldiers in policing was officially approved. "[Lobo] has deployed the military to carry out joint operations with the police on several occasions, and in late November 2011, the Honduran National Congress approved a decree to temporarily allow military personnel to carry out raids, make arrests, disarm people, and act against police officers that are involved in criminal activities."[51] Lobo appointed Juan Carlos Bonilla Valladares, known as "El Tigre," as head of Honduras's police in May 2010. Bonilla, who was accused of having participated in death squads, became the "US government's go-to man in Honduras for the war on drug trafficking."[52] This is the CARSI-funded war, which flared up again in 2010, as efforts to disrupt drug traffickers became a priority in a country where state institutions and legitimacy are already extremely weak. As elsewhere, the drug war provided a powerful pretext to increase the number of soldiers in the streets. In October 2013, the first contingent of militarized cops, named the Military Police for Public Order, hit the streets. "The new military police are better armed than the civilian police they will replace in this mission. For example, they will be armed with Israeli Galil ACE 21 assault rifles carrying 35-round magazines, capable of firing 700 rounds per minute."[53] Honduran police and soldiers have been trained by Colombian and Chilean armed forces as security cooperation has increased between South America and Central America.

Political Resistance via LIBRE

In the four and a half years following the coup, through the presidency of Porfirio Lobo, Hondurans saw the birth of a new political party: LIBRE, which stands for Libertad y Refundación (Freedom and Refoundation), was born in 2011 through an agreement between broad segments of the resistance movement and Liberal party members who opposed the coup. Deposed president Zelaya, who had just returned from exile, became head of the party and his wife, Xiomara Castro, was selected as their candidate for president. LIBRE is a democratic socialist party, which promised voters a break with the past and a focus on education and health. In addition, the social-movement forces within the party proposed a "refoundational project," which would include the writing of a new constitution.

Five years after the coup, election day in Tegucigalpa kicked off with the feel of a carnival, a rare sensation in a city where the vast majority of residents are faced with grinding poverty, regular gang extortions, and a murder rate that is among the world's highest. In front of each voting station, tents from the various political parties provided shade, blaring music at each other from huge speakers as groups of youth and volunteers hung around. Police, army, and masked military police oversaw the crowds, cars honked, and people waved Honduran and political party flags as their vehicles crawled through the fray. But for Marta de Jesús Raudales Varela, who lives in a small house on a steep unpaved street, it was a heart-wrenching day. In January, her son Ángel Francisco Durón Raudales, an activist with the LIBRE Party, was murdered along with five others around the corner from the family home in the Las Ayestas neighborhood.

I interviewed Raudales on a stoop under the shade of a tree in front of her house. The three local activists that took us to meet her insisted on staying nearby, saying that my photographer and I could be in danger were we to be left alone in the area. "[The killers] told them to lie face down, so they lay face down, and they emptied their pockets so that they could pretend it was a robbery. [The killers] had their faces covered, but everyone could see what happened," said Raudales. The killers shot all six in their backs and heads as they lay with their faces to the sidewalk. Two days after the massacre, street gangs posted signs and handed out pamphlets warning residents they were imposing a 7 p.m. curfew. Almost a year after the massacre, no one dares to mention gang involvement in the killings for fear of reprisals. A tough-as-nails grandmother, Raudales Varela was robbed at gunpoint four times in a single year while she walked home from selling lottery tickets a few blocks from her house. She cried quietly during our interview, wiping her eyes with her apron. Durón Raudales was a construction worker who organized a local base committee and made flags in support of the LIBRE Party. His mother thinks he may have been targeted because of his political activity. "I'm going to go vote this evening, but I really don't feel like going," she said. "I feel bad today." The murder of Durón Raudales was one of at least thirty-eight killings of people actively involved in electoral campaigns leading up to November's election. Among the parties, the hardest hit by the violence has been LIBRE. The intense political violence reflects an overall trend in Honduras, where according to the United Nations Development Program, the murder rate climbed from 37 per 100,000 in 2004 to 77.5 in 2010—the highest in Latin America by over ten points. By 2013, it was the highest in the world.

Official results posted by electoral authorities gave LIBRE 29 percent of the vote, and with it, almost a third of the seats in Congress. The National Party claimed 37 percent, the Liberals claimed 20 percent and almost 14 percent went to the new Anti-Corruption Party. "This has no precedent," said Noé, referring to the break with bipartisan rule. The afternoon after election day, several hundred red-flag-waving protesters marched through the streets of Tegucigalpa in support of Xiomara Castro, the woman they claimed was the rightful president of the country. The next day, hundreds of students took to the streets against election fraud, staving off police and teargas. And the following morning, even more students poured into the streets, adding their voices to the crescendo of outrage that has roiled the country amid allegations of vote buying by the winning party, election fraud, and ongoing murders of opposition supporters. Honduras's November 24, 2013 election was supposed to have been a signal moment, the first time since the US–backed military coup that citizens had a meaningful opportunity to express their political will.

All signs point to a deepening of the war on drugs in order for the state to maintain control over the people and their movements. During his inauguration speech in January 2014, Honduras's new president, Juan Orlando Hernández, said that approximately 70 percent of homicides in the country are linked to drug trafficking. The reality, however, is otherwise. According to a recent report put out by human rights organizations, only 1 percent of crimes in Honduras are followed up by a police investigation.[54] What Juan Orlando doesn't want to admit is that an important number of killings in Honduras are politically or ideologically motivated attacks on peasants, poor people, political activists, journalists, and queer and trans people. Outside an opulent conference room in the Hotel Maya, the most prestigious accommodation in Tegucigalpa, I spoke with Rossana Guevara, one of Honduras's three new vice presidents, on the day she was elected. Her argument in favor of the presence of US troops in Honduras was blunt in a way that would be considered unacceptable in sovereign countries in most of the world. "They have to fight it; why should we be victims when we aren't even considered a large market for drugs; the main market is North America, so I think they are the ones with a historical responsibility to help fight drug trafficking, and really help, not just with little things," she said. The Pentagon is heeding the call, with new US military bases under construction in various locations in the country.

Regardless of the new opposition force, President Hernández is entrenching the status quo. Similar to recent reforms in Mexico, in Honduras major reforms to the energy sector were undertaken immediately following the elections, before the new government took power. "The outgoing Congress passed the General Law of the Electrical Industry in a single debate on January 20, literally on the eve of the transition of Congress. The law mandates the conversion of the National Electrical Energy Company (ENEE) into a private corporation and then into separate generation, transmission, and distribution companies—all by mid-2015."[55] In addition, the state telephone company, HonduTel, was set on the path to privatization, and a handful of public-private partnerships were announced.

Gang Control and Murders

Tegucigalpa, Honduras's bustling capital, is an example of how modern mafia control functions in the Americas. During the day, there's plenty of activity in the streets, but once night falls the place goes eerily quiet. Taxis, which can be hired as shared vehicles (at about 50¢ a ride) or privately, proliferate. Typically taxi drivers are a source of information only for the laziest of journalists, but in this city, it makes perfect sense to seek out their views. For one thing, taxi drivers are among the only residents who will talk about the gangs, as drivers are required to pay quotas, usually weekly, to either (and sometimes both) the Mara Salvatrucha (MS-13) or the 18 Street Gang (M-18), the two most important street gangs in the city.

Whenever I was alone in a cab, I asked the driver about the quotas. All the drivers were forthcoming, and said the consequence for not paying is simple: death. I met one young driver who paid US$200 a month in extortion, a weekly payment of $25 to each of M-13 and M-18. It was, he said, more than his monthly rent payment. But pay he did, every Saturday, in both of the taxi sites he worked from. Cab drivers are far from the only segment of Honduran society living in fear of street gangs, but they are the only people I met with the privacy to talk about it in their workplaces. Gangs regularly extort small and medium-sized businesses and working people throughout Tegucigalpa and San Pedro Sula, Honduras's second city. People in these environments don't dare to even hint that they're being extorted, for fear they will be overheard. So they pay, and they try to get on with their lives. The biggest shops, US fast food chains and grocery stores, are the only ones that seem to get away without paying the so-called "war tax" to gangs. According to the UN Office on Drugs and Crime, in 2012 there were an estimated 12,000 gang members in Honduras affiliated with MS-13 and M-18.

A critical mass of politicians, prosecutors, and police are in the business themselves, taking a cut of the illicit earnings in return for turning a blind eye to gang activity. Marvin Ponce, the former vice president of Congress, said in 2011 that at least 40 percent of Honduran police are involved in organized crime. A 2014 article in the mainstream Honduran newspaper *El Heraldo* explores the illicit activities of Honduran police, noting that their participation in illicit activity is carried out under the supervision of high-ranking officers. "These public servants put the power, the uniform and the weapons the state gave them to protect the citizenry in the service of the darkest part of drug trafficking and organized crime, in many cases with the complicity and tolerance of the high command."[56] An internal police report released to the media linked officers of various ranks to "drug trafficking, organized crime, money laundering and illicit wealth, the commission of a rosary of crimes including hired killings, kidnappings, assassinations, bank robberies, extortion, selling drugs, drug dealing, car theft, robbery from drug traffickers and congresspeople."[57]

Police are also accused of participation in death squads and in hate crimes against queer and transgendered people. Human Rights Watch points out that "according to local rights advocates, more than 70 members of the lesbian, gay, bisexual, and transgender (LGBT) population were killed between September 2008 and March 2012. The alleged involvement of members of the Honduran police in some of these violent abuses is of particular concern." In addition to the role of police in criminal activity, "the military has been linked to drug trafficking in Honduras since the 1980s, and recent reports suggest some sectors continue to engage in illicit activities."[58] Military-grade arms, like grenades, anti-tank weapons, and assault rifles sold to the Honduran military, have later been seized in the possession of drug runners in Mexico and Colombia.[59]

The pressure that gang and police violence puts on the poor is intense. In 2013, I interviewed a thirty-three-year-old Honduran man, as he sat under a tree beside the railroad tracks in Coatzacoalcos, Veracruz, waiting for a cargo train to take its leave toward the north. He only gave me his first name, Alexander, which he backed up by showing me a battered copy of his student identification. Alexander was leaving a full-time job at a maquiladora in San Pedro Sula, fed up with paying the "war tax" to gang members every week on his $100 weekly salary. Others that I met along the way admitted that part of the reason they were leaving Honduras was because of the violence and extortion. Without remittances from Honduran migrants working outside the country (mostly in the United States), poverty would be much worse, according to Noé, the former finance minister. In 2012, he said, migrants sent home around $2.8 billion; in 2013, $3.15 billion. "That is almost the equivalent of two-thirds of the central government's budget," he told me. Today over 700,000 people of Honduran origin live in the United States; only about two in ten are US citizens. This brings us back to how the discrimination faced by this community in the United States has led Honduras to where it is today.

Gang activity in Honduras has a history that reaches back across the border to the United States. People deported to Central America from the United States initiated both the MS-13 and M-18 gangs. The number of gang members grew dramatically in cities like Tegucigalpa, as a Clinton-era policy of double punishment (deporting undocumented migrants after they'd served a prison sentence, even if they'd spent nearly their whole lives in the United States) came into play in 1996. The imposition of the prison system on jailed youth, followed by deportations, and with increasing poverty, rising unemployment, and the unplanned growth of urban areas in Honduras has swelled the ranks of these groups. This stands out especially in a comparison of gang membership between Honduras, Guatemala, and El Salvador, with Nicaragua. The US Government Accountability Office reports that "Nicaragua has a significant number of gang members, but does not have large numbers of MS-13 or M-18 members, perhaps due to the fact that Nicaragua has had a much lower deportation rate from the United States than the 'northern triangle' countries."

Though far more established than many cartels, street gangs are often portrayed as junior players to Mexican drug trafficking organizations, like Los Zetas. Here's an example, from the United Nations Office on Drugs and Crime: "The Zetas are chronically short of manpower, and so may recruit *mareros* [gang members] with promise, but on an institutional level, they will most likely continue to use the *maras* instrumentally." Being there in Tegucigalpa, trying to do interviews with people about the violence, I couldn't help but notice uncanny similarities between gang-controlled areas and places said to be run by groups like Los Zetas: residents and victims terrorized into silence, the charging of regular extortion payments, the involvement of local police in criminal activities, and surveillance on a street-corner-to-street-corner level. But the Maras have a much longer history than a group like Los Zetas, which has existed as a totally independent organization for less than a decade. In so many ways, it seems like rather than the Zetas attempting to integrate gang members into their membership, it's the Central American street gangs that provide a model for territorial control and for building a long-term economic strategy that is not tied to drug shipments. That said, gangs are also involved in drug trafficking; the UN Office on Drugs and Crime reported in 2012 that drug traffickers in the Aguán region allegedly contracted members of a gang denominated Mara 61 to defend their operations.

In any case, it is gangs and drug traffickers who take the brunt of the blame for violence in Honduras, when economic conditions and the activities of state security forces are major contributors to insecurity. "By blaming urban youth, gangs, and the poor, the state silences other possible definitions of violence that might include critiques of the policies that perpetuate structural violence in the form of extreme inequality," writes scholar Sarah England. "By denying any social or political content to current crime rates and trends, the state can institute such policies as the 'iron-fist,' which allows for arrests without due process of young people who appear to belong to gangs without the public's seeing this as a return to state terrorism."[60] Though England was writing specifically about El Salvador, much of this is true in Honduras and Guatemala as well. The Honduran state has adopted anti-gang legislation that allows police to pre-emptively arrest people based on their social networks, the fact that they have a tattoo, or one of many other subjective accusations left to the discretion of police, prosecutors, and judges. "We passed the 'anti-maras' law. It's actually an illicit association law. What it is, in layman's terms, is conspiracy to commit a crime," Oscar Álvarez, Honduras's former minister of security, told InSight Crime. On October 23, 2013, Honduran military police raided the home of Edwin Espinal, a member of the LIBRE Party and a widely known community activist. The warrant authorizing the raid allowed police to enter Espinal's house to search for drugs and weapons (neither was found during the raid), and specifically mentioned a LIBRE flag in his residence. Activists criticized the government for using drugs as a pretext for political persecution, further pointing to language used in the warrant to evidence their claims.

Rural Violence and Social Control

As I traveled through the interior of Honduras, I was constantly surprised at the large stands of forests and the strong-flowing rivers cutting through the landscape, which stood in stark contrast to the extreme poverty of the urban areas. In some rural areas of the country, things are quieter, and murder and violence is considered a city problem. In others, however, especially where state security forces as well as US forces have been deployed with the stated purpose of fighting against drug trafficking, the sensation of war is present. "Drug trafficking has been a pretext to militarize, because in reality the amount of trafficking hasn't fallen, but because of narco activity there are now military bases in La Mosquitia, for example, and there are more bases than ever. [It's a] US occupation, and narcotrafficking is the pretext," COPINH's Cáceres told me during a short interview in Siguatepeque, a small city in central Honduras. For Cáceres and others involved in struggles against oil drilling, mining companies, hydroelectric projects, wind farms, large-scale forestry, and the exploitation of petrified wood, the militarization of Honduras brings with it direct and deadly consequences. Three of her four children are living outside of the country because of fears for their safety. When I spoke with Cáceres in late 2013, she was keeping a low profile, having been arrested and held on trumped-up charges she described as an attempt to keep her from participating in resistance movements. She was later released, but still had an arrest warrant pending, which has since been dropped.

US assistance to Honduras in combating the drug war has already had deadly consequences, including the 2012 massacre in Ahuas, in the Mosquitia region of Honduras, when four Indigenous people were shot at from a helicopter and killed in an incident overseen by the US DEA. No one denies there are clandestine landing strips in the region that are used by drug traffickers to move their product, but this activity has traditionally taken place on the edges of daily life for most people in the area, who live from fishing, the dangerous practice of lobster diving, and agriculture. Times are changing, however, as drug traffickers begin to take a more active role in displacing people from their lands. According to two journalists who traveled to the Mosquitia region in 2013, drug traffickers are on the front lines of dispossession, forcing local people from their lands. They write: "On our last visits to the region, the dynamics of narco-dispossession were impossible to ignore. Residents recounted story after story of being coerced—by money or violence—to give up their lands. In the Miskitu town of Brus Laguna (population 11,000), for example, few residents plant their fields any more, since most agricultural lands were bought up by a narco. If locals wish to fish in the town's lagoon, they must get traffickers' permission. In another community, a trafficker pressured an Indigenous landowner to sell. When the landowner refused, he was killed by hitmen. His terrorized wife then sold the land at a very low price. In the Río Plátano Biosphere Reserve, whole communities have abandoned their lands following threats from traffickers."[61]

A report written by US solidarity activists who visited Ahuas shortly after the massacre states: "In general, the policy of increased militarization of drug interdiction policies is negatively perceived in the Moskitia region, and places communities already vulnerable due to their isolation and extreme poverty at much greater risk. This is particularly concerning at a time when there is growing focus on the exploitation of natural resources Miskitu communities defend."[62] Following the coup d'état, six military bases were built in Honduras. "One of the bases is in the Moskitia, where President Chávez, may he rest in peace, was planning to work with Honduras on oil extraction; in addition in this area there is natural gas," said Carla García from the Black Fraternal Organization of Honduras (OFRANEH) during a panel on the drug war hosted by the Centre for Constitutional Rights.[63] "Basically this Indigenous community is simply a stone in the shoe of those who want to continue with giving away [the resources]. The United States has always denied the participation of their soldiers in the massacre, but we are victimized because we are poor, because we are Indigenous, and because we are standing in the way of these investments."

Indigenous and campesino peasant movements are the most steadfast sectors of the resistance in Honduras, refusing to bow down even when faced with assassinations, threats, and incarceration. The

Chicago Religious Leadership Network on Latin America released a report documenting 229 politically related murders in Honduras during Porfirio Lobo's presidency.[64] In addition, local campesino organizations calculate that more than 3,000 peasant farmers in Honduras are facing criminal charges linked to land struggles. "After the coup d'état, the Congress and de facto government implemented a series of laws and mechanisms to persecute and criminalize the organizations and spaces that are active in territory struggles … [those] who have used blockades as an alternative in facing down large transnationals and large megaprojects," Aurelio Molina from COPINH told a delegation of US election observers. In addition to the truckloads of soldiers traveling on rural roads and secondary highways, a striking feature of the Honduran countryside is the number of rivers and amount of freshwater in the country: according to Molina, the government of Honduras has handed out a total of 800 mining concessions and 70 dam concessions in rural areas.

One of the most watched rural battles in Honduras is taking place in the lush, forested valleys of the country's midwest, where an Indigenous community's fight against a dam promises to continue. "The Lenca people have taken the decision to defend the Gualcarque River against the construction of a hydroelectric project called Agua Zarca," said Molina, who along with Cáceres and one other faced criminal charges for their efforts to support the community's fight against the dam. Tomás García was killed and another wounded when the army opened fire on the community's blockade in July 2013. In March 2014, García's sister was attacked and wounded by men with machetes, as were her husband and son, who rushed to defend her. When he spoke in November 2013, Molina said he feared the worst was yet to come, saying, "There have been high-level meetings where it has been determined that after the elections they are going to remove us, dead or alive, from Río Blanco so that the hydroelectric project can be built."

Meanwhile, in the fertile Aguán region along the country's north coast, peasant organizations have occupied twenty-six farms on 3,000 hectares of land. The Aguán is a verdant river valley that butts up against the Caribbean Sea. In 2010, more than 2,000 peasant families began to occupy lands granted to them through a government program. By the time I visited in November 2013, 113 participants in the land occupations had been murdered. We entered La Confianza, one of the largest occupations, after a short check by community guards on a hot, humid weekday afternoon. There was a sense of tranquility in the settlement, where residents were beginning to erect concrete houses beside their original houses with roofs and walls of palm. Community members were working to organize into a cooperative to harvest the fruits of the palm plants, but all of this self-organization by marginalized peasant farmers has ruffled palm oil magnate Miguel Facussé's feathers. The region is militarized, in part, under the pretext that the government needs to fight against drug trafficking. It is not uncommon to see civilians bearing arms in Honduras, nor is it illegal, but in the department of Colón, where the Aguán is located, a new law introduced in August of 2012 prevents the carrying of weapons—but it does not apply to police, soldiers, or private security guards. The role of private security cannot be underestimated: the United Nations Working Group on Mercenaries notes that private security guards outnumber police in Honduras five to one.

"Security forces apply the law unequally, criminalizing campesinos while providing protection to local businessmen, some reported to engage in drug trafficking," according to a report by Rights Action, a social justice group with a long history of supporting grassroots struggles in Central America.[65] In this region, there is a blurred line between just who are the police; who are military; and who are private security guards, paramilitaries, or death squad members. One warm afternoon in La Ceiba, part of the same Atlantic region used by drug traffickers, I sat on a large couch facing the wooden desk of the second in command of the National Office of Criminal Investigation (DNIC). As Inspector Miguel Enrique Suazo complained about how his men don't have enough vehicles or equipment to do their jobs, he shuffled the same stack of papers over and over again. Even though we both knew violence related to the drug trade had rocked the region, he casually told me that drug trafficking and violence wasn't much of an issue. As we neared the end of our interview, he leaned forward and said, "If someone goes out drinking every day in the streets, and has a bohemian life, it's not that nothing bad will happen to them." His statement came across as a suggestion that it would be fine by the police if so-called bohemians were killed off on the streets. Maybe he sensed that, and he stopped for a moment before adding: "Not that I am justifying murders."

There are also Honduran special forces, organized into the 15th Battalion and the Joint Task Force Xatruch III, some of whom have been trained by the United States, though it is Colombians who play a prominent role as trainers of private security guards and police in Honduras. "We don't know if they just dress up in the uniforms, or if they are police, or soldiers, or criminals," said Yoni Rivas, a leader of the Unified Campesino Movement of the Aguán who ran unsuccessfully with LIBRE for a Congress seat. I interviewed Rivas in a one-room cement office, the air conditioning working on full against the humid, sunbaked heat. Rivas told me that around sixty men dressed in military uniforms kidnapped one of his comrades. Later, German Alfaro Escalante, who was then the commander of Joint Task Force Xatruch III, said the kidnappers were part of a criminal group. The crossover between soldiers, police, and private security is common in this area. According to the UN Working Group on Mercenaries, the day five people were massacred at the El Tumbador farm, "Members of the 15th Battalion were seen with Orion security guards at the site and some of them reportedly took off their military uniforms and changed into Orion uniforms before the shooting began."[66]

Along with their attacks on members of the land occupations in the Aguán, security forces are accused of participating directly in drug trafficking. Locals say the army participates in drug smuggling up the coast. "In October we were organizing a press conference, and that same day a small airplane supposedly loaded with drugs crash-landed on a clandestine air strip on one of Miguel Facussé's properties. Then twenty-five men, dressed in military fatigues, went in five vehicles, took the drugs, and burned the airplane," said Rivas, who himself has survived five assassination attempts. Reports of military activity in drug trafficking go back to 1978, and investigations by the DEA found army officers participating in trafficking, including in one instance moving fifty tons of cocaine during a fifteen-month period.[67] The US and Honduras governments did little to punish the army's actions, fearing a crackdown could impact the Honduran army's role in supporting Nicaraguan Contras.[68] The United States began using the Soto Cano air force base in central Honduras in the early 1980s, and continued funding the Honduran army even as it was known to participate in trafficking in order to have continued access to the base. To this day, "military officers and their immediate and extended families have formed a powerful elite largely isolated from the rule of law. Accordingly, they have been in a unique position to work closely with traffickers, protecting shipments, carrying drugs in diplomatic pouches, and serving as vital cogs in transshipment schemes."[69]

Amid the confusion and the proliferation of armed actors in Honduras are US soldiers and special forces. US Special Operations Command South operates in the Aguán and other parts of the country, and the US Air Force runs the region's key Southern Command base at Soto Cano, near Tegucigalpa. There are a handful of US bases under construction in Honduras, and funding under the Central America Regional Security Initiative has boosted anti-drugs efforts in Honduras under US watch. In 2014, the State Department requested just over $54 million for Honduras, $5 million of which is specifically meant to finance the military and military training programs. All of these factors together—political violence, gangs, the war on drugs, US military presence, and curtailment of civil rights—have created a maze of militarization and impunities that ultimately results in further barriers for Hondurans living in urban centers and those organizing in rural areas to ensure their continued ability to access clean water, wood from the forests, and meet other needs. It also undermines any attempts at political freedom and it disproportionately impacts the poorest sectors of the population.

THINKING THROUGH PEACE IN WARTIME

THIS book is a sprawling project, and the process of researching and writing has left me with even more questions than I had when I set out on this journey nearly four years ago. This text represents my best attempt to introduce readers to the systems at work when warfare is introduced throughout the hemisphere under the pretext of fighting drugs. Drug war capitalism differs from previous repressive drug war initiatives internationally because it takes place during overarching policy, legislative and foreign aid frameworks enshrined in Plan Colombia, the Mérida Initiative, the Central America Regional Security Initiative, and other state initiatives. Throughout this book, I argue that there are three principal mechanisms through which the drug war advances the interests of neoliberal capitalism: through the imposition of rule of law and policy changes, through formal militarization, and through the paramilitarization that results from it. The violence and forced displacement resulting from the drug war are experienced most acutely by poor and working people and migrants, often in resource rich or geographically strategic areas. Other central impacts of the drug war include restrictions on mobility and harsh limitations on free expression in the media or through public activities and protest. The insights that I have used to guide the process of understanding, theorizing, and writing about drug war capitalism have come through years of conversations and dozens of reporting trips to regions affected by the drug war. They are not mine alone, rather they belong to the many people who have shared their time and space with me over the past four years.

As I neared completion of this book in the spring of 2014, I found that I was meeting more and more people who shared an analysis similar to that included within these pages. The trip I made to Colombia in February of 2014 laid bare the impact of the drug war and Plan Colombia there. The people I interviewed clearly articulated the connections between Plan Colombia and preparing the terrain for foreign direct investment and the extractive industries. A few months later, during a visit to Nuevo Laredo, Mexico, I met a young man who explained how he thought the violence there was related to the eventual exploitation of gas through fracking in the region. It was, he said, the only explanation that he and his friends could come up with for why things had gotten so bad in the border region just south of Laredo, Texas, where the Eagle Ford shale deposit is located. But it was the very last interview I did for the book, with Carlos Fazio, a professor at the Autonomous University of Mexico City (UACM), that helped me summarize some of my own thinking about the issue. Under the bold fluorescent lights of a university conference room, Fazio shared with me his vision of what the drug war represents in Mexico. "I think what is being hidden by this war is a phase of present day imperialism that has to do with displacement, and a form of neo-colonization, which has to do with the appropriation of land and territories, with considering the land as a form of merchandise, and opening that land to industrial agriculture, to the exploitation of African palm and rare wood products, but it also has to do with the land and the subsoil, with mining." This war is about control over territory and society, much more so than it is about cocaine or marijuana.

But voices like Fazio's remain marginal in Mexico and elsewhere, as media discourse and so called experts on the drug war focus almost exclusively on inter-cartel violence and state successes in reigning in criminals. The binary between state and criminals deployed by the media is perhaps the central methodological weakness in press reports and mainstream analysis about the drug war. This binary casts state security forces as legitimate actors for good (bringing security), and highly organized, nefarious drug cartels as completely separate from the state. The image of the benevolent state against the bad drug traffickers provides a frame through which governments can justify rising military spending and attacks on unarmed civilians as necessary for national security. Most journalism fails to make the connections or allow readers to see these events in context, and instead isolates the police officers, soldiers, or bankers and bureaucrats that are discovered facilitating or participating in the activities of criminal groups as bad apples. Social theorist Immanuel Wallerstein writes that if issues like globalization and terrorism are "defined in limited time and scope, we tend to arrive at conclusions that are as ephemeral as the newspapers."[1] This prevents us, he says, from understanding how these themes and events fit into a larger context. I would not hesitate to add the war on drugs to Wallerstein's list, and this book is about attempting to understand this brand of war across time and from a wide analytical scope.

The lines between governments and organized criminal groups are blurred enough to force a complete reassessment of the very categories used to explain what is taking place in Mexico. An alternative framework through which to understand the drug war need not be revolutionary. Acknowledging how and when perpetrators of violence are linked to the state, as well as how structural impunity functions to permit terror and violence would help to clarify what is actually taking place in regions impacted by violence. In doing so, we could begin to escape from the logical and ethical quagmires presented by sticking to the official line on the drug war.

Official discourse in Colombia has shifted toward emphasis on the fact that the country is now in a peace process, that paramilitaries have demobilized, that President Santos is a drug policy reformer, and that the war is as good as over. My reporting in the chapter on Colombia pokes holes in this discourse, but it remains a difficult discourse to counter when the media, think tanks, governments, and elite sectors continue to promote it. When I traveled to Arauca to report on the ongoing violence there, I met with the leaders of an occupation of land belonging to the Colombian Ministry of Defense, who live in a war-like context. "The problem is that Arauca is considered a red zone in Colombia, and any leader who teaches people, who even just teaches them how to go to city hall [to manage their paperwork], that's enough to say they're a guerrilla and hunt them until they kill them," said Jhon Carlos Ariza Aguilar, the vice president of the squatted community of Héctor Alirio Martínez. His words brought me back to a description of the functions of terror in Guatemala, as described by writers Gomis, Romillo, and Rodríguez in the early 1980s.

> With domination through terror, in addition to the physical elimination of those who oppose the interests of the regime, there is also the pursuit of 'the control of a social universe made possible through the intimidation induced by acts of destruction ... (and with) acts of terror there is an overall impact on the social universe,—at a social and generalized level—, of a whole series of

psychosociological pressures which impose an obstacle to possible political action.'[2]

Ariza Aguilar's story reminded me of Francisco Chavira's description of how acts of terror carried out at city halls in Tamaulipas carried a strong message for residents, which was to avoid demanding transparency from local governments.

State and paramilitary terror continues to be used against broad swaths of the population in Mexico, Colombia, Honduras, and Guatemala, as well as in regions outside the scope of this book. Official discourses have begun to shift toward peace and prosperity; the mainstream media and governments would have us believe that peace has been achieved in Colombia and that things have calmed down in Mexico. Anyone taking a longer view, as suggested by Wallerstein, realizes that a city like Juárez, where over 10,000 people were killed in a handful of years, does not simply get better overnight. To begin with, the murders have not stopped, rather they carry on through to today. Then there are tens of thousands of children orphaned by violence, as well as widows who lost their partners and mothers and fathers grieving their murdered children. The near total impunity with which these crimes were committed prevents closure for friends and families of victims. In addition, the underlying social conditions in Juárez, including harsh inequality in the service of multinational corporations, a lack of educational and career opportunities for residents, and safe, regular transportation for workers, have not changed. Though Juárez became the murder capital of the world, it is but one example of a place where peace remains a faraway promise. For Francisco Ramírez, the Colombian union lawyer who investigates links between displacement and corporate activity, the most active voices promoting peace are the ones responsible for disrupting it, and who use it to rebrand their image. "Those who talk about being post-conflict are the intellectual authors of the crimes: the governments of developed countries, the spokespeople for multinationals, the spokespeople for the establishment, etcetera. They talk about being post-conflict, because they want to say to the people, 'Shut your eyes, that is over now, that already happened, we're going to forgive, look at those dogs who did that, we're good people.'"

Untangling hegemonic discourses of peace and prosperity is greatly complicated by self-censorship by members of the press, as well as attacks on journalists. It is hard to know what is taking place in remote and rural areas impacted by the drug war. But getting at the social, political, and economic transformations that accompany drug war policies remains a critical task as these wars drag on. In this respect, this book feels very much like a preliminary work, and hopefully one of many emerging efforts to extend our understanding and analysis of the economic and political factors that drive the drug war. It seems inevitable that over time more evidence of the collusion of corporate interests and drug war capitalism will emerge; in any case it is a constantly evolving story that requires ongoing attention. In June 2014, as I finished the final edits on this text, secondary legislation linked to the energy reforms, which facilitate the expropriation of lands on behalf of energy companies, was approved by Mexico's Senate. The reform was debated for only fifty-five minutes, as World Cup soccer dominated television screens across the nation. According to Senator Alejandro Encinas, "It is a shame that the Senate supports ejido members and community members being obliged to hand over their lands to foreign companies, with the threat that if they don't their lands will be appropriated with great celerity, and on top of that, that they can be paid [for their land] in-kind or via jobs." That this legislation was passed following more than six years of extreme violence and terror is not a mere coincidence. This book is an attempt to explain how the violence of the drug war laid the foundation for the expansion of neoliberal capitalism in Mexico, Central America, and Colombia. I hope it will help to nourish future actions and thinking in defense of the land and of autonomous spaces outside of or in contradiction to capitalism.

The ongoing, daily resistances of communities throughout Mexico, Central America, and Colombia are under attack by the drug war, yet they carry on, day after day. This book may leave some readers filled with a sense of despair or hopelessness, but it would be dishonest to pretend that there is a unified resistance movement taking on the the drug war in the hemisphere. Rather, it is from many autonomies and from many communities that the strongest challenges to capitalism are being mounted. I hope this book incites more meaningful discussions about the drug war and reveals more spaces from which communities as well as allies can fight back.

ACKNOWLEDGMENTS

I first had the idea that I wanted to write *Drug War Capitalism* in late 2010. Since then, I've traveled far and wide, gathering information on the meager income of a freelancer working primarily for alternative media. This book would not have been possible without the generous support of my family, friends, and independent journalists in Canada, the US, Mexico, Guatemala, Honduras, Colombia, and elsewhere. Dozens of people helped in so many ways with this text, and have helped me out immensely over the years. Special thanks are due to Chelsea Elizabeth Manning, whose brave actions provided critical information for this and so many other projects.

Thanks to the crew at AK Press, especially Zach Blue, and my editor Charles Weigl, for believing in this project and helping to improve and shape the final work. Lorna Vetters shone through toward the end of the process with incredibly helpful suggestions. Thanks to Amélie Trudeau, Shannon Young, Isaac Oommen, Stefan Christoff, Sandra Cuffe, Zara Snapp, Luis Solano and especially Myles Estey for their feedback on previous versions of the manuscript. That being said, any mistakes in the book are my own.

Without my friends and colleagues at the Media Co-op and *The Dominion* I wouldn't have made it through; thanks especially to Tim McSorley for being there through thick and thin. Cyril Mychalejko at *Upside Down World* is an encouraging editor and a good friend, and Ben Dangl at *Toward Freedom* shared with me many tips as I wrote and pitched the book. Delores Broten at *Watershed Sentinel*, Mark Karlin at *Truth Out*, and Dianne Feely at *Against the Current* have been incredibly supportive. Thanks to Harsha Walia for her important work, writing, and early support of this book, to Nemer Narchi for believing in my work, and to Anthony Fenton for his critical eye. Nicolas Olucha Sánchez in Berlin has artfully translated an unending stream of my articles over the years. Gracias.

This work was informed by hundreds of chats, discussions, arguments, and otherwise in Mexico City. Luis Arroyo, Gladys Tzul, Dave

O. Mitchell, Daniel Hernández, Laura Carlsen, Andalusia Knoll, Beto Paredes, Clayton Conn, and Pablo Pérez were important sources of friendship, critical thought, advice, and ideas. Thanks to Koko Medina in Chihuahua, Leobardo Alvarado, Héctor Padilla, Connie Gutiérrez, and especially Julián Cardona in Juárez, as well as Molly Molloy in Las Cruces, New Mexico. It deeply saddens me that Charles Bowden passed away suddenly before this book went to print. His support for this project was whole, and made a world of difference. He is deeply missed. Without Francisco Chavira and the families that supported me in Reynosa and Tampico, my reporting in Tamaulipas would not have been possible. Dr. Guadalupe Correa-Cabrera, who wrote the foreword, helped me think through many late night doubts about the nature of events in northern Mexico. Gustavo Castro, Miguel Mijangos, and Ruben Figueroa helped ground my understanding of events in Chiapas, Guerrero, and Tabasco. Bernardo Vásquez in Oaxaca was a key influence in forming my understanding around territory and conflict before he was tragically murdered in March 2012. In Puebla, Dr. Raquel Gutiérrez has been a rock and a role model. I am inordinately excited to be working with her on my next project. Eva Hershaw helped me out in many ways, and is dearly missed in Mexico. Amélie Trudeau and Fallon Poisson have been a source of deep inspiration, as they continue to struggle inside prison walls. Kath, Mau, Dai, Nacho, and Citlali were amazingly patient roomies as I shut myself in to write, day in, day out, for weeks and months. Abraham Muñoz and *la banda* at Surf in Cabo helped me get the fresh air I needed to make this project happen. I owe a very deep thanks to *mis lobas* in Mexico: Zara Snapp, Isis Goldberg, Adriana Paz, Moravia de la O, Mandeep Dhillon, and Juanita Sundberg. You were all there with me through the good times and the bad times too. From the bottom of my heart, thank you for your company and your friendship.

In Guatemala, Luis Solano has been a constant help and encouragement. His work is an inspiration. Through earlier reporting projects in Guate I met photographer James Rodríguez, who has long since become a close friend and colleague. Thanks to Grahame Russell and Nate Einbinder, two of the coolest men I know, for waking up early and staying up late drinking Gallo alongside me in Guatemala and elsewhere over the years. Daniele Volpe was also a great help in Guatemala City. Sandra Cuffe, my partner in crime and frequent co-writer, provided comic relief, and incredible insight on Honduras and life in general. Annie Bird and Karen Spring were both great resources in

Honduras. Thanks to Murray Bush, I'll never think of Tapachula the same way again. In Colombia, Blandine Fuchs at the Red de Hermandad y Solidaridad con Colombia is an outstanding resource and a dear friend. Thanks to Manuel Rozental and Vilma Almendra for the time spent and ideas shared in Cauca, in Canada, and in México. I hope I have more opportunities to work and write together with all of you over the coming years.

Thanks to my friends and co-conspirators in Canada and the US, who never let me feel alone, even on the hardest days of writing and research for this project. In Montréal, Amy Miller, Aaron Lakoff, Andrea Rideout, and the folks at Alma House provided friendship, kitchen table talks, and a safe, welcoming space when I needed it most. Frédéric Dubois, Maya Rolbin-Ghanie, Dru Oja Jay, Arij Riahi, Stefan Christoff, and Shannon Walsh helped me talk through my ideas at various stages of this project. Malcolm Rogge provided warm companionship in Ecuador and in Ontario, and was always ready to discuss a new angle or a complicated problem. My discussions with Egla Martínez Salazar and Jamie Kneen in Ottawa were crucial in informing this project. In Peterborough, Rachelle Sauvé is a permanent inspiration. In Toronto, Justin Podur provided invaluable insight at the beginning of the writing process, as did Naomi Klein. In the Bay Area, Isabeau Doucet and David Zlutnik have been solid co-conspirators, in addition to being all-around inspiring, and the Institute for Anarchist Studies provided a small grant toward part of the research in the Honduras chapter.

In Vancouver, occupied Coast Salish Territories, where I have spent a good part of the last decade, I am incredibly blessed to have many friends, allies and longtime supporters. First off, thanks to all the brave people who took a stand against the 2010 Olympics in Vancouver. The organizing and friendships fostered in the lead-up to those protests planted in me the seeds of anarchy and rebellion, which are still growing. To my habibi Isaac Oommen, shukran for everything we have shared. I am lucky to have had many conversations with brilliant thinkers and organizers like Swathi Lakshmi, Gord Hill, Macdonald Stainsby, and Harjap Grewal. Thanks to Freda Huson, Dini Togestiy, Mel Bazil, Ambrose Williams, and all the folks at the Unist'ot'en Camp, who teach not only through words but through powerful actions. Ann and Emma Turner, Darius Kinney, Janice Westlund, and Dave Turner have fostered in me a spirit of justice and friendship since I can remember. Carel Moiseiwitsch has been a mentor and a dear friend, and has helped me become a stronger writer and a more ba-dass woman. Sara Kendall and Margo Chapman Kendall repeatedly opened their homes and their hearts to me as I completed the man-uscript. Megan H. Stewart was a crucial confidante and a wonderful host during many of my visits to Vancouver. Donald McPherson at the Canadian Drug Policy Coalition was an early supporter of the project. Dr. Mary Lynn Young of UBC Journalism has been an ongoing advo-cate for my work over the years, as has David Beers, who is a master storyteller. Thanks to everyone who came to the East Van *tertulia*; your presence, encouragement, and ideas made finishing this book possible. Extra special thanks are due to Marla Renn and Ahseea Ahmed, who contributed so generously to this project, and who I love dearly.

This book would never, ever have been possible without the life-long, ongoing support of my parents, Valerie and Larry Paley, and my brother, William Paley. The discipline of hard work and intense play, and the spirit of adventure and curiosity that all three of them instilled in me is what pushed me to become a writer, and to try to understand the world around me. To them, my deepest gratitude is due.

NOTES

FOREWORD

1   Karl Marx, *Critique of the Gotha Program*, Marxist Internet Archive, accessed August 15, 2014, https://www.marxists.org/archive/marx/works/1875/gotha/ch01.htm.
2   Ibid.
3   Interview with Richard Heffner on *The Open Mind* television program, December 7, 1975.
4   Bertrand Russell, "Freedom in Society," *Harper's Magazine*, 1926, 33.

CHAPTER I: DRUG WAR CAPITALISM

1   Inter-American Commission on Human Rights, "Case No. 12.416 Santo Domingo Massacre Colombia." Inter-American Commission on Human Rights, 14, https://www.cidh.oas.org/demandas/12.416ENG.pdf.
2   Ibid., 11.
3   Christian T. Miller, "A Colombian Town Caught in the Crossfire," *Los Angeles Times*, March 17, 2002, http://articles.latimes.com/2002/mar/17/news/mn-33272/3.
4   Ibid.
5   InfoMil Prensa, "Aeronaves de Inteligencia en Colombia: C-337 Skymaster," http://www.webinfomil.com/2012/05/aeronaves-de-inteligencia-en-colombia-c.html.
6   Mats Berdal and David M. Malone, introduction to *Greed & Grievance: Economic Agendas in Civil Wars*, eds. Mats Berdal and David M. Malone (Boulder: Lynne Rienner, 2000), http://web.idrc.ca/openebooks/421-5/.
7   Ibid.
8   "Cartel," *New Oxford American Dictionary*, http://www.oxforddictionaries.com/us/definition/american_english/cartel.
9   Marcus Rediker and Peter Linebaugh, *The Many-Headed Hydra: Sailors, Slaves, Commoners and the Hidden History of the Revolutionary Atlantic* (Boston: Beacon Press, 2000), 53.
10 D. Hernández, "Calderón's War on Drug Cartels: A Legacy of Blood and Tragedy," *Los Angeles Times*, December 1, 2012, http://articles.latimes.com/2012/dec/01/world/la-fg-wn-mexico-calderon-cartels-20121130.
11 Raul Zibechi, *Territories in Resistance: A Cartography of Latin American Social Movements* (Oakland: AK Press, 2012), 39.
12 David Harvey, *Spaces of Global Capitalism* (New York: Verso, 2006), 91.
13 David Harvey, *A Brief History of Neoliberalism* (Oxford: Oxford University

Press, 2005), 159.

14 Doug Stokes, *America's Other War: Terrorizing Colombia* (London: Zed Books, 2013), 121.

15 John McCain, "Speech by Sen. John McCain (R-Arizona)," June 6, 2002, http://archive.is/WNO9d#selection-273.112-273.469.

16 Jasmin Hristov, *Blood and Capital: The Paramilitarization of Colombia* (Toronto: Between the Lines, 2009).

17 Laleh Khalili, "The Location of Palestine in Global Counterinsurgencies," *International Journal of Middle East Studies* 42, no. 13 (2010): 413–414.

18 Consulate Monterrey, "Mexico: Tracking Narco-grenades," March 3, 2009, http://cablegatesearch.net/cable.php?id=09MONTERREY100#para -3961-4.

19 Dawn Paley, "Strategies of a New Cold War," *Toward Freedom*, December 20, 2012, http://www.towardfreedom.com/31-archives/americas/2997-strategies-of-a-new-cold-war-us-marines-and-the-drug-war-in-guatemala.

20 Naomi Klein, *The Shock Doctrine: The Rise of Disaster Capitalism* (Toronto: Knopf, 2007), 248–249.

21 Donna Chollett, "From Sugar to Blackberries: Restructuring Agro-export Production in Michoacán, Mexico," *Latin American Perspectives* 36, no. 3 (May 2009): 79.

22 Tom Barry, *Zapata's Revenge: Free Trade and the Farm Crisis in Mexico* (Boston: South End Press, 1995), 43.

23 Judith Teichman, *Privatization and Political Change in Mexico* (Pittsburgh: University of Pittsburgh, Digital Research Library, 2009), http://digital. library.pitt.edu/cgi-bin/t/text/text-idx?idno=31735055592376;view=toc;c= pittpress.

24 Juan Carlos Moreno-Bird, "La Economía Mexicana Frente a la Crisis Internacional," *Nueva Sociedad* 220 (March–April 2009): 64.

25 Petro Strategies Inc., "World's Largest Oil and Gas Companies," http://www. petrostrategies.org/Links/worlds_largest_oil_and_gas_companies.htm.

26 S. McCrummen, "Mexican President Proposes Historic Changes to State-owned Pemex Oil Monopoly," *Washington Post,* August 12, 2013, http:// www.washingtonpost.com/world/mexican-president-proposes-historic -changes-to-state-owned-pemex-oil-monopoly/2013/08/12/7f848d4c-0380- 11e3-bfc5-406b928603b2_story.html.

27 Carlos Slim, "5. ¿Es cierto que Carlos Salinas de Gortari le vendió Telmex a cambio de un favor?," http://www.carlosslim.com/05.html.

28 U.S. State Department, "08MEXICO2187, Who Are Mexico's Wealthiest Business Leaders?," July 16, 2008, http://wikileaks.org/cable/2008/07/ 08MEXICO2187.html#par21.

29 The bone-dry border region near Tucson, Arizona is, the single deadliest area for migrants—6,029 of whom died attempting to cross the Southwest border between 1998 and 2014, according to the US Customs and Border Patrol.

30 Elinor Comlay, "Mexico Becoming Nissan's Export Hub for Americas: CEO," Reuters, November 12, 2013, http://www.reuters.com/article/2013/11/13/us-autos-mexico-nissan-idUSBRE9AC03G20131113.

31 IDMC, "Briefing Paper by the Norwegian Refugee Council's Internal Displacement Monitoring Centre on Forced Displacement in Mexico Due to Drug Cartel Violence," December 2010, http://internal-displacement.org/p. 1briefing/mexico/.

32 William I. Robinson, *Promoting Polyarchy: Globalization, US Intervention and Hegemony* (Cambridge: Cambridge University Press, 1996), 33.

33 William I. Robinson, *Latin America and Global Capitalism: A Critical Globalization Perspective* (Baltimore: The Johns Hopkins University Press, 2008), 15.

34 Molly Molloy, "Q & A with Frontera List's Molly Molloy," *Frontera List*, August 22, 2014, http://fronteralist.org/2014/08/22/q-a-with-frontera-lists-molly-molloy/.

35 US Department of Defense, "News Transcript," March 27, 2012, http://www.defense.gov/transcripts/transcript.aspx?transcriptid=5000.

36 William Booth and Nick Miroff, "Mexico's Drug War is at a Stalemate as Calderón's Presidency Ends," *Washington Post*, November 27, 2012, http://www.washingtonpost.com/world/the_americas/calderon-finishes-his-six-year-drug-war-at-stalemate/2012/11/26/82c90a94-31eb-11e2-92f0-496af208bf23_story.html.

37 Instituto Nacional de Estadística y Geografía, "Boletín de Prensa núm. 288/13," July 30, 2013, http://www.inegi.org.mx/inegi/contenidos/espanol/prensa/Boletines/Boletin/Comunicados/Especiales/2013/julio/comunica9.pdf.

38 Georgina Saldierna, "Van 21 mil homicidios dolosos este sexenio," *La Jornada*, March 1, 2014, http://www.jornada.unam.mx/2014/03/01/politica/012n2pol.

39 SEGOB, "PROGRAMA Nacional de Derechos Humanos 2014–2018," April 30, 2014, http://www.dof.gob.mx/nota_detalle.php?codigo=5343071&fecha=30/04/2014.

40 INEGI, "Encuesta Nacional de Victimización y Percepción sobre Seguridad Pública 2013 (ENVIPE)," September 30, 2013, http://www.inegi.org.mx/inegi/contenidos/espanol/prensa/boletines/boletin/comunicados/especiales/2013/septiembre/comunica15.pdf., 21.

41 CNDH, "Informe Especial sobre secuestro de migrantes en México," February 2011, http://www.cndh.org.mx/sites/all/fuentes/documentos/informes/especiales/2011_secmigrantes_0.pdf, 12.

42 Movimiento Migrante Mesoamericano, "Caravana de Madres Centroamericanas 2012," October 9, 2012, http://www.movimientomigrantemesoamericano.org/caravana-de-madres-centroamericanas-2012-2/.

43 Instituto Nacional de Estadística y Geografia, "Índice de percepción sobre la seguridad pública: Cifras durante diciembre de 2011," January 5, 2012, http://www.inegi.org.mx/inegi/contenidos/espanol/prensa/Boletines/Boletin/Comunicados/Percepci%F3n%20sobre%20Seguridad%20P%FAblica/2012/enero/comunica.pdf.

44 UNODC, "Global Study on Homicide, 2011," 2011, http://www.unodc.org/documents/data-and-analysis/statistics/Homicide/Globa_study_on_homicide_2011_web.pdf, 23.

45 Melissa Dell, "Tracking Networks and the Mexican Drug War," December 2012, http://scholar.harvard.edu/files/dell/files/121113draft.pdf, 2.

46 Ibid., 3.

47 Ioan Grillo, *El Narco: Inside Mexico's Criminal Insurgency* (New York: Bloomsbury, 2011), 61.

48 Univision, "Los cárteles se multiplicaron en la sexenio de Calderón, dice fiscal," December 20, 2012, http://noticias.univision.com/narcotrafico/noticias/article/2012-12-19/los-carteles-se-multiplicaron-en-sexenio-de-calderon#axzz2FdDn53NS.

49 The collaboration of local police forces and the army with Zetas and other cartels can take numerous forms, which will be examined later in the text. In Guatemala, the funeral of José Luis Fernández Ligorría provides an example of high-level state authorities' recognition of Zetas: Fernández himself was the leader of the Zetas before his death, and at his funeral in January 2011, Otto Pérez Molina's minister of government, Mauricio López Bonilla, gave the eulogy and presented Fernández's widow with a commemorative beret from the Kaibil elite special forces.

50 As an example, take the municipal police force of San Fernando, Tamaulipas, whose members are accused of protecting the Zetas while they pulled passengers from buses, murdered them, and buried them in mass graves. Rubén Mosso, "Detienen a 16 policías por proteger matanzas de Los Zetas en San Fernando," *Milenio*, April 13, 2011, http://www.entretodos.com.mx/notacompleta.php?id=57608.

51 Yolanda Figueroa, *El Capo del Golfo: Vida y captura de Juan García Abrego* (Mexico: Avelar Editores, 1996), 137. Figueroa, her husband, and their three children were murdered less than six months after her book was released.

52 Gary Fields, "White House Czar Calls for End to 'War on Drugs'," *Wall Street Journal*, May 14, 2009, http://online.wsj.com/news/articles/SB124225891527617397.

53 Embassy Mexico, "Ambassador's Private Dinner With President-elect Calderon," September 29, 2006, https://cablegatesearch.wikileaks.org/cable.php?id=06MEXICO5607#para-4964-1.

54 Colleen Cook, Rebecca Rush, and Clare Ribando Seelke, "Mérida Initiative: Proposed U.S. Anticrime and Counterdrug Assistance for Mexico and Central America," *Congressional Research Service*, March 18, 2008, http://fpc.state.gov/documents/organization/103694.pdf, 1.

55 ECLAC, "Statistical Yearbook for Latin America and the Caribbean, 2011," United Nations, http://www.eclac.cl/publicaciones/xml/7/45607/LCG2513b.pdf, 81.

56 Shannon O'Neill, "Refocusing U.S.-Mexico Security Cooperation," *Council on Foreign Relations*, June 18, 2013, http://www.foreign.senate.gov/imo/media/doc/ONeil_Testimony.pdf.

57 William Brownfield, "Remarks at the Council of the Americas," March 22, 2013, http://www.state.gov/j/inl/rls/rm/2013/207231.htm.

58 John Feeley, "U.S.-Mexico Security Cooperation: An Overview of the Mérida Initiative, 2008–Present," May 13, 2013, http://docs.house.gov/meetings/FA/FA07/20130523/100907/HHRG-113-FA07-20130523-SD001.pdf, 2. Clare Ribando Seelke, "Mérida Initiative for Mexico and Central America: Funding and Policy Issues," Congressional Research Service, April 19, 2010, http://fpc.state.gov/documents/organization/141560.pdf.

59 Hristov, *Blood and Capital*, 202.

60 Sharon Ennis, Merarys Ríos-Vargas, and Nora Albert, "U.S. Census Bureau: The Hispanic Population, 2010 Census Briefs," May 2011, http://www.census.gov/prod/cen2010/briefs/c2010br-04.pdf.

61 Stop the Injunctions Coalition, "Our Oakland, Our Solutions," in *Life During Wartime: Resisting Counterinsurgency*, eds. Kristian Williams, Lara Messersmith-Glavin, and William Munger (Oakland: AK Press, 2013), 150.

62 Dawn Paley, "Interview: Dr. William I. Robinson on Power, Domination and Conflicts in Mexico," *Upside Down World*, December 7, 2010,

http://upsidedownworld.org/main/mexico-archives-79/2811-interview-dr
-william-i-robinson-on-power-domination-and-conflicts-in-mexico.

63 Equipo Bourbaki, "El Costo Humano de la Guerra por la Construction
del Monopolio del Narcotrafico en Mexico, 2008–2009," February 2011,
http://redporlapazyjusticia.org/directorioinfo/InformeBourbaki.pdf.

64 Howard Campbell, *Drug War Zone: Frontline Dispatches From the Streets
of El Paso and Juárez* (Austin: University of Texas Press, 2009), 6.

65 Dawn Paley, "Insight Crime & the Mexicanization of Cartel War Discourse," March 11, 2013, http://dawnpaley.tumblr.com/post/45119662682/
insight-crime-the-mexicanization-of-cartel-war.

66 In 2011, two people in Veracruz were charged with terrorism for their
Twitter and Facebook status updates, in which they mistakenly reported
a hostage-taking at a school. Charges against them were later dropped.
BBC News, "Mexico 'Twitter terrorism' Charges Dropped," September 22,
2011, http://www.bbc.co.uk/news/world-latin-america-15010202.

67 Carlos Lauría and Mike O'Conner, "Silence or Death in Mexico's Press:
Cartel City," Committee to Protect Journalists, September 8, 2010, http://
cpj.org/reports/2010/09/silence-death-mexico-press-cartel-city.php.

68 Articulo 19, *Informe 2013,* March 2014, http://www.articulo19.org/
wp-content/uploads/2014/03/Art19_Informe2013web.pdf, 30.

69 Redacción, "Panismo: 102 periodistas asesinados o desaparecidos," *Con-
tralínea,* September 13, 2011, http://contralinea.info/archivo-revista/index.
php/2011/09/13/panismo-102-periodistas-asesinados-o-desaparecidos/.

70 Committee to Protect Journalists, "Getting Away With Murder: CPJ's 2013
Impunity Index," May 2, 2013, https://www.cpj.org/reports/impunity_index
2013.pdf.

71 Hristov, *Blood and Capital,* 27. Stratfor was hacked, and five million internal emails were released to Wikileaks in early 2012. "The most striking revelation from the latest disclosure is not simply the military-industri-
al complex that conspires to spy on citizens, activists and trouble-causers,
but the extremely low quality of the information available to the highest
bidder," wrote Pratap Chatterjee ("WikiLeaks' Stratfor Dump Lifts Lid
on Intelligence-industrial Complex," *Guardian,* February 28, 2012, http://
www.guardian.co.uk/commentisfree/cifamerica/2012/feb/28/wikileaks
-intelligence-industrial-complex.

72 As students at the Masters in Journalism program at the University of British Columbia, we were taught once and again that statements from police
and officials are key primary sources—enough to anchor a story on. During
a brief stint at the *Globe and Mail,* Canada's paper of record, I was made
aware that police press releases were akin to gospel—not to be questioned
or fact-checked before being reformatted and printed in the newspaper. The
status quo media's reliance on police and official sources, combined with
threats, harassment, or elimination of journalists and photographers who
dare operate outside this discourse ensure a near-picture-perfect reproduc-
tion of the official line on the drug war.

73 German Alfonso Palacio Castañeda, "Institutional Crisis, Parainstitutionality, and Regime Flexibility in Colombia: The Place of Narcotraffic and
Counterinsurgency," in *Vigilantism and the State in Modern Latin America: Essays on Extralegal Violence,* ed. Martha Huggins (Portsmouth, NH:
Greenwood Publishing Group, 1991), 108.

74 Bureau of Western Hemisphere Affairs, "The Central America Regional Security Initiative: A Shared Partnership," April 25, 2013, http://www.state.gov/p/wha/rls/fs/2013/208592.htm.

75 The Caribbean Basin Security Initiative (CBSI) covers Antigua and Barbuda, the Bahamas, Barbados, Belize, Dominica, the Dominican Republic, Grenada, Guyana, Haiti, Jamaica, Montserrat, Saint Lucia, St. Kitts and Nevis, St. Vincent and the Grenadines, Suriname, and Trinidad and Tobago.

76 Gian Carlo Delgado-Ramos and Silvina Maria Romano, "Political-Economic Factors in U.S. Foreign Policy: The Colombia Plan, the Mérida Initiative, and the Obama Administration," *Latin American Perspectives* 38, no. 4 (July 2011): 93, 94.

77 Executive Office of the President of the United States, "National Drug Control Strategy, 2012," http://www.whitehouse.gov/sites/default/files/ondcp/2012_ndcs.pdf 32.

78 Correo, "Destinarán US$ 300 millones a lucha contra terrorismo y narcotráfico," *Diario Correo*, December 19, 2012, http://diariocorreo.pe/movil/ultimas/noticias/2732815/edicion+lima/destinaran-us-300-millones-a-lucha-contra-t.

79 Charlie Savage and Thom Shankar, "U.S. Drug War Expands to Africa, a Newer Hub for Cartels," *New York Times*, July 21, 2012, http://www.nytimes.com/2012/07/22/world/africa/us-expands-drug-fight-in-africa.html?_r=0.

CHAPTER 2: DEFINING THE DRUG WAR

1   Julia Buxton, *The Political Economy of Narcotics: Production, Consumption & Global Markets* (Black Point, NS: Fernwood Publishing, 2006), 62.

2   David Courtwright, *Dark Paradise: A History of Opiate Addiction in America* (Cambridge: Harvard University Press, 2001), 163.

3   Matthew Robinson and Renee Scherlen, *Lies, Damned Lies, and Drug War Statistics* (Albany: State University of New York Press, 2007), 25.

4   "Historians agree that efforts to limit opium smoking grew out of an effort to control Chinese immigrants and their influence on (white) Americans." Ibid., 20.

5   Drug Enforcement Administration, "DEA History," http://www.justice.gov/dea/about/history.shtml.

6   Beriah Empie and Lydia Anne Bartholow, "Raze the Walls," in *Life During Wartime*, 189.

7   Courtwright, *Dark Paradise*, 168.

8   Ibid., 165.

9   Buxton, *The Political Economy of Narcotics*, 61.

10 Ibid.

11 Kate Doyle, "Operation Intercept: The Perils of Unilateralism," National Security Archive, April 13, 2003, http://www2.gwu.edu/~nsarchiv/NSAEBB/NSAEBB86/.

12 Ibid.

13 Ted Carpenter, "Bad Neighbor Policy: Washington's Futile War on Drugs in Latin America," (Basingstoke, UK: Palgrave, 2003), 29.

14 Ibid., 37.

15 Robinson and Scherlen, *Lies, Damned Lies, and Drug War Statistics*, 31 (emphasis in original).

16 John Gibler, *To Die in Mexico: Dispatches from Inside the Drug War* (San Francisco: City Lights Books, 2011), 43.

17 Michelle Alexander, *The New Jim Crow: Mass Incarceration in the Age of Colorblindness* (New York: New Press, 2010), 15.

18 Federal Bureau of Prisons, "Offenses," February 22, 2014, http://www.bop. gov/about/statistics/statistics_inmate_offenses.jsp.

19 Drug Enforcement Administration, "A Tradition of Excellence: 1970–1975," http://www.justice.gov/dea/about/history/1970-1975.pdf.

20 Drug Enforcement Administration, "DEA History."

21 Amy Goodman, "'Drugs Aren't the Problem': Neuroscientist Carl Hart on Brain Science & Myths About Addiction," *Democracy Now!*, http://www. democracynow.org/2014/1/6/drugs_arent_the_problem_neuroscientist_carl.

22 John Strang, Thomas Babor, Jonathan Caulkins, et al. "Drug Policy and the Public Good: Evidence for Effective Interventions," *The Lancet* 379, no. 9810 (January 7, 2012): 71–83, www.thelancet.com/pdfs/journals/lancet/PIIS0140673611616747.pdf.

23 Paul Gootenberg, "Talking About the Flow: Drugs, Borders, and the Discourse of Drug Control," *Cultural Critique* 71 (Winter 2009): 36–37.

24 Holder, Eric. "Retroactive Application of Department Policy on Changing Mandatory Minimum Sentences and Recidivist Enhancements in Certain Drug Cases." Office of the Attorney General. August 29, 2013. http://www.fd.org/docs/select-topics/sentencing-resources/august-29-2013-holder-memo-on-retroactivity-of-mandatory-minimum-charging-policy.pdf?sfvrsn=4.

25 Evan Munsing and Christopher Lamb, "Joint Interagency Task Force–South: The Best Known, Least Understood Interagency Success," *Institute for National Strategic Studies, Strategic Perspectives* 5 (July 2011), http://www.ndu.edu/press/lib/pdf/strategic-perspectives/Strategic-Perspectives-5.pdf, 7–8.

26 Paley, Dawn. "Repressive Memories: Terror, Insurgency and the Drug War." *Occupied London*. Fall, 2013. dawnpaley.ca/2013/10/27/repressive-memories-terror-insurgency-and-the-drug-war/.

27 David Courtwright, *Forces of Habit: Drugs and the Making of the Modern World*, (Cambridge: Harvard University Press, 2001), 3.

28 Ibid., 4–5.

29 Paul Gootenberg, "Talking About the Flow," 16.

30 Ibid.

31 Ibid., 21.

32 Paul Gootenberg, "Cocaine in Chains," in *From Silver to Cocaine: Latin American Commodity Chains and the Building of the World Economy, 1500–2000*, eds. Steven Topik, Carlos Marichal, and Zephyr Frank (Durham: Duke University Press, 2006), 323.

33 Courtwright, *Forces of Habit*, 34.

34 Peter Andreas, "Illicit Globalization: Myths, Misconceptions, and Historical Lessons," *Political Science Quarterly* 126, no. 3 (2011): 7.

35 Ibid., 8.

36 Gootenberg, "Cocaine in Chains," 330.

37 Ibid., 325.

38 Ibid., 329.

39 Courtwright, *Forces of Habit*, 78.

40 Joseph Spillane, "Making a Modern Drug: The Manufacture, Sale, and

Control of Cocaine in the United States, 1880–1920," in *Cocaine: Global Histories*, ed. Paul Gootenberg (London: Routledge, 1999), 21.

41 Patrick O'Day, "Mexican Army as Cartel," *Journal of Contemporary Criminal Justice* 17, no. 3 (2001): 284.

42 Ibid., 286.

43 Drug Enforcement Administration, "A Tradition of Excellence."

44 Ibid.

45 Ibid.

46 Ioan Grillo, *El Narco*, 49.

47 Ibid.

48 Moritz Tenthoff, "Coca, Petroleum and Conflict in Cofán Territory," *Transnational Institute*, Drug Policy Briefing #23, September 2007, http://www.tni.org/sites/www.tni.org/files/download/brief23.pdf, 2.

49 Asociación de familiares de detenidos, desaparecidos, *Colombia, nunca más: Crímenes de lesa humanidad* Zona 14a 1966, Tomo 1 (Bogata: Asfaddes, 2000), 117.

50 Peter Andreas, "Illicit Globalization," 5.

51 Oeindrila Dube, Omar García-Ponce, and Kevin Thom, "From Maize to Haze: Agricultural Shocks and the Growth of the Mexican Drug Sector," February 2014, http://www.cgdev.org/sites/default/files/maize-haize-agricultural-shocks-growth-mexican-drug-sector_0.pdf.

52 Peter Dale Scott, *Drugs, Oil and War: The US In Afghanistan, Colombia and Indochina* (Oxford: Bowman & Littlefield Publishers, 2003), 75.

53 Arthur Benavie, "Drugs: America's Holy War," (London: Routledge, 2009), 37.

54 John Kelly, "Posture Statement of General John F. Kelly, United States Marine Corps Commander, United States Southern Command: Before the 113th Congress House Armed Services Committee," February 26, 2014, http://www.southcom.mil/newsroom/Documents/2014_SOUTHCOM_Posture_Statement_HASC_FINAL_PDF.pdf, 6.

55 Ibid., 7.

56 Natalie Southwick, "Venezuela Destroys 17 Cocaine Labs Near Colombia Border," *InSight Crime*, October 23, 2013, http://www.insightcrime.org/news-briefs/venezuela-destroys-17-cocaine-labs-near-colombia-border.

CHAPTER 3: A LOOK SOUTH TO COLOMBIA

1 Consejo Municipal de Recetor, "Acuerdo No. 007," August 24, 2011, http://cdim.esap.edu.co/BancoMedios/Documentos%20PDF/recetorcasanarepiu20082011.pdf, 22.

2 Fabian Laverde Doncel, "Perfiles de algunos municipios de la zona," in *Casanare: exhumando el genocidio*, ed. Javier Giraldo Moreno (Colombia: Editorial Códice, 2009), 68.

3 Scott, *Drugs, Oil and War*, 75.

4 Ibid., 74.

5 William O. Walker, *Drug Control in the Americas* (Albuquerque: University of New Mexico Press, 1989), 221.

6 Noam Chomsky, *Rogue States* (Cambridge, MA: South End Press, 2000), 62.

7 Forrest Hylton, "Plan Colombia: The Measure of Success," *Brown Journal of World Affairs* 17, no. 1 (2010), http://democracyinamericas.org/pdfs/Hylton.pdf.

8   Peter Chalk, *The Latin American Drug Trade: Scope, Dimensions, Impact and Response* (RAND Corporation [Project Air Force], 2011), 89. http://www.rand.org/content/dam/rand/pubs/monographs/2011/ RAND_MG1076.pdf.

9   US Government Accountability Office, "PLAN COLOMBIA: Drug Reduction Goals Were Not Fully Met, but Security Has Improved; US Agencies Need More Detailed Plans for Reducing Assistance," October 2008, http://www.gao.gov/new.items/d0971.pdf, 17.

10 Dana Priest, "Covert Action in Colombia," *The Washington Post*, December 13, 2013, http://www.washingtonpost.com/sf/investigative/2013/12/21/covert-action-in-colombia/.

11 Oeindrilla Dube and Suresh Naidu, *Bases, Bullets and Ballots: The Effects of U.S. Military Aid on Political Conflict in Colombia*, December 2013, https://files.nyu.edu/od9/public/papers/Dube_bases_bullets.pdf, 2.

12 Alvaro Sierra, "Seis miliones de victimas y contando," *Semana*. February 6, 2014, http://www.semana.com/nacion/multimedia/seis-millones-de-victimas-contando/376351-3.

13 Hugh O'Shaunessy, "Colombia: Chemical Spraying of Coca Poisoning Villages," *The Observer*, June 17, 2001, http://www.corpwatch.org/article.php?id=11081.

14 Santos was elected for a second term in June 2014.

15 Juan Forero, "Congress Approves Doubling U.S. Troops in Colombia to 800," *New York Times*. October 11, 2004, http://www.nytimes.com/2004/10/11/international/americas/11colombia.html.

16 United Nations Human Rights Council, "Promotion and Protection of All Human Rights, Civil, Political, Economic, Social and Cultural Rights, Including the Right to Development," February 16, 2009, http://www2.ohchr.org/english/bodies/hrcouncil/docs/10session/A.HRC.10.21.Add3.pdf, 17.

17 Verdad Abierta. "Estadísticas Parapolítica." February 2013. http://www.verdadabierta.com/cifras/3826-estadisticas-parapolitica.

18 Nick Reding, *Methland: The Death and Life of an American Small Town*, (New York: Bloomsbury, 2009), 157.

19 Ibid.

20 Hristov, *Blood and Capital*.

21 Inter-American Court of Human Rights, "Case of the 'Mapiripán Massacre' v. Colombia: Judgment of September 15, 2005," http://www.corteidh.or.cr/docs/casos/articulos/seriec_134_ing.pdf, 37.

22 Ibid., 38.

23 Javier Giraldo, *Colombia: Genocidal Democracy* (Monroe, ME: Common Courage Press, 1996), 17.

24 Castañeda Palacios, "Institutional Crisis, Parainstitutionality, and Regime Flexibility in Colombia," in *Vigilantism and the State in Modern Latin America*, 110.

25 Ibid.

26 Ibid.

27 Jaun Diego E. Restrepo, "Álvaro Uribe, entre las 'Convivir' y las AUC," *Semana*, September 19, 2013, http://www.semana.com/opinion/articulo/alvaro-uribe-entre-convivir-las-auc-opinion-juan-diego-restrepo/358144-3.

28 U.S. Government Accountability Office, "Drug Control: US Counternarcotics Efforts in Colombia Face Continuing Challenges," February 1998, http://www.gao.gov/archive/1998/ns98060.pdf, 6.

29 Ibid., 28.

30 Bureau of Western Hemisphere Affairs, "The Colombia Strategic Development Initiative (CSDI)," April 12, 2012, http://www.state.gov/p/wha/rls/fs/2012/187926.html.

31 US Government Accountability Office, "PLAN COLOMBIA: Drug Reduction Goals Were Not Fully Met," 17.

32 Ibid., 4.

33 Just the Facts, "Grant Aid to Colombia through International Narcotics Control and Law Enforcement," http://justf.org/Program_Detail?program=International _Narcotics_Control_and_Law_Enforcement&country=Colombia. Bureau of International Narcotics and Law Enforcement, "2012 INCSR: Country Reports—Colombia," March 7, 2012, http://www.state.gov/j/inl/rls/nrcrpt /2012/vol1/184098.htm#Colombia.

34 David Maher and Andrew Thomson, "The Terror That Underpins the 'Peace': The Political Economy of Colombia's Paramilitary Demobilisation Process," *Critical Studies on Terrorism* 4, no. 1 (2011): 96.

35 Geoff Simons, *Colombia: A Brutal History* (London: Saqi Books, 2004), 322.

36 María Victoria Uribe, "Dismembering and Expelling: Semantics of Political Terror in Colombia," *Public Culture* 16, no. 1 (2004), 91.

37 Ibid., 80.

38 Ana Maria Ibánez and Carlos Eduardo Vélez, "Civil Conflict and Forced Migration: The Micro Determinants and Welfare Losses of Displacement in Colombia," *World Development* 36, no. 4 (2008): 661.

39 Alvaro Sierra, "Seis millones de victimas y contando," *Semana*, February 6, 2014, http://www.semana.com/nacion/multimedia/seis-millones-de-victimas -contando/376351-3.

40 Camilo Olarte, "La Guerra y la desmemoria en Colombia," *America Economía*, January 21, 2014, http://www.americaeconomia.com/analisis -opinion/la-guerra-y-la-desmemoria-en-colombia

41 Maher and Thomson, "The Terror that Underpins the 'Peace,'" 96.

42 United Nations Human Rights Council, "Promotion and Protection of All Human Rights, 12.

43 National Security Archive, "The Chiquita Papers," April 7, 2011, http:// www.gwu.edu/~nsarchiv/NSAEBB/NSAEBB340/index.html.

44 Inter-American Court of Human Rights, "Case of the 'Mapiripán Massacre' v. Colombia," 45.

45 Ibid., 47.

46 Ibid., 44.

47 Comisión Intereclesial de Justicia y Paz, "Colombia: Banacol, empresa implicada en paramilitarismo y acaparamiento de tierras en Curvaradó y Jiguamiandó," May 2012, http://www.askonline.ch/fileadmin/user_up-load/documents/Thema_Wirtschaft_und_Menschenrechte/Lebensmittel_ Landwirtschaft/Chiquita/Banacol-Estudio-de-Caso-ES-final.pdf, 4.

48 US Department of Justice, "Chiquita Brands International Pleads Guilty to Making Payments to a Designated Terrorist Organization and Agrees to Pay $25 Million Fine," March 19, 2007, http://www.justice.gov/opa/pr/2007/ March/07_nsd_161.html.

49 Mario A. Murillo, "Fronting for Paramilitaries: Holder, Chiquita and Colombia," *CounterPunch*, November 19, 2008, http://www.counterpunch. org/2008/11/19/holder-chiquita-and-colombia/.

50 Curt Anderson, "Chiquita Accused of Funding Colombia Terrorists," Associated Press, May 31, 2011, http://www.cbsnews.com/news/chiquita-accused-of-funding-colombia-terrorists/.

51 "United States of America v. Chiquita Brands International Inc.," http://www2.gwu.edu/~nsarchiv/NSAEBB/NSAEBB217/indictment.pdf, 4.

52 William Moore, "Para-Business Gone Bananas: Chiquita Brands in Colombia," *Council on Hemispheric Affairs*, August 18, 2011, http://www.coha.org/para-business-gone-bananas-chiquita-brands-in-colombia/.

53 James Bargent, "Chiquita Republic," *In These Times* (January 7, 2013), http://inthesetimes.com/article/14294/chiquita_republic.

54 Ibid.

55 William Moore, "Para-Business Gone Bananas."

56 Geoff Simons, *Colombia: A Brutal History*, 324.

57 Phillip MacLean, "Colombia," in *Energy Cooperation in the Western Hemisphere*, ed. Sidney Weintraub (Washington, DC: CSIS Press, 2007), 196–197. Cerrejón, "Nuestra Empresa," http://www.cerrejon.com/site/nuestra-empresa.aspx.

58 Observatorio Social de Empresas Transnacionales Megaproyectos and Derechos Humanos, *Pica y Pala: Conflictos del modelo extractivista en los sectores de la minería y los agrocombustibles* (Bogatá, Ediciones Desde Abajo, 2011), 143.

59 Oficina de las Naciones Unidas contra la Droga y el Delito, "Colombia: Monitoreo de Cultivos de Coca 2012," June 2013, http://www.unodc.org/documents/colombia/2013/Agosto/censo_de_cultivos_de_coca_2012_BR.pdf, 11.

60 Observatorio Social de Empresas Transnacionales Megaproyectos, *Pica y Pala*, 143.

61 Colombia Solidarity Campaign, "La Colosa: A Death Foretold Alternative Report about the AngloGold Ashanti Gold Mining Project in Cajamarca, Tolima, Colombia," December, 2013, retrieved February 16, 2014, https://www.colombiasolidarity.org.uk/attachments/article/612/LA%20COLOS-A_A%20Death%20Foretold.pdf. Fedeagromisbol, "Communiqué to National and International Public Opinion: Continued Extermination of Members of Fedeagromisbol," February 18, 2010, http://londonminingnetwork.org/2010/02/killings-of-smallscale-miners-in-colombia/

62 Observatorio Social de Empresas Transnacionales Megaproyectos, *Pica y Pala*, 143.

63 UNHCR, "2012 UNHCR Country Operations Profile – Colombia," http://www.unhcr.org/pages/49e492ad6.html.

64 CODHES, "Desplazamiento creciente y crisis humanitaria invisibilizada," CODHES Boletín 79. March 2012, http://nasaacin.org/informativo-nasaacin/contexto-colombiano/4038-desplazamiento-creciente-y-crisis-humanitaria-invisibilizada, 2.

65 International Platforms and Organizations, "Report for the Universal Periodic Review: The Situation of Human Rights and Humanitarian Law in Colombia 2008–2013," May 2013, http://www.forum-menschenrechte.de/cms/upload/PDF/ab_02_2012/120920_UPR_English_final_con_firmas.pdf, 6.

66 US Leap, "Background: Violence Against Trade Unionists in Colombia," http://www.usleap.org/usleap-campaigns/colombia-murder-and-impunity/more-information-colombia/background-violence-against-

67 International Platforms and Organizations, "Report for the Universal Periodic Review," 11.
68 Ibid., 6–7.
69 James Bargent, "Toxic Mix of Drug Lords, Corruption and Trade Fuels Disorder In Colombian Port City," *Alternet*, March 5, 2014, http://www.alternet.org/world/toxic-mix-drug-lords-corruption-and-trade-fuels-disorder-colombian-port-city.
70 Jesús González Bolaños and Nelson Franco Díaz, "Compilación y analisis sobre crisis humanitaria en el municipio de Buenaventura," *Arquidiocesis de Cali*, April 3, 2013.
71 Simon Romero, " Cocaine Wars Make Port Colombia's Deadliest City," *New York Times*, May 22, 2007, http://www.nytimes.com/2007/05/22/world/americas/22colombia.html.
72 Bolaños and Díaz, "Compilación y analisis sobre crisis humanitaria."
73 International Platforms and Organizations, "Report for the Universal Periodic Review," 117.
74 ONIC, "Palabra Dulce, Aire de Vida," 2010, http://www.abcolombia.org.uk/downloads/C6D_Final_ONIC_report_-_Palabra_Dulce.pdf, 8, 11.
75 Venezuela has the highest homicide rate in South America. "Global Study on Homicide, 2011," 2011, http://www.unodc.org/documents/data-and-analysis/statistics/Homicide/Globa_study_on_homicide_2011_web.pdf, 23.
76 US Government Accountability Office, "PLAN COLOMBIA," 90.
77 Jess Ford, "International Programs Face Significant Challenges Reducing the Supply of Illegal Drugs but Support Broad U.S. Foreign Policy Objectives," US Government Accountability Office, July 21, 2012, http://www.gao.gov/products/GAO-10-921T.
78 Ibid.
79 Embassy Bogota, "Revision: Colombia—2009 Investment Climate Statement," February 11, 2009, https://cablegatesearch.wikileaks.org/cable.php?id=09BOGOTA437&q=cooperative%20location%20security
80 US Government Accountability Office, "PLAN COLOMBIA," 101.
81 Banco de la Republica, "Flujos de inversion extranjera directa (IED) en Colombia – Balanza De Pagos," 2011, http://www.banrep.gov.co/economia/flujos/C2Flujo_Paises_2007.xls.
82 Julia Gordon, "PDAC-Colombia to award mining concessions gradually," Reuters, March 5, 2012, http://www.reuters.com/article/2012/03/05/canada-mining-pdac-colombia-idUSL2E8E57EP20120305.
83 Schipani, Andres, "Colombia: Making Many Millionaires," *Financial Times*. October 21, 2013, retrieved August 27, 2014, http://blogs.ft.com/beyond-brics/2013/10/21/colombia-making-many-millionaires/
84 Simons, *Colombia: A Brutal History*, 327.
85 Hristov, *Blood and Capital*, 17.
86 Globalize This, "Colombia and the IMF: Policies that Worsen Problems," *Committee for the Abolition of Third World Debt*, January 2002, http://cadtm.org/Colombia-and-the-IMF-Policies-that.
87 Ibid.
88 MacLean, "Colombia," in *Energy Cooperation in the Western Hemisphere*, 206.
89 National Planning Department of Colombia, Department of Security and

Justice of Colombia. "Plan Colombia Progress Report, 1999–2005," September 2006, http://www.dnp.gov.co/Portals/0/archivos/documentos/DJS/DJS_Documentos_Publicaciones/bal_plan_Col_ingles_final.pdf, 9.

90 Banco de la Republica, "Flujos de inversion extranjera directa (IED) en Colombia." The Economist, "Gushers and Guns: A Boom, and Threats to It," *The Economist*, March 17, 2012. http://www.economist.com/node /21550304.

91 Scott, *Drugs, Oil and War*, 72.

92 MacLean, "Colombia," in *Energy Cooperation in the Western Hemisphere*, 194.

93 Simons, *Colombia: A Brutal History*, 320–321.

94 World Construction Network, "Colombia to Construct $3.5 Billion Oil Pipeline," March 20, 2010, http://www.worldconstructionnetwork.com/news/colombia_to_construct_35_billion_oil_pipeline_100323/. The information in this paragraph was drawn from: Dawn Paley, "Oil, Gas, and Canada-Colombia Free Trade," *NACLA* (August 11, 2010), https://nacla.org/node/6694.

95 Luke Burgess, "Colombian Oil Stocks Are Set to Run: The World's Hottest Oil Frontier," *Energy & Capital*, May 17, 2010, http://www.energyandcapital .com/articles/colombia-oil-stocks/1150

96 Thad Dunning and Leslie Wirpsa, "Oil and the Political Economy of Conflict in Colombia," in *The Geopolitics of Resource Wars: Resource Dependence, Governance and Violence*, ed. Philippe Le Billon (New York: Routledge, 2005), 84.

97 US Government Accountability Office. "Security Assistance: Efforts to Secure Colombia's Caño Limón-Coveñas Oil Pipeline Have Reduced Attacks, but Challenges Remain," September 2005, www.gao.gov/cgi-bin/getrpt ?GAO-05-971, 2.

98 Ibid., 8.

99 Paley, "Oil, Gas, and Canada-Colombia Free Trade."

100 El Pais, "Colombia tendrá aviones no tripulados y radar militar en el 2015," October 25, 2012, http://www.elpais.com.co/elpais/judicial/noticias/colombia -tendra-aviones-tripulados-y-radar-militar-2015.

101 Gary Leech, "Plan Petroleum in Putumayo," *Colombia Reports*, May 10, 2004, http://web.archive.org/web/20070606213622/http://www.colombiajournal .org/colombia184.htm.

102 This section is partly dervied from: "Global Capitalism, Oil, and the Canada-Colombia Free Trade Agreement," a speech delivered by the author at the Parkland Institute's fourteenth annual conference, November 2010, http://dawnpaley.files.wordpress.com/2010/11/parkland_paley_2010.pdf.

103 Ibáñez and Vélez, "Civil Conflict and Forced Migration," 661–662.

104 Sistema de Información Indígena de Colombia, "Pueblo Cofán," http:// www.siidecolombia.gov.co/CMS/media/32636/pueblo_cof_n.pdf.

105 Mortiz Tenthoff, "Coca, Petroleum and Conflict in Cofán Territory (Drug Policy Briefing #23)," *Transnational Institute*, September 2007, http://www. tni.org/sites/www.tni.org/files/download/brief23.pdf, 2.

106 Before becoming Colombia's biggest private oil baron, Pacific Rubiales's CEO, Ronald Pantin, worked in the Venezuelan oil industry for over twenty years, eventually becoming president of PDVSA, the state-owned oil company. He was also president of Enron Venezuela until he left the country after Hugo Chávez's election.

107 John Otis, "Pioneering CEO of the Year: Ronald Pantín—Oil Expert Striking Success Anew," *Bravo.* September 29, 2010, http://bravo.latintrade.com/2010/09/pioneering-ceo-of-the-year-ronald-pantin-oil-expert-striking-success-anew/.

108 Chris Arsenault, "Digging Up Canadian Dirt in Colombia," *Colombia Journal* (November 6, 2006), http://colombiajournal.org/digging-up-canadian-dirt-in-colombia.html.

109 Haynes Boone, "The Oil and Gas Industry in Colombia and the Ecopetrol Partial Privatization," March 18, 2008, http://www.haynesboone.com/files/Publication/9e5a1219-cf5e-4c8b-b06f-f34b3754bf57/Presentation/PublicationAttachment/22bb9393-f485-4bdc-aa0f-f945ea93f3bc/The%20Oil%20and%20Gas%20Industry%20in%20Columbia.pdf, 13.

110 Embassy Bogota, "Assistant Secretary Shannon's July 7 Meeting With President Uribe," July 15, 2008, http://cablegatesearch.net/cable.php?id=08BOGOTA2568&q=cooperative%20location%20security.

111 Ben Dangl, "U.S. Bases in Colombia Rattle the Region," *The Progressive*, March 2010, http://progressive.org/danglmarch10.html.

112 John Lindsay-Poland, "Pentagon Building Bases in Central America and Colombia: Despite Constitutional Court Striking Down Base Agreement," January 27, 2011, http://forusa.org/blogs/john-lindsay-poland/pentagon-building-bases-central-america-colombia/8445.

113 International Platforms and Organizations, "Report for the Universal Periodic Review," 15.

114 Hillary Clinton, "Remarks at the Central American Security Conference (SICA)," June 22, 2011, http://www.state.gov/secretary/rm/2011/06/166733.htm.

115 US State Department, "Congressional Budget Justification Foreign Operations Annex: Regional Perspectives 2014," http://www.state.gov/documents/organization/208291.pdf, 636.

CHAPTER 4: MEXICO'S DRUG WAR REFORMS

1 Dawn Paley, "Off the Map in Mexico," *The Nation* (May 4, 2011), http://www.thenation.com/article/160436/map-mexico.

2 Clare R. Seelke, "Mérida Initiative for Mexico and Central America: Funding and Policy Issue," Congressional Research Service, April 19, 2010, http://fpc.state.gov/documents/organization/141560.pdf.

3 US GAO, "Mérida Initiative: The United States Has Provided Counternarcotics and Anticrime Support but Needs Better Performance Measures," July 21, 2010, http://www.gao.gov/products/GAO-10-837, 27.

4 110th Congress, 2d Session, "An Act to authorize law enforcement and security assistance, and assistance to enhance the rule of law and strengthen civilian institutions, for Mexico and the countries of Central America, and for other purposes," June 11, 2008, http://www.govtrack.us/congress/bills/110/hr6028/text, 17.

5 US State Department, "Mérida Initiative," http://www.state.gov/j/inl/merida/m.

6 110th Congress, 2d Session. "AN ACT to authorize law enforcement."

7 Take, for example, the arrival of the US Navy in Guatemala in August 2012: approximately 200 US Marines arrived before the agreement was reached. A special session was called in Guatemala in so that the agreement could be

approved and become legal.

8   US State Department. "Mérida Initiative."

9   BBC News, "Clinton Says Mexico Drug Crime Like an Insurgency," September 9, 2010, http://www.bbc.co.uk/news/world-us-canada-11234058.

10   David Morgan, "US Military Chief Backs Counter-insurgency for Mexico," March 6, 2009, http://www.reuters.com/article/2009/03/07/idUSN06397194.

11   Vincente L. Rafael, "Targeting Translation: U.S. Counterinsurgency and the Politics of Language," in *Life During Wartime*, 277–278.

12   John Feeley, "U.S.-Mexico Security Cooperation: An Overview of the Mérida Initiative, 2008–Present," Hearing before the House Foreign Affairs Subcommittee on the Western Hemisphere, May 13, 2013, http://docs.house.gov/meetings/FA/FA07/20130523/100907/HHRG-113-FA07-Wstate-FeeleyJ-20130523.pdf, 2–3.

13   Morena, "Mural 27: Alerta a todos los mexicanos!," *Regeneración* 27 (February 2013): 4–5.

14   Chalk, *The Latin American Drug Trade*, 60.

15   Just the Facts, "Military and Police Aid, All Programs, Entire Region, 2009–2014," undated, http://justf.org/All_Grants_Country.

16   World Bank, "Global Economic Prospects: Latin America and the Caribbean," undated, http://www.worldbank.org/en/publication/global-economic-prospects/regional-outlooks/lac. Sam Perlo-Freeman and Corina Solmirano, "Trends in World Military Expenditure, 2013." SIPRI Fact Sheet, April 2014, http://books.sipri.org/files/FS/SIPRIFS1404.pdf.

17   Chalk, *The Latin American Drug Trade*, 61.

18   International Crisis Group, "Peña Nieto's Challenge: Criminal Cartels and the Rule of Law in Mexico," *Latin America Report* 48 (March 19, 2013), http://www.crisisgroup.org/~/media/Files/latin-america/mexico/048-pena-nietos-challenge-criminal-cartels-and-rule-of-law-in-mexico.pdf, ii.

19   Clare R. Seelke and K. Finklea, "CRS Report for Congress Prepared for Members and Committees of Congress U.S.-Mexican Security Cooperation: The Mérida Initiative and Beyond," *Congressional Research Service*, April 8, 2014, http://fas.org/sgp/crs/row/R41349.pdf, 7.

20   P. Meyer and Clare R. Seelke, "Central America Regional Security Initiative: Background and Policy Issues for Congress," GAO, February 21, 2012, http://www.fas.org/sgp/crs/row/R41731.pdf. Voice of America, "Mérida's New Direction," March 3, 2012, http://www.voanews.com/policy/editorials/MERIDAS-NEW-DIRECTION-141416863.html (This represents a far better ability on the part of the US to leverage Mexican funds as compared to the Colombian commitment under Plan Colombia, which was closer to 2 to 1). See: National Planning Department of Colombia, Department of Security and Justice of Colombia, 9.

21   Meyer and Seelke, "Central America Regional Security Initiative, 17.

22   United States Government Accountability Office, "Status of Funding, Equipment, and Training for the Caribbean Basin Security Initiative," March 20, 2013, http://www.gao.gov/assets/660/653173.pdf, 3.

23   Clare R. Seelke, "Mérida Initiative for Mexico and Central America: Funding and Policy Issue," Congressional Research Service, April 19, 2010, http://fpc.state.gov/documents/organization/141560.pdf, 2.

24   William Brownfield, "Remarks at the Council of Americas," *US State Department*, March 22, 2013, http://www.state.gov/j/inl/rls/rm/2013/207231.htm.

25 Berdal and Malone, "Introduction," 91.

26 UNODC, "World Drug Report, 2010," 2010, http://www.unodc.org/documents/wdr/WDR_2010/World_Drug_Report_2010_lo-res.pdf, 18.

27 Global Commission on Drug Policy. "Taking Control: Pathways to Drug Policies that Work." September, 2014. P. 13.

28 What I describe as the first component includes the "Pillars" called "Institutionalize Reforms to Sustain Rule of Law and Respect for Human Rights" and "Build Strong and Resilient Communities." US GAO, "Mérida Initiative," 33.

29 USAID. "US AID History." June 11, 2012. Retrieved December 21, 2012, http://www.usaid.gov/who-we-are/usaid-history.

30 USAID, "The State Department and USAID Budget," http://www.usaid.gov/sites/default/files/documents/9276/FactSheet_StateUSAIDBudget.pdf.

31 US State Department, "Congressional Budget," 620.

32 Ibid.

33 Ibid.

34 Eva Hershaw, "Aztec Tiger," *Ozy* (December 5, 2013), http://www.ozy.com/fast-forward/mexico-preps-for-a-comeback/4093.article.

35 Victor Renuart Jr. and Biff Baker, "U.S.-Mexico Homeland Defense: A Compatible Interface," *Strategic Forum*, National Defense University, February 2010, http://usacac.army.mil/cac2/call/docs/11-23/ch_10.asp.

36 T. Padgett, "Mexico's Peña Nieto Talks to *TIME*: 'We Can Move Beyond the Drug War'," *Time* (November 30, 2012), http://world.time.com/2012/11/30/mexicos-pena-nieto-talks-to-time-we-can-move-beyond-the-drug-war/#ixzz2PvNnOdBf.

37 US GAO, "Mérida Initiative," 29.

38 USAID Mission to Mexico, "Competitiveness Program: 2nd Quarter FY 2010," January–March 2010, http://pdf.usaid.gov/pdf_docs/PDACR720.pdf.

39 USAID. "USAID/Mexico Annual Program Statement (APS)," January 30, 2012, http://www07.grants.gov/search/downloadAtt.do;jsessionid=TJgHRLlPMVzGSg2cXvSMjwRHSvGsBKD7hGGqCPfrv8VQ5BnXCrGW!-861966415?attId=113385, 11.

40 Magdalena Lara Monroy, ed., *Acciones Cruciales en competencia y regulación*, Centro de Investigación para el Desarrollo, A.C., 2011, http://accionescruciales.cidac.org/documentos/acciones.pdf.

41 USAID, "Mexico: Country Overview," http://transition.usaid.gov/mx/index.html.

42 Monroy, *Acciones Cruciales*.

43 Abt Associates, "Mexico Competitiveness Program," http://www.abtassociates.com/Websites/2012/Mexico-Competitiveness-Program.aspx. Abt has its roots firmly planted in defense and war: "Abt Associates focused on transferring defense-related technology and systems to civilian application, such as the nation's War on Poverty," according to the firm's website ("Our History," http://www.abtassociates.com/About-Us/Our-History.aspx). Abt also provided reports forecasting cocaine availability in the Americas for the US Office of National Drug Control Policy in 2002 (https://www.ncjrs.gov/ondcppubs/publications/pdf/cocaine2002.pdf).

44 Casals & Associates, "Building More Effective and Efficient Government in Mexico," http://www.casals.com/2010/03/building-more-effective-and-efficient-government-in-mexico/.

45 DynCorp, "About Us," http://www.dyn-intl.com/about-us/overview.aspx. And Abt Associates, "Our History."

46 Evensen Dodge International, "About Us," http://www.dodgeglobal.com/our_clients.html.

47 S. Goldfarb, "U.S. Center at COP-16: U.S. and Mexico Bi-National Cooperation on Climate Change and Development," *Dipnote*, December 9, 2010, http://blogs.state.gov/index.php/site/entry/us_center_mexico_cooperation.

48 Kristian Williams, "Life during Wartime: Resisting Counterinsurgency," in *Life During Wartime*, 104.

49 Elizabeth Malkin and Randal Archibold, "A New Leader Pushes a Different Side of Mexico," *New York Times*, November 27, 2012, http://www.nytimes.com/2012/11/28/world/americas/mexico-seeks-to-recast-relationship-with-us.html?_r=1&.

50 The center-left Democratic Revolution Party (PRD) left the Pact for Mexico in the lead-up to the energy reform.

51 Luis Hernández Navarro, "Las mentiras sobre la reforma educative," *La Jornada*, January 15, 2013, http://www.jornada.unam.mx/2013/01/15/opinion/017a1pol.

52 ProMéxico, *México: La puerta de aceso al mundo*, October 2012, http://www.promexico.gob.mx/es/mx/boletin-promexico-comparte.

53 Anthony Wayne, "Ambassador Wayne's Remarks to the U.S. Mexico Chamber of Commerce Breakfast attended by CODEL Sessions, Cuellar, McCaul, and Polis," December 1, 2012, http://mexico.usembassy.gov/eng/ebio_ambassador/texts/ambassador-waynes-remarks-to-the-us-mexico-chamber-of-commerce-breakfast-attended-by-codel-sessions-cuellar-mccaul-and-polis.html.

54 International Monetary Fund, "IMF Renews $73 Billion Credit Line for Mexico," December 11, 2012, www.imf.org/external/pubs/ft/survey/so/2012/car121112a.htm.

55 International Monetary Fund, "Transcript of a IMF Western Hemisphere Department Press Briefing," April 19, 2013, http://www.imf.org/external/np/tr/2013/tr041913.htm.

56 Ben Bain and Natacha Cattan, "Mexico Credit Rating Upgraded by Fitch to BBB+; Peso Rallies," *Bloomberg News*, May 8, 2013, http://www.bloomberg.com/news/2013-05-08/mexico-credit-rating-upgraded-by-fitch-to-bbb-currency-rallies.html.

57 Luis Videgaray, "Palabras del Secretario de hacienda y crédito pùblico, Dr. Luis Videgaray Caso, en la presentación de la iniciativa de reforma financiera," May 8, 2013, http://www.shcp.gob.mx/SALAPRENSA/doc_discurso_funcionarios/secretarioSHCP/2013/lvc_reforma_financiera_08052013.pdf.

58 Manuel Sánchez González, "Economía Mexicana: Una mirada de largo plazo," Banco de México, March 8, 2012, http://www.banxico.org.mx/publicaciones-y-discursos/discursos-y-presentaciones/presentaciones/%7B694E563B-9721-B4A2-3023-D914148CCC91%7D.pdf, 24.

59 Ibid., 22.

60 Amy Guthrie, "Mexico Proposes Financial Reform in Effort to Boost Lending," *Wall Street Journal*, May 8, 2013, http://online.wsj.com/article/BT-CO-20130508-713157.html.

61 Reyes Retana, Roberto Arena, et al, "Mexico's Large-scale Financial Reform: Greater Availability of Credit, Lower Costs and Certainty of Legal Remedies,"

Lexology, May 22, 2013, 2013, http://www.lexology.com/library/detail .aspx?g=3d7aaeaa-792e-4b8c-8d02-e1a03b0c32d7.

62 Dawn Paley, "Til Debt Do Us Part," CIP Americas Program, August 8, 2013, http://www.cipamericas.org/archives/10229.

63 Ejidos are communally owned lands used for agriculture. Community members farm specific parcels, with some sections of the ejido designated specifically to be farmed communally.

64 Amy Guthrie, "Mexico Proposes Financial Reform."

65 International Monetary Fund, "Transcript of a Press Briefing by G24 Ministers," October 10, 2013, https://www.imf.org/external/np/tr/2013/ tr101113.htm.

66 Daniel Hernández, "Saving Mexico? Selling Mexico? Slaying Mexico?," *Vice* (February 21, 2014), http://www.vice.com/read/saving-mexico-selling -mexico-slaying-mexico.

67 James Taylor and Mike Shannon, "How Mexico Can Rescue Its Brand," May 9, 2012, http://vianovo.com/news/how-mexico-can-rescue-its-brand.

68 Thomas L. Friedman, "How Mexico Got Back in the Game," *New York Times*, February 23, 2013, http://www.nytimes.com/2013/02/24/opinion/ sunday/friedman-how-mexico-got-back-in-the-game.html?_r=0.

69 Enrique Pena Nieto, "U.S., Mexico Should Develop Their Economic Bond," *Washington Post*, November 23, 2012, http://www.washingtonpost.com/ opinions/enrique-pena-nieto-us-mexico-should-develop-their-economic- bond/2012/11/23/248b8ec4-3589-11e2-9cfa-e41bac906cc9_story.html.

70 Ashley Southall, "Obama to Visit Mexico and Costa Rica in May," *New York Times*, March 27, 2013, http://thecaucus.blogs.nytimes.com/2013/03/27/ obama-to-visit-mexico-and-costa-rica-in-may/.

71 Todd Miller, "Senate Disguises Militarization as Immigration Reform," *Salon.com*, July 11, 2013, http://www.salon.com/2013/07/11/the_u_s_mexi- can_border_is_ground_zero_for_a_domestic_surveillance_state_partner/.

72 As evidenced recently with the implementation of austerity measures in Spain, Portugal, Italy, and Greece.

73 Maracio Schettino, "El mito de la energía en México," *Nueva Sociedad* 220 (March–April 2009): 146.

74 Flavia Krause-Jackson and Nacha Cattan, "Mexican Presidential Candidate Seeks Private Investment in Oil Industry," *Bloomberg*, November 17, 2012, http://www.bloomberg.com/news/2011-11-17/pena-nieto-pledges-mexi- can-oil-opening-calderon-found-elusive.html.

75 Diana Férnandez, "PEMEX Can Be More Competitive," April 2, 2012, http://eng .fundsamericas.com/news/business/8845/PEMEX-can-be-more-competitive.

76 Adam Thompson, "Mexico-US: Let's Talk Trade," *Financial Times*, March 28, 2013, http://blogs.ft.com/beyond-brics/2013/03/28/mexico-us -lets-talk-about-trade/?#axzz2VGI7jPbo.

77 Esther Arzate and Maribel Zavala, "Bienvenido: El Abanico Energético," *Petroleo y Energia* (December 2013–January 2014):19.

78 Mexico is the largest silver producer in Latin America, and the second largest in the world, and is the third copper producer in Latin America, according to ProMéxico. ProMéxico, *México: La puerta de aceso al mundo*, 2013.

79 Ralph Cuervo-Lorens, "Commentary: A Better Response to Mexico's New Mining Taxes," *The Northern Miner*, February 24, 2014, http://www.northernminer

.com/news/commentary-a-better-response-to-mexicos-new-mining-taxes/1002929894/?ref=rss&ctid=1002929894.

80 The Economist, "Mexico: The Sovereign Take," *The Economist* (November 2, 2013), http://www.economist.com/news/americas/21588891-new-royalty-rattles-investors-sovereign-take.

81 Cuervo-Lorens, "Commentary."

82 V. Espinosa, B. Bain, and N. Cattan, "Mexico Credit Rating Raised After Oil Industry Opened," *Bloomberg News*, February 5, 2014, http://www.bloomberg.com/news/2014-02-05/mexico-rating-raised-to-a3-by-moody-s-after-oil-industry-opened.html.

83 World Bank, "Mexico," undated, http://data.worldbank.org/country/mexico.

84 Embassy of the United States in Mexico, "U.S. Ambassador Wayne and Attorney General Morales Launch Training Program for Prosecutors and Investigators," February 7, 2012, http://mexico.usembassy.gov/press-releases/us-ambassador-wayne-and-attorney-general-morales.html.

85 Dawn Paley, "Legal Battles in Mexico," *Upside Down World*, 2011, http://upsidedownworld.org/main/mexico-archives-79/3353-legal-battles-in-mexico.

86 Gustavo Castillo, "Evolución de la delincuencia sorprendió al sistema de justicia: Murillo Karam," http://www.jornada.unam.mx/ultimas/2014/01/08/evolucion-de-la-delincuencia-sorprendio-al-sistema-de-justicia-murillo-karam-3326.html.

87 Poiré's candid comments came during a talk sponsored by the Council on Foreign Relations, the powerful US organization that publishes *Foreign Affairs* magazine: The Economist, "Shannon O'Neil and Alejandro Poiré: Disrupting the drug war," *The Economist* (November 7, 2012), https://www.youtube.com/watch?v=X1V54Rw-HNQ.

88 Paley, "Legal Battles in Mexico."

89 UN Mission to Mexico. "Report of the Special Rapporteur on the Independence of Judges and Lawyers," April, 2011, retrieved October 10, http://daccess-dds-ny.un.org/doc/UNDOC/GEN/G11/129/33/PDF/G1112933.pdf?OpenElement, 12.

90 Deborah Weissman, "Remaking Mexico: Law Reform as Foreign Policy," *Cardozo Law Review* 4, no. 354 (2014): 18.

91 Rodger Garner, "Statement by USAID Mission Director to Mexico, Rodger D. Garner on USAID/Mexico's Role in the Mérida Initiative," March 10, 2009. http://www.usaid.gov/news-information/congressional-testimony/statement-usaid-mission-director-mexico-rodger-d-garner.

92 Deborah Weissman, "Remaking Mexico," 18, 28.

93 Martha Huggins, "U.S. Supported State Terror: A History of Police Training in Latin America," in *Vigilantism and the State in Modern Latin America*, 265.

94 CMDPDH/Red SOS-Tortura, "Arraigo Made in Mexico: A Violation to Human Rights," October 2012, http://www2.ohchr.org/english/bodies/cat/docs/ngos/CMDPDH_OMCT_Mexico_CAT49_en.pdf.

95 Organization of American States, "IACHR Wraps Up Visit to Mexico," September 2011, http://www.oas.org/en/iachr/media_center/PReleases/2011/105.asp.

96 Malkin and Archibold, "A New Leader Pushes a Different Side of Mexico."

97 Jason Lange, "Mexico sees 2010 FDI bouncing back," Reuters, May 4, 2010, http://www.reuters.com/article/2010/05/04/us-latam-summit-mexico-investment-idUSTRE64351D20100504.

98 Comisión Nacional de Inversiones Extranjeras, "Informe estadístico sobre el comportamiento de la inversion extranjera directa en México," http://www .economia.gob.mx/files/comunidad_negocios/comision_nacional/Informe _2011_IV.pdf.

99 Ibid.

100 Shannon O'Neil, "Refocusing U.S.-Mexico Security Cooperation."

101 US State Department. "Congressional Budget Justification," 687.

102 UNODC, "World Drug Report, 2010," United Nations, 2010, http://www. unodc.org/documents/wdr/WDR_2010/World_Drug_Report_2010_lo-res. pdf, 18.

103 Dominic Rushe and Jill Treanor, "HSBC's Record $1.9bn Fine Preferable to Prosecution, US Authorities Insist," The Guardian, December 11, 2012, http://www.guardian.co.uk/business/2012/dec/11/hsbc-fine-prosecution -money-laundering?CMP=twt_fd&CMP=SOCxx2I2.

104 New York Times, "Too big to indict," New York Times, December 11, 2012, http://www.nytimes.com/2012/12/12/opinion/hsbc-too-big-to-indict. html?_r=0. Matt Taibbi, "Outrageous HSBC Settlement Proves the Drug War is a Joke," Rolling Stone, December 13, 2013, http://www.rollingstone. com/politics/blogs/taibblog/outrageous-hsbc-settlement-proves-the-drug- war-is-a-joke-20121213#ixzz2vZpnNZ7o.

105 Rajeev Sayal, "Drug Money Saved Banks in Global Crisis, Claims UN Advisor," December 13, 2009, http://www.theguardian.com/global/2009/dec/13/ drug-money-banks-saved-un-cfief-claims.

106 Perhaps the most famous case is that of Tomás Yarrington Ruvalcaba, who was mayor of Matamoros, Tamaulipas, and who went on to be governor of Tamaulipas and a presidential candidate for the PRI. According to documents filed in a Texas court, between 1998 and 2005, Yarrington—now a fugitive of justice—"acquired millions of dollars in payments while holding elected office from large-scale drug organizations operating in and through the Mexican State of Tamaulipas, and from various extortion or bribery schemes." United States District Court Southern Division of Texas, "U.S.A. v. Real Property," May 22, 2012, http://www.ice.gov/doclib/news/releases /2012/120522brownsville.pdf.

107 Alberto Nájar, "El gran negocio del lavado de dinero en México," BBC News, http://www.bbc.co.uk/mundo/noticias/2013/07/130717_mexico_negocio_ lavado_de_dinero_ley_an.shtml.

108 Barney Jopson, "Walmart Tackled on Laundering Concerns," Financial Times, August 15, 2012, http://www.ft.com/intl/cms/s/0/0c949a9a-e6f1- 11e1-8a74-00144feab49a.html#axzz333RM46B9.

109 N. Miroff and W. Booth, "Mexico's 2012 Vote is Vulnerable to Narco Threat," The Washington Post, January 15, 2012, http://articles.washington- post.com/2012-01-15/world/35440426_1_luisa-maria-calderon-drug-cartel -leader-pri-candidate.

110 It was reported in 2012 that a van used for trafficking drugs through Nicaragua was registered to the television empire. Televisa officials denied wrongdoing. Homero Campa, "Admite Televisa que vehículos confiscados en Nicaragua podrían estar a su nombre," Proceso, September 12, 2012, http://www.proceso.com.mx/?p=319672.

CHAPTER 5: PLAN MEXICO AND MILITARIZATION

1   Christopher Hooks, "Q&A with Molly Molloy: The Story of the Juarez Femicides Is a 'Myth'," *Texas Observer*, January 11, 2014, http://www.texas observer.org/qa-molly-molloy-story-juarez-femicides-myth/.

2   Melissa Wright, "Necropolitics, Narcopolitics, and Femicide: Gendered Violence on the Mexico-U.S. Border," *Signs* 36, no. 3 (Spring 2011): 713–714.

3   Victor Quintana, "Sordera calderoniana, movilización ciudadana," *La Jornada*, December 2009.

4   Molly Molloy, "The Mexican Undead: Toward a New History of the 'Drug War' Killing Fields," August 21, 2013, http://smallwarsjournal.com/jrnl/art/the-mexican-undead-toward-a-new-history-of-the-%E2%80%9Cdrug-war%E2%80%9D-killing-fields.

5   Human Rights Watch, "Mexico's Disappeared: The Enduring Cost of a Crisis Ignored," February 2013, http://www.hrw.org/sites/default/files/reports/mexico0213_ForUpload_0_0.pdf,

6   Organization of American States, "IACHR Wraps Up Visit to Mexico," September 2011, http://www.oas.org/en/iachr/media_center/PReleases/2011/105.asp.

7   US State Department, "Ecuador's Push for Conditions-free Foreign Assistance Has Major Implications for Usg Operations," February 24, 2010, http://cablegatesearch.net/cable.php?id=10QUITO101#para-6706-12

8   Ibid.

9   Martha Huggins, *Political Policing: The U.S. and Latin America* (Durham: Duke University Press, 1998), 4.

10 Huggins, "U.S. Supported State Terror," 219.

11 US GAO, "FOREIGN AID: Police Training and Assistance," March 1992, http://www.gao.gov/products/145909

12 G. Thompson, "U.S. Widens Role in Battle Against Mexican Drug Cartels," *New York Times*, August 6, 2011, http://www.nytimes.com/2011/08/07/world/07drugs.html?pagewanted=all.

13 William Brownfield, "The Future of Mexico-US Relations," May 20, 2014, http://www.state.gov/j/inl/rls/rm/2014/226345.htm.

14 C. Hawley, "U.S. Training Bolsters Mexico's War on Drugs," *USA Today*, October 29, 2009, http://www.usatoday.com/news/world/2009-10-28-mexico-police-training_N.htm.

15 Beth Asch, et al, "Mitigating Corruption in Government Security Forces: The Role of Institutions, Incentives, and Personnel Management in Mexico," 2011, Rand Corporation, http://www.rand.org/content/dam/rand/pubs/technical_reports/2011/RAND_TR906.pdf, xii.

16 Ioan Grillo, "Mexican Police Attacked CIA Officers, Ambush Likely: sources," Reuters, August 29, 2012, http://www.reuters.com/article/2012/08/29/us-mexico-shooting-idUSBRE87S19K20120829.

17 Insyde, "¿Cuántos policías hay en México?," September 12, 2010, http://www.insyde.org.mx/shownews.asp?newsid=319.

18 Ibid.

19 The highest-ranking federal police officer in Mexico today was trained in the United States, Israel, and Spain.

20 Michael Evans, "Mexico Fusion Center: NSA Refuses to Acknowledge 'Existence or Non-existence' of Documents on U.S. Intelligence Facility," February 11, 2014, http://migrationdeclassified.wordpress.com/2014/02/11/mexico

-fusion-center-nsa-refuses-to-acknowledge-existence-or-non-existence
-of-documents-on-u-s-intelligence-facility/.

21 Anthony Wayne, "Ambassador's Remarks for Opening Ceremony of International Gang Training Conference," June 10, 2013, http://mexico.usembassy
.gov/eng/ebio_ambassador/texts/ambassadors-remarks-for-opening
-ceremony-of-international-gang-training-conference.html.

22 Puebla Noticias, "Puebla contará con la mejor Academia de Profesionalización Policial del mundo," February 21, 2012, http://pueblanoticias.com.mx/noticia
/puebla-contara-con-la-mejor-academia-de-profesionalizacion-policial
-del-mundo-17149/.

23 Academia de Formación y Desarrollo Policial Puebla Iniciativa Mérida Gral. Ignacio Zaragoza, "Oferta Educativa," undated, http://www.academianacional
puebla.mx/oferta-educativa.php.

24 Anthony Wayne, "Ambassador's Remarks at Tactical Village Ribbon Cutting," December 10, 2013, http://mexico.usembassy.gov/eng/ebio_ambassador
/texts/ambassadors-remarks-at-tactical-village-ribbon-cutting.html.

25 Patrick Corcoran, "Mexico, Colombia Talk Security, Tied by Drug Trade," Insight Crime, August 3, 2011, http://insightcrime.org/insight-latest-news/
item/1338-mexico-colombia-talk-security-tied-by-drug-trade.

26 Staff, "Capacitará Colombia a 12 mil policías mexicanos en lucha antidroga," Animal Politico, April 13, 2012, http://www.animalpolitico.com/2012/04/
capacita-colombia-12-mil-policias-mexicanos-en-lucha-antidroga/.

27 EFE, "Jefes de la Gendarmería mexicana reciben capacitación de Francia y Colombia," March 3, 2014, http://www.efe.com/efe/noticias/usa/mexico/jefes
-gendarmeria-mexicana-reciben-capacitacion-francia-colombia
/5/50038/2255439.

28 Belén Zapata, "Un exdirector de la policía de Colombia asesora a Peña Nieto en seguridad," CNN Español, June 14, 2012, http://mexico.cnn.com/
nacional/2012/06/14/un-exdirector-de-la-policia-de-colombia-asesora-a-pena
-nieto-en-seguridad.

29 Human Rights Watch, "Neither Rights nor Security," November 2011, http://www.hrw.org/reports/2011/11/09/neither-rights-nor-security-0, 5.

30 Ibid., 6.

31 Ibid., 7.

32 Ibid., 16.

33 German Alfonso Palacio Castañeda, "Institutional Crisis, Parainstitutionality, and Regime Flexibility in Colombia: The Place of Narcotraffic and Counterinsurgency," in Vigilantism and the State in Modern Latin America.

34 Yolanda Figueroa, El Capo del Golfo, 31. Sierra Gúzman and Jorge Luis, El Enemigo Interno: Contrainsurgencia y Fuerzas Armadas en México (Madrid: Plaza y Valdes, 2003), 120. Reporte Indigo, "La DEA detrás de exgobernadores," Excelsior, February 11, 2012, http://www.vanguardia.com.
mx/ladeadetrasdeexgobernadores-1216637.html. La Redaccion, "Exmiembro de Los Zetas incrimina a exgobernadores de Tamaulipas con el narco," Proceso, February 2, 2012, http://www.proceso.com.mx/?p=296970.

35 T. Poppa, Drug Lord (New York: Pharos Books, 1998), 167.

36 See, for example, Consulate Monterrey, "Border Violence Spreads to Nuevo Leon," February 26, 2010, http://wikileaks.org/cable/2010/02/10MON
TERREY43.html#par9.

37 Rubén Mosso, "Detienen a 16 policías por proteger matanzas de Los Zetas

en San Fernando," *Milenio*, April 13, 2012, http://www.milenio.com/cdb/doc/noticias2011/434f5cc48739b1e6f2b64e6cf286ba60.

38 By its own admission the US trained at least one of their members: US State Department, "Subject: Setting the Record Straight on Zetas and U.S. Military Training," August 21, 2009, http://wikileaks.org/cable/2009/08/09MEXICO2473.html.

39 Ibid.

40 Paley, "Strategies of a New Cold War."

41 Kim Murphy and Ken Ellingwood, "Mexico Demands Answers on Guns," *Los Angeles Times*, March 11, 2011, http://articles.latimes.com/2011/mar/11/nation/la-naw-mexico-guns-20110311.

42 Bill Conroy, "US Court Documents Claim Sinaloa 'Cartel' Is Protected by US Government," *Borderland Beat*, July 31, 2011, http://www.borderlandbeat.com/2011/07/us-court-documents-claim-sinaloa-cartel.html.

43 Guadalupe Correa-Cabrera, "Desigualdades y flujos globales en la frontera noreste de México," http://www.desigualdades.net/Resources/Working_Paper/64-WP-Correa-Cabrera-Online.pdf?1393595421.

44 The first time I met Fong, whose father was a renowned activist in Chihuahua, was at the Autonomous University of Ciudad Juárez (UACJ).

45 Jorge Balderas Dominguez, *Discursos y narrativas sobre violencia, miedo e inseguridad en Mexico* (University of Leiden: Doctoral Thesis, 2012), 123.

46 Marcos Muedano, "A prisión, 10 policías federales," *El Universal*, September 29, 2011, http://www.eluniversal.com.mx/nacion/189396.html.

47 Carlos Huerta, "Tribunal confirma la participación de militares en crimen de juarense," *Norte Digital*, January 21, 2014, http://www.nortedigital.mx/59211/tribunal_confirma_la_participacion_de_militares_en_crimen_de_juarense/.

48 Instituto Nacional de Estadística y Geografía, "Mortalidad: Conjunto de datos: Defunciones por homicidios," 2011, http://www.inegi.org.mx/lib/olap/consulta/general_ver4/MDXQueryDatos.asp?#Regreso&c=2882.

49 Steven Dudley, "Juarez After the War," *InSight Crime*, February 13, 2013, http://www.insightcrime.org/reports/juarez.pdf, 6.

50 Balderas Dominguez, *Discursos y narrativas sobre violencia, miedo e inseguridad en México*, 123.

51 Seguridad, Justicia y Paz. "La violencia en los municipios de México, 2012," February 1, 2014, http://www.seguridadjusticiaypaz.org.mx/biblioteca/finish/5-prensa/164-la-violencia-en-los-municipios-de-mexico-2012/0.

52 R. Fausset, "Federal Police in Mexico Accused of Being Part of Kidnapping Ring," *Los Angeles Times*, October 8, 2013, http://www.latimes.com/world/worldnow/la-fg-wn-mexico-federal-police-kidnapping-ring-20131008,0,5728960.story.

53 William Brownfield, "Security Cooperation in Mexico: Examining the Next Steps in the U.S.-Mexico Security Relationship," Hearing Before the Senate Foreign Relations Committee Subcommittee on the Western Hemisphere and Global Narcotics Affairs, June 18, 2013, http://www.foreign.senate.gov/imo/media/doc/Brownfield_Testimony.pdf, 2.

54 International Centre for Prison Studies, "Mexico," January 2013, http://www.prisonstudies.org/info/worldbrief/wpb_country.php?country=83.

55 Ibid.

56 US Department of State, "Public Notice of a Grant Award to Colorado

Department of Corrections," July 5, 2011, http://www.state.gov/r/pa/prs/ps/2011/07/167594.htm.

57 Kirk Mitchell, "Afghan General, Wardens Learn U.S. Prison Tactics at Canon City Center," *Denver Post*, September 23, 2012, http://www.denverpost.com/ci_21610507/afghan-general-wardens-learn-u-s-prison-tactics.

58 Kirk Mitchell, "Mexican Federal Prison Officers Train in Colorado to Combat Drug-gang Attacks," *Denver Post*, September 13, 2011, http://www.denverpost.com/ci_16059581.

59 N. Casey, "U.S. Shifts Mexico Drug Fight," *Wall Street Journal*, September 17, 2012, http://online.wsj.com/article/SB10000872396390443720204578000463890865962.html.

60 US Embassy Mexico, "Fact Sheet – Corrections Reform," August 2013, http://photos.state.gov/libraries/mexico/310329/agosto2013/factsheet-correctionsreform%20-%200813.pdf.

61 Less than 13 percent of the Mexico-U.S. border is militarized on both sides. US GAO, "Border Patrol Strategy: Progress and Challenges in Implementation and Assessment Efforts," May 8, 2012, http://www.gao.gov/assets/600/590687.pdf.

62 Laleh Khalili, "The Location of Palestine in Global Counterinsurgencies," *International Journal of Middle East Studies* 42 (2010): 420.

63 B. McCaffrey and R. Scales, "Texas Border Security: A Strategic Military Assessment," September 2011, http://texasagriculture.gov/Portals/0/DigArticle/1623/46982_Final%20Report-Texas%20Border%20Security.pdf.

64 Ibid.

65 Harsha Walia, *Undoing Border Imperialism* (Oakland: AK Press, 2013).

66 Ibid., 31.

67 Bloomberg, "Mexico's Ferrari on Foreign Investment, Economy," *Bloomberg*, August 22, 2011, http://www.bloomberg.com/video/74229052/ (at 19:45, his comments were made in English).

68 North American Production Sharing, Inc., "Manufacturing in Mexico: Industrial Real Estate," March 8, 2013, http://news.cision.com/kindling-media/r/manufacturing-in-mexico--industrial-real-estate,c9382673.

69 Renuart and Baker, "U.S.-Mexico Homeland Defense: A Compatible Interface."

70 P. Engardio and G. Smith, "The Other Mexico: A Wave of Investment," *Businessweek*, April 9, 2009, http://www.businessweek.com/magazine/content/09_16/b4127034232864.htm.

71 G. Smith, "Doing Business in Harm's Way," *Businessweek*, April 9, 2009, http://www.businessweek.com/magazine/content/09_16/b4127034241721.htm.

72 Ed Vulliamy, *Amexica: A War Along the Borderline* (New York: Farrar, Straus and Giroux, 2010), 39.

73 Riodoce, "Secuestra el Ejército a 12 pobladores de Vascogil, Durango," *Riodoce*, 2009, http://riodoce.mx/?joomla=/content/view/2687/67/.

74 M3 Engineering and Technology, "Metates Gold-Silver Project: Updated Preliminary Economic Assessment," Chesapeake Gold Corp, April 21, 2011, http://chesapeakegold.com/downloads/Metates%20PEA%20Update%20April%202011.pdf, 49.

75 Ibid., 21.

76 Ibid., 13.

77 *Vice*, "Mexican Vigilantes Stand Up Against Crime," April 29, 2013, https://www.youtube.com/watch?v=8XiSnCt9fDc.

78 Ibid.

79 Jaime Quintana, "Oro y plata detrás de la persecución militar contra la policía comunitaria," *Desinformémonos*, August 2013, http://desinformemonos. org/2013/08/minerales-detras-de-la-persecucion-militar-contra-la-policia -comunitaria/.

80 Vandana Felbab Brown, "Peña Nieto's Piñata: The Promise and Pitfalls of Mexico's New Security Policy Against Organized Crime," *Brookings Institute*, February 2013, http://www.brookings.edu/research/papers/2013/02/ mexico-new-security-policy-felbabbrown, 7.

81 Peter Chalk, "Mexico's New Strategy to Combat Drug Cartels: Evaluating the National Gendarmerie," Combatting Terrorism Centre at West Point, May 23, 2013, http://www.ctc.usma.edu/posts/mexicos-new-strategy -to-combat-drug-cartels-evaluating-the-national-gendarmerie.

82 *The Economist*. "The Feds Ride Out." August 23, 2014. http://www.economist .com/news/americas/21613312-mexico-gets-new-police-force-it-needs-new- policing-strategy-feds-ride-out.

CHAPTER 6: MEXICO, PARAMILITARIZATION & THE DRUG WAR

1 One of Beltran Leyva's claims to fame was his participation in the bribery of Noe Ramirez Mandujano, Calderón's head of anti-drug intelligence: Ken Ellingwood, "Mexico Traffickers Bribed Former Anti-drug Chief, Officials Say," *Los Angeles Times*, November 22, 2008, http://www.latimes.com/news/ nationworld/world/latinamerica/la-fg-bribe22-2008nov22,0,5384359.story.

2 Dube and Naidu, "Bases, Bullets and Ballots," 3.

3 Huggins, *Political Policing*, 18–21.

4 Vulliamy, *Amexica*, 127–128.

5 Guadalupe Correa-Cabrera, "Flujos de Inversión, Desarrollo Empresarial y Seguridad en México: Las Empresas Mexicanas y Extranjeras en un Entorno Violento," *1er Congreso Internacional: Gestión y Administración Empresarial para el Siglo* 21 (February 2012): 18–19.

6 Marcela Turati, "Juárez: Tiendas cerradas, ollas vacías," *Proceso*, June 28, 2011, http://www.proceso.com.mx/?p=274273.

7 Diana Washington Valdezz, "Mexican Businessman Who Lost Feet to Violence Going on Bike Journey," *El Paso Times*, October 9, 2013, http://www.elpasotimes.com/latestnews/ci_24272527/mexican-business man-who-lost-feet-violence-going-bike.

8 Correa-Cabrera, "Flujos de Inversión, Desarrollo Empresarial y Seguridad en México," 22.

9 Carlos Lauría and Mike O'Conner, "Cartel City: Silence or Death in Mexico's Press," Committee to Protect Journalists, September 8, 2010, http://cpj. org/reports/2010/09/silence-death-mexico-press-cartel-city.php.

10 Figueroa, *El Capo del Golfo*, 29.

11 Between 1996 and 1998, the USG trained 422 GAFEs, one of that last instances of unit-level training of Mexican soldiers by the US. The USG didn't start keeping a database of Mexican soldiers trained by the US until 1996, by which time the Zetas had already begun to form. According to the US State Department, Fort Bragg also didn't keep records on foreign nationals

in training until 1996, http://wikileaks.org/cable/2009/08/09MEXICO2473. html.

12 US Attorney's Office, "Osiel Cardenas-Guillen, Former Head of the Gulf Cartel, Sentenced to 25 Years' Imprisonment," February 24, 2010, http://www.fbi.gov/houston/press-releases/2010/ho022410b.htm.

13 Oddly, in the US. Federal Prisons Database, Osiel's first name is misspelled Oziel, as if in homage to his legacy (Zeta means "Z" in Spanish).

14 Carlos Resa Nestares, "El comercio de drogas ilegales en México: Los Zetas: de narcos a mafiosos," April 2003, http://www.uam.es/personal_pdi/economicas/cresa/nota0403.pdf.

15 Francisco Gómez, "Ejecución de 'El Concord' detonó guerra en Tamaulipas," *El Universal*, March 7, 2010, http://www.eluniversal.com.mx/nacion/176125. html.

16 Daniel B. Madrigal, "Policías daban clases de tiro a Zetas y eran espías," *Crónica*, April 23, 2011, http://www.cronica.com.mx/notas/2011/574313. html.

17 Bruce Williamson, "10Monterrey43, Border Violence Spreads to Nuevo Leon," US State Department, February 26, 2011, http://wikileaks.org/cable /2010/02/10MONTERREY43.html#par8.

18 Dawn Paley, "Drug War Capitalism," *Solidarity*, July/August, 2012, http://www.solidarity-us.org/node/3652.

19 Roberto Garduño, "Diputado: fin a la movilidad poblacional por la violencia," *La Jornada*, February 8, 2014, 11.

20 Comisión Nacional de los Derechos Humanos, "Informe especial sobre secuestro de migrant es en México," 12, 26.

21 Genaro Sánchez, "Ejecutan a dos mujeres migrantes en Palenque," *Tabasco Hoy*, May 30, 2013, http://www.tabascohoy.com/2/notas/index. php?ID=130334.

22 Ibid.

23 Noé Zavaleta, "Asaltan a migrantes en Veracruz; Duarte lo tergiversa: 'fue una riña' Asaltan a migrantes en Veracruz; Duarte lo tergiversa: 'fue una riña'," *Proceso*, May 2, 2013, http://www.proceso.com.mx/?p=340766.

24 USGS, "Assessment of Undiscovered Oil and Gas Resources of the Burgos Basin Province, Northeastern Mexico, 2003," http://pubs.usgs.gov/fs/2004/3007/fs-2004-3007.pdf.

25 Milenio, "Llegan 8 mil soldados a Tamaulipas para reforzar seguridad," http://www.zocalo.com.mx/seccion/articulo/llegan-8-mil-soldados-a -tamaulipas-para-reforzar-seguridad.

26 IDMC, "Briefing paper by the Norwegian Refugee Council's Internal Displacement Monitoring Centre on forced displacement in Mexico due to drug cartel violence," December 2010, http://www.refworld.org/docid/4d2714522. html, 3.

27 US District Court for the Southern District of Texas, Houston Division, "Pemex Condensate Theft Ring Lawsuit (Complaint)," http://www.archive.org/download/PemexCondensateTheftRingLawsuitcomplaint/PEP.PDF.

28 Noticias Televisa, "México descubre yacimientos de gas natural en frontera con EU," http://noticierostelevisa.esmas.com/nacional/355102/mexico-descubre-yacimientos-gas-natural-frontera-con-eu.

29 Servicio Mexicano de Geologia, "Panorama Minero del Estado de Chihuahua," July 2011, http://www.sgm.gob.mx/pdfs/CHIHUAHUA.pdf, 8.

30 Ibid.

31 Ibid., 5.

32 James Munson, "Before the Rush: The Rancher's Rebellion," *Ipolitics. ca*, http://www.ipolitics.ca/2013/03/04/before-the-rush-the-ranchers-rebellion-2/. A board member for MAG Silver hinted that Solorio was involved in criminal activity—an insinuation that, in Mexico, is enough to suggest that victims of violence are somehow deserving of their fate.

33 Dan MacInnis, personal communication, March 28, 2013.

34 Rogelio Agustín Esteban, "Investigan escalada de violencia en zona minera," May 16, 2013, http://www.milenio.com/cdb/doc/noticias2011/9f20 e3acb061086cf7606c9c464e2422.

35 Notinfomex, "Guerrero: encuentran dos ejecutados en el KL. 170 de la carretera Iguala-Chilpancingo," July 18, 2013, http://www.notinfomex. info/2013/07/guerrero-encuentran-dos-ejecutados-en.html.

36 Sergio Ocampo and Héctor Briseño, "La violencia en Tierra Caliente, por 'alianza' del gobierno con el hampa para explotar minas," *La Jornada*, July 21, 2013, http://www.jornada.unam.mx/2013/07/21/politica/010n1pol.

37 Brisa Araujo, "Te sumas al narco, te vas, o te mueres: desplazados en Guerrero," *Desinformemonos*, July 2013, http://desinformemonos.org/2013/07/ te-sumas-al-narco-te-vas-o-te-mueres-desplazados-en-guerrero/.

38 Ibid.

39 Redacción, "Carbón, nueva actividad del narco en Coahuila: Moreira," *El Universal*, October 26, 2012, http://www.eluniversal.com.mx/notas/879116.html.

40 Channel 4 News, "On the Trail of a Mexican Drug Lord," January 28, 2014, https://www.youtube.com/watch?v=jX7dbLW-47M.

41 José Juan Estrada Serafín, "Estamos en defensa de nuestras familias y de la comunidad indígena: San Miguel Aquila," *Subversiones*, June 2013, http:// www.agenciasubversiones.org/?p=8080.

42 El Consejo de Autodefensa de Aquila, Michoacán, "Primer Comunicado del Grupo de Autodefensa de Aquila, Michoacán," January 19, 2014, http:// elenemigocomun.net/es/2014/01/autodefensa-aquila-michoacan/.

43 IDMC, "Briefing Paper By the Norwegian Refugee Council's Internal Displacement Monitoring Centre on Forced Displacement in Mexico Due to Drug Cartel Violence," December 2010, http://www.refworld.org/docid/4d2714522.html, 6.

44 Melissa del Bosque, "The Deadliest Place in Mexico," *The Texas Observer*, February 29, 2013, http://www.theinvestigativefund.org/investigations/ international/1615/the_deadliest_place_in_mexico/.

45 Prudential Real Estate Investors, "2011 Sustainability Report," 2011, http:// www3.prudential.com/prei/pdf/2011_PREI_Sustainability_Report.pdf, 19.

46 Sandra Rodríguez, "Nueva ciudad en San Agustín," April 19, 2011, http:// zuelos.com/blog/nueva-ciudad-en-san-agustin/.

47 Diana Washington, "$400M Development Planned for Area in Juárez Valley," *El Paso Times*, May 23, 2011, http://www.elpasotimes.com/ ci_18118303.

48 Harold L. Sirkin, Michael Zinser, and Douglas Hohner, "Made in America, Again Why Manufacturing Will Return to the U.S.,"*BCG.com*, August 2011, http://www.bcg.com/documents/file84471.pdf, 12.

49 Sandra Rodríguez, "Demandan no convertir en otro Riberas del Bravo a San

Agustín," *El Diario de Juárez*, April 20, 2011, http://www.skyscrapercity. com/showthread.php?p=75966555.

50 Nicholas Casey and Alexandra Berzon, "Mexico Tourism Feels Chill of On-going Drug Violence," *Wall Street Journal*, June 8, 2011, http://online.wsj. com/news/articles/SB10001424052702304432304576367710290674534.

51 Adriana Covarrubias, "Confirman violación a seis turistas españolas en Acapulco," *El Universal*, February 4, 2013, http://www.eluniversal.com. mx/notas/900731.html.

52 Gay Nagel Myers, "Acapulco Fights Image Woes as It Seeks Return to Glory," *Travel Weekly*, May 16, 2012, http://www.travelweekly.com/Mexico-Travel /Acapulco-fights-image-woes-as-it-seeks-return-to-glory/.

53 Ibid.

54 Dolia Estevez, "Can Billionaire Carlos Slim Return Acapulco to its Past Glory?," *Forbes*, February 12, 2013, http://www.forbes.com/sites/doliaestevez /2013/02/12/can-billionaire-carlos-slim-return-acapulco-to-its-past-glory/.

55 Castillo García, "Tamaulipas enfrenta diáspora de ganaderos por causa del narco," *La Jornada*, November 13, 2010, http://www.jornada.unam. mx/2010/11/13/index.php?section=politica&article=003n1pol.

56 Editor, "Otros ganaderos abandonan sus ranchos en Tamaulipas," *Milenio*, November 24, 2010, http://www.milenio.com/cdb/doc/noticias2011/ d9733f1d182257206a2cdeac4ff310a5.

57 Los Zetas have forcibly recruited Central Americans, in addition to Guatemalan special forces who work with the cartels.

58 Donna Chollett, "From Sugar to Blackberries: Restructuring Agro-export Production in Michoacán, Mexico," *Latin American Perspectives* 36, no. 3 (May 2009): 79.

59 Aguilar Valenzuela, Rubén, "Cártel de los Valencia," *El Economista*, August 30, 2011, http://eleconomista.com.mx/columnas/columna-especial-politica /2011/08/30/cartel-valencia.

60 The first state where Felipe Calderón sent troops was Michoacán, his home state.

61 Arturo Cano, "'Me llaman templario mayor por revancha política', asegura alcalde de Tepalcatepec," *La Jornada*, February 8, 2014, 9.

62 Humberto Padgett, "Aguacate: el 'oro verde' de los Templarios," *Sin Embargo*, October 11, 2013, http://www.sinembargo.mx/11-10-2013/780868.

63 Marcela Salas Cassani, "Hablan las mujeres de Cherán, protagonistas de la insurrección," *Desinformemonos*, April, 2012, http://desinformemonos. org/2012/04/mujeres/.

64 Administrador, "Fotos limoneros emboscados por los Caballeros Templarios," April 10, 2013, http://www.historiasdelnarco.com/2013/04/fotos-limoneros -emboscados-por-los.html.

65 La Policiaca, "Veta crimen a limoneros," April 14, 2013, http://www.lapoliciaca .com/nota-roja/veta-crimen-a-limoneros/.

66 Redaccion, "Acusan a guardias comunitarias de Michoacán de obedecer al Cártel de Jalisco," *Proceso*, May 2, 2013, http://www.proceso.com.mx /?p=340789.

67 Paula Chouza, "El infierno también está en Michoacán," *El Pais*, October 28, 2013, http://internacional.elpais.com/internacional/2013/10/28/actualidad /1382921848_799992.html.

68 Ibid.

69 Patrick Corcoran, "Counterinsurgency is not the Answer for Mexico," *In-Sight Crime*, September 26, 2011, http://www.insightcrime.org/news-analysis/counterinsurgency-is-not-the-answer-for-mexico.

CHAPTER 7: DRUG WAR CAPITALISM IN GUATEMALA

1 FAO, "The Continuing Need for Land Reform: Making the Case for Civil Society," FAO Land Tenure Series: Concept Paper, volume 1, http://www.landcoalition.org/sites/default/files/legacy/legacydocs/odfaomon2guate.htm.

2 Mexican painter Diego Rivera depicts the scene in a painting titled "Gloriosa Victoria": Allen Dulles, who was on the board of the United Fruit Company, stands beside his brother John Foster, the US secretary of state, who shakes the hand of Castillo Armas, Washington's choice for president. A bomb in front of the men is painted with the face of Dwight Eisenhower, then president of the United States. The US ambassador and the Archbishop of Guatemala stand by, giving their blessings to the coup. In the background, Guatemalan laborers carry stems of bananas onto a waiting cargo ship; the foreground is littered with dead bodies. Ernesto "Ché" Guevara, who was in Guatemala when the coup took place, fled to the relative safety of Mexico with other progressives, and it was there he would meet Fidel Castro.

3 Luis Solano, "En manos de quién estará la seguridad en el futuro gobierno PP?," *Enfoque*, November 28, 2011, http://www.albedrio.org/htm/documentos/EnfoqueAnalisisSituacion182011.pdf, 5.

4 Dawn Paley, "Conflict, Repression, and Canadian Mining & Oil Companies in Guatemala," May 14, 2012, http://dawnpaley.tumblr.com/post/23043137951/conflict-repression-and-canadian-mining-oil.

5 Paula Worby, "America's Country of Origin Series: Guatemala Background Paper," United Nations High Commissioner for Refugees, October 2013, http://www.refworld.org/pdfid/53832fe84.pdf, 14.

6 InSight Crime, "Special Series: The Zetas in Guatemala," *InSight Crime*, September 2011, http://www.insightcrime.org/special-series/the-zetas-in-guatemala.

7 Romina Ruiz-Goireina and Martha Mendoza, "200 US Marines Join Anti-Drug Effort in Guatemala," August 29, 2012, http://bigstory.ap.org/article/200-us-marines-join-anti-drug-effort-guatemala.

8 CNN Wire Staff, "Guatemala's President Calls on Troops to 'Neutralize' Organized Crime," January 16, 2012, http://articles.cnn.com/2012-01-16/americas/world_americas_guatemala-military_1_alta-verapaz-peten-civil-war?_s=PM:AMERICAS.

9 Rodrigo Baires Quezada, "Presupuesto: más represión que investigación y justicia," *Plaza Publica*, November 7, 2012, http://www.plazapublica.com.gt/content/presupuesto-mas-represion-que-investigacion-y-justicia.

10 Department of Defense, "Western Hemisphere Defense Policy Statement," October 2012, http://www.defense.gov/news/WHDPS-English.pdf, 6.

11 Ibid., 8.

12 Annie Bird and Alex Main, "Collateral Damage in the Drug War: The May 11 Killings in Ahuas and the Impact of the US War on Drugs in La Moskitia, Honduras," August 2012, http://www.cepr.net/documents/publications/honduras-2012-08.pdf, 20.

13 Carlos Hernández, "Estados Unidos concluye 'Operación Martillo' en el país,"

Diario de Centro América, October 23, 2012, http://www.dca.gob.gt/index.php/
template-features/item/5940-estados-unidos-concluye-%E2%80%9Coperaci
%C3%B3n-martillo%E2%80%9D-en-el-pa%C3%ADs.html. Further proof
of the whereabouts of US Marines during Operation Martillo is based on visual
evidence posted by US Southern Command and the US Embassy in Guatemala.
Note that the image of Santa Elena is mislabeled with the dateline RETALHU-
LEU: http://www.flickr.com/photos/ussouthcom/7979820592/in/photostream/.
The same dateline issue appears here: http://www.2ndmaw.marines.mil/Photos
.aspx?mgqs=2207160. Puerto Quetzal: http://www.flickr.com/photos/ussouth
com/7979821816/in/photostream. Guatemala City: http://www.flickr.com/
photos/usembassyguatemala/sets/72157631809378179/.

14   The media silence around the deployment of US combat troops to Guatemala has been deafening. To illustrate, a *Los Angeles Times* article purport-
ing to review US involvement in anti-narcotics activities in Central America
left it out entirely. See: Tracy Wilkinson and Richard Fausset, "US Gingerly
Expands Security Role in Central America," *Los Angeles Times*, December
4, 2012, http://www.latimes.com/news/nationworld/world/la-fg-us-central-
america-20121205,0,7198665,full.story.

15   The original 1949, 1954, and 1955 agreements (in Spanish) are available here:
https://s3.amazonaws.com/TowardsFreedom/1949+agreement.pdf; https://s3
.amazonaws.com/TowardsFreedom/1954+agreement.pdf; https://s3.amazo
naws.com/TowardsFreedom/1955+Agreement.pdf

16   Organismo Ejecutivo. "Acuerdo por Canje de Notas entre el Gobierno de
la Republica de Guatemala y el Gobierno de Estados Unidos de America
Relativo a la Operacion Martillo," *Diario de Centro América* 18, tomo
CCXCV (August 20, 2012), https://s3.amazonaws.com/TowardsFreedom/
Canje+De+Notas+Martillo+2012.pdf.

17   Ibid. Recall that, in February 2011, a US Air Force cargo plane arriving in
Argentina for joint police training exercises was found to contain weapons
and morphine that were not declared by the US soldiers: CNN Wire Staff,
"Cargo Sparks Dispute between Argentina, US," February 16, 2011, http://
www.cnn.com/2011/WORLD/americas/02/15/argentina.us.spat/index.
html. The agreement allowing US Marines arriving in Guatemala prevents
Guatemalan agents from revising the contents of aircraft or other vehicles
entering the country.

18   Greg Wolf, "After Partnering to Disrupt Trafficking, Detachment Martillo Departs Guatemala," October 16, 2012, http://www.hqmc.marines.
mil/News/NewsArticleDisplay/tabid/3488/Article/128618/after-partner-
ing-to-disrupt-trafficking-detachment-martillo-departs-guatemala.aspx.

19   Central Intelligence Agency, "Official History of the Bay of Pigs Operation:
Participation in the Conduct of Foreign Policy, Volume II," October 1979,
http://www.gwu.edu/~nsarchiv/NSAEBB/NSAEBB353/bop-vol2-part1.pdf,
13–14.

20   US Northern Command, or NORTHCOM, is responsible for Mexico, as well
as the US Virgin Islands, Puerto Rico, the Bahamas, Canada, and the US.

21   United States Southern Command, "Beyond the Horizon, New Horizons
2012," June 19, 2012, http://www.southcom.mil/newsroom/Pages/Beyond-
the-Horizon--New-Horizons-2012.aspx.

22   Southcom, "Seabees, Preventive Medicine Specialists Team Up in Guatemala,"
October 22, 2012, http://www.navy.mil/submit/display.asp?story_id=70228.

23 Ruiz-Goireina and Mendoza, "200 US Marines Join Anti-Drug Effort."

24 Leon E. Panetta, "Speech: Hampton Roads Chamber of Commerce," October 19, 2012, http://www.defense.gov/speeches/speech.aspx?speechid=1729.

25 Center for Hemispheric Defense Studies, "12 Questions for Deputy Assistant Secretary of Defense for Western Hemisphere Affairs Frank Mora," January 2012, http://www.ndu.edu/chds/news.cfm?action=view&id=57&lang=PT.

26 William Brownfield, "Regional Security Cooperation: An Examination of the Central America Regional Security Initiative and the Caribbean Basin Security Initiative," June 19, 2013, http://docs.house.gov/meetings /FA/FA07/20130619/101032/HHRG-113-FA07-Wstate-Brownfield W-20130619.pdf.

27 Ibid., 40.

28 Ralph Espach, et al., "Criminal Organizations and Illicit Trafficking in Guatemala's Border Communities," *CNA Analysis and Solutions*, December 2011, http://www.cna.org/sites/default/files/research/IPR%2015225.pdf.

29 Julie López, "Guatemala's Crossroads: The Democratization of Violence and Second Chances," in *Wilson Center Reports on the Americas* 29: 151, http://www.wilsoncenter.org/sites/default/files/LAP_single_page.pdf.

30 Democracy Now!, "Genocide-Linked General Otto Pérez Molina Poised to Become Guatemala's Next President," *Democracy Now!*, September 15, 2011, http://www.democracynow.org/2011/9/15/genocide_linked_general_otto _prez_molina. In March 2011, Harbury filed a lawsuit in Guatemala against President Pérez Molina, alleging his role in the disappearance, torture, and assassination of her husband, guerrilla commander Efraín Bámaca. See: Corelia Orantes, "Jennifer Harbury acciona contra Pérez Molina," *Prensa Libre*, March 23, 2011, http://prensalibre.com.gt/noticias/Acciona -Perez_0_449355088.html.

31 Elyssa Pachico, "How Much Is Guatemala Arming the Zetas?," *InSight Crime*, http://www.insightcrime.org/news-analysis/how-much-is-guatemala-arming-the-zetas.

32 Siglo21, "Fiscal dice que ex kaibil capturado dirigió massacre," May 19, 2011, http://www.s21.com.gt/node/39187.

33 Cpl. Daniel Negrete, "Marines Sweat It Out With Guatemalan Kaibiles," *Marines*, September 18, 2010, http://www.2ndmaw.marines.mil/News/ ArticleView/tabid/357/Article/32610/marines-sweat-it-out-with-guatemalan -kaibiles.aspx. Tim Padgett, "Guatemala's Kaibiles: A Notorious Commando Unit Wrapped Up in Central America's Drug War," *Time*, July 14, 2011, http://world.time.com/2011/07/14/guatemalas-kaibil-terror-from-dictators -to-drug-cartels/#ixzz2EguGbDZW.

34 Sylvia Gereda Valenzuela, "El capítulo negro de Fernández Ligorría," *El Periodico*, January 15, 2011, http://www.elperiodico.com.gt/es/20110115/ opinion/188624.

35 Douglas Gámez, "Crearán Fuerza de Tarea militar contra el narcotráfico," March 30, 2012, http://goldcorpoutnews.wordpress.com/2012/03/30/crearan -fuerza-de-tarea-militar-contra-el-narcotrafico/.

36 Elyssa Pachico, "Key Zetas Ally Walther Overdick Arrested in Guatemala," *Insight Crime*, April 3, 2012, http://www.insightcrime.org/news-analysis/ key-zetas-ally-walther-overdick-arrested-in-guatemala.

CHAPTER 8: DRUG WAR CAPITALISM IN HONDURAS

1   Hillary Clinton, "Remarks at her Meeting With Central American Foreign Ministers," September 27, 2012, http://www.state.gov/secretary/20092013clinton/rm/2012/09/198315.htm.
2   Peter Meyer, "Honduras-US Relations," *Congressional Research Service.* July 24, 2013, http://www.fas.org/sgp/crs/row/RL34027.pdf, 21.
3   Ibid.
4   Clinton, Hillary, "Remarks at her Meeting With Central American Foreign Ministers,"
5   Observatorio de la Violencía, "Mortalidad y Otros," January 2013, http://iudpas.org/pdf/Boletines/Nacional/NEd28EneDic2012.pdf.
6   Ibid.
7   Observatorio de la Violencía, "Mortalidad y Otros," May 2006, http://iudpas.org/pdf/Boletines/Nacional/NEd01EneDic2005.pdf.
8   Observatorio de la Violencía, "Mortalidad y Otros," February 2014, http://iudpas.org/pdf/Boletines/Nacional/NEd32EneDic2013.pdf.
9   Darío Euraque, *Reinterpreting the Banana Republic: Region and State in Honduras, 1870–1972* (Chapel Hill: University of North Carolina Press, 1996), 43–44.
10 Marvin Barahona, *Honduras en el siglo XX: Una síntesis histórica* (Tegucigalpa: Editorial Guaymaras, 2009), 72.
11 Alison Acker, *Honduras: The Making of a Banana Republic* (Toronto: Between the Lines, 1988), 74.
12 Ibid.
13 John Booth, Christine Wade, and Thomas Walker, *Understanding Central America: Global Forces, Rebellion and Change*, Fourth Edition, (Boulder, Colorado: Westview Press, 2006), 135.
14 Euraque, *Reinterpreting the Banana Republic*, 73–74.
15 Booth, Wade, and Walker, *Understanding Central America*, 135, 218.
16 Walter LaFeber, *Inevitable Revolutions: The United States in Central America*, Second Edition (New York: W.W. Norton and Company, 1983), 182. Tim Merrill, *Honduras: A Country Study* (Washington, DC: GPO for the Library of Congress, 1995), 147.
17 Noam Chomsky, *Turning the Tide: The US and Latin America*, Second Edition (Montréal: Black Rose Books, 1987), 40
18 Edelberto Torres Rivas, *History and Society in Central America* (Austin: University of Texas Press, 1993), 104.
19 Booth, Wade, and Walker, *Understanding Central America*, 135, 218.
20 Alcides Hernández, *El Neoliberalismo en Honduras* (Tegucigalpa: Editorial Guaymuras, 1983), 93.
21 Meyer, "Honduras-US Relations."
22 William I. Robinson, *Promoting Polyarchy*, 62.
23 Tom Barry and Kent Norsworthy, *Honduras: A Country Guide* (Albuquerque: The Resource Center, 1990), 17.
24 Torres-Rivas, *History and Society in Central America*, 127.
25 William I. Robinson, *Transnational Conflicts: Central America, Social Change and Globalization* (New York: Verso, 2003), 123.
26 Booth, Wade, and Walker, *Understanding Central America*, 135, 218.
27 Ibid.

28   Robinson, *Transnational Conflicts*, 125.

29   Booth, Wade, and Walker, *Understanding Central America*, 135, 137.

30   Jorge L. Fernández and Luis M. Martínez, *A veinte años del auge de la maquila en Honduras: La situación de los derechos humanos laborales de las trabajadoras y los trabajadores* (El Progreso, Yoro: Comunicaciones Comunitarios, 2009), 32.

31   Jack R. Binns, *The United States in Honduras, 1980–1981: An Ambassador's Memoir* (Jefferson, NC: McFarland & Company, 2000), 2.

32   Robinson, *Transnational Conflicts*, 118, 125.

33   Ibid., 125.

34   Ibid., 118, 125.

35   Raymond Robertson, Drusilla Brown, Gaëlle Pierre, and María Laura Sanchez-Puerta, *Globalization, Wages and the Quality of Jobs: Five Country Studies* (Washington, DC: World Bank Publications, 2009), 177.

36   Robinson, *Transnational Conflicts*, 129. Booth, Wade, and Walker, *Understanding Central America*, 135, 144.

37   SICE. "Honduras: Exports to Partner Countries 1980–2002," *SICE*, 2005. http://www.sice.oas.org/tradedata/HND_e.asp.

38   Alcides Hernández, *Del reformismo al ajuste structural* (Tegucigalpa: Editorial Guaymuras, 2007), 75.

39   Ibid., 60.

40   Robinson, *Transnational Conflicts*, 130.

41   Meyer, "Honduras-US Relations."

42   Mark J. Ruhl, "Redefining Civil-Military Relations in Honduras," *Journal of Interamerican Studies and World Affairs* 38, no. 1 (Spring,1996): 49.

43   Booth, Wade, and Walker, *Understanding Central America*, 135, 145.

44   Ibid., 135, 145.

45   Morgan Lee and Alexandra Olson, "Honduran Coup Shows Business Elite Still in Charge," The Associated Press. August 6, 2009, http://www.utsandiego.com/news/2009/Aug/06/lt-honduras-coup-elite-backlash-080609/.

46   Economist Intelligence Unit, "Honduras Politics: Mixed Report Card for Zelaya," *The Economist* (May 10, 2007).

47   COHEP, "Press Release," Consejo Hondureño de la Empresa Privada, June 29, 2009, http://narcosphere.narconews.com/userfiles/70/PressRlease-JuneCohep.2009.pdf.

48   ANDI, "Comunicado: Golpe de Estado? Manuel Zelaya Rosales ya lo habia llevado a cabo," Asociación Nacional de Industriales de Honduras, July 1, 2009, http://nacerenhonduras.com/2009/06/golpe-de-estado-manuel-zelaya-rosales.html

49   COHEP, "Documento de Posición," Consejo Hondureño de la Empresa Privada, August 19, 2009, http://narcosphere.narconews.com/userfiles/70/PositionPaper.pdf.

50   Adrián Burgos Padilla, "Honduras: promoción y protección de la inversion," July 4, 2012, http://www.centralamericalink.com/es/Legales/Honduras_promocion_y_proteccion_de_la_inversion/.

51   Meyer, "Honduras-US Relations," 13.

52   Alberto Arce, "AP Exclusive: Honduras Chief Denies Death Squads," The Associated Press, November 2, 2013, http://bigstory.ap.org/article/ap-exclusive-honduras-chief-denies-death-squads.

53   Rosemary Joyce and Russell Sheptak, "Re-militarizing the Police: Turning the

Clock Back in Honduras," *Upside Down World*, October 7, 2013, http://
upsidedownworld.org/main/honduras-archives-46/4495-re-militarizing-the-
police-turning-the-clock-back-in-honduras.

54 Kaitlin Owens, *Honduras: Periodismo bajo la sombra de impunidad* (Toronto: IHRP/Pen Canada, 2014), 7, defensoresenlinea.com/cms/documentos/
Honduras_Periodismo_sombra_impunidad.pdf.

55 Sandra Cuffe, "Congress' Last Stand: Privatizations among New Laws in
Honduras," *Upside Down World*, January 28, 2014, http://upsidedownworld
.org/main/honduras-archives-46/4668-congress-last-stand-privatizations-
among-new-laws-in-honduras.

56 Redaccion, "Honduras: Redes del narcotráfico penetraron a altos oficiales,"
El Heraldo, February 5, 2014, http://www.elheraldo.hn/Secciones-Principales/
Al-Frente/Honduras-Redes-del-narcotrafico-penetraron-a-altos-oficiales.

57 Redaccion, "Honduras: La lista de policías vinculados a delitos es escalof-
riante," *El Heraldo*, February 5, 2014, http://www.elheraldo.hn/content/
view/full/217348.

58 Meyer, "Honduras-US Relations," 11.

59 G. Ramsey, "Cable: Honduran Military Supplied Weaponry to Cartels,"
InSight Crime, April 25, 2011, http://www.insightcrime.org/news-analysis/
cable-honduran-military-supplied-weaponry-to-cartels.

60 Sarah England, "'Worse than the War': Experiences and Discourses of Violence in Postwar Central America," *Latin American Perspectives* 39, no. 6
(November 2012), 246–247.

61 K. McSweeny and Z. Pearson, "Prying Native People from Native Lands:
Narco Business in Honduras," *NACLA*, February 4, 2014, http://nacla.org/
news/2014/2/4/prying-native-people-native-lands-narco-business-honduras.

62 Annie Bird and Alex Main, "Collateral Damage of a Drug War," *Center for
Economic and Policy Research*, August 2012, http://www.cepr.net/documents
/publications/honduras-2012-08.pdf.

63 "The Drug War: Policing and US Militarism at Home and Abroad," event,
February 20, 2014.

64 CRLN, "229 Politically Related Murders in Honduras Under President
'Pepe' Lobo," *Chicago Religious Leadership Network on Latin America*,
November 20, 2013, retrieved March 11, 2014, http://www.crln.org/story
/229_Murders_Honduras.

65 Annie Bird, "Human Rights Violations Attributed to Military Forces in the
Bajo Aguan Valley in Honduras," February 20, 2013, http://rightsaction.
org/sites/default/files/Rpt_130220_Aguan_Final.pdf, 4.

66 UN Working Group on Mercenaries, "Report of the Working Group on the
Use of Mercenaries as a Means of Violating Human Rights and Impeding
the Exercise of the Right of Peoples to Self-determination on its Mission to
Honduras," *UNHR*, 18–22 February 2013, 13.

67 Michael R. Fowler, "Honduras," in *Bribes, Bullets and Intimidation*, eds.
Julie Bunck and Michael Fowler (University Park, PA: Penn State University
Press, 2012), 265.

68 Ibid., 273.

69 Ibid., 307.

CONCLUSION: THINKING THROUGH PEACE IN WARTIME

1   Immanuel Wallerstein, *World-Systems Analysis: An Introduction* (Durham, NC: Duke University Press, 2004), ix.

2   R. Gomis, M. Romillo, and I. Rodríguez, "Reflexiones sobre la politica del terror: El caso de Guatemala," *Cuadernos de Nuestra América*, Vol 1. (1983).

INDEX

AK Press is small, in terms of staff and resources, but we also manage to be one of the world's most productive anarchist publishing houses. We publish close to twenty books every year, and distribute thousands of other titles published by like-minded independent presses and projects from around the globe. We're entirely worker-run and democratically managed. We operate without a corporate structure—no boss, no managers, no bullshit.

The Friends of AK program is a way you can directly contribute to the continued existence of AK Press, and ensure that we're able to keep publishing books like this one! Friends pay $25 a month directly into our publishing account ($30 for Canada, $35 for international), and receive a copy of every book AK Press publishes for the duration of their membership! Friends also receive a discount on anything they order from our website or buy at a table: 50% on AK titles, and 20% on everything else. We have a Friends of AK ebook program as well: $15 a month gets you an electronic copy of every book we publish for the duration of your membership. You can even sponsor a very discounted membership for someone in prison.

Email FRIENDSOFAK@AKPRESS.ORG for more info, or visit the Friends of AK Press website: HTTPS://WWW.AKPRESS.ORG/FRIENDS.HTML.

There are always great book projects in the works—so sign up now to become a Friend of AK Press, and let the presses roll!